Second Language Writing

CAMBRIDGE LANGUAGE EDUCATION
Series Editor: Jack C. Richards

This series draws on the best available research, theory, and educational practice to help clarify issues and resolve problems in language teaching, language teacher education, and related areas. Books in the series focus on a wide range of issues and are written in a style that is accessible to classroom teachers, teachers-in-training, and teacher educators.

Second Language Writing

Ken Hyland
City University of Hong Kong

CAMBRIDGE
UNIVERSITY PRESS

PUBLISHED BY THE PRESS SYNDICATE OF THE UNIVERSITY OF CAMBRIDGE
The Pitt Building, Trumpington Street, Cambridge, United Kingdom

CAMBRIDGE UNIVERSITY PRESS
The Edinburgh Building, Cambridge CB2 2RU, UK
40 West 20th Street, New York, NY 10011-4211, USA
477 Williamstown Road, Port Melbourne, VIC 3207, Australia
Ruiz de Alarcón 13, 28014 Madrid, Spain
Dock House, The Waterfront, Cape Town 8001, South Africa

http://www.cambridge.org

© Ken Hyland 2003

First published 2003

Printed in the United States of America

Typefaces Times New Roman 10.5/12.5 pt. *and* Helvetica Neue   *System* LaTeX 2_ε [TB]

A catalog record for this book is available from the British Library.

Library of Congress Cataloging in Publication Data

Hyland, Ken.
Second language writing / Ken Hyland.
    p.   cm. – (Cambridge language education)
Includes bibliographical references and index.
ISBN 0-521-82705-1 – ISBN 0-521-53430-5 (pb.)
1. Language and languages – Study and teaching.   2. Rhetoric – Study and teaching.
3. Second language acquisition.   I. Title.   II. Series.
P53.27.H95   2003
808′.042–dc21   2003041957

ISBN 0 521 82705 1 hardback
ISBN 0 521 53430 5 paperback

Contents

PERMISSIONS ACKNOWLEDGEMENTS

The publishers and I are grateful to authors, publishers, and software developers who have given permission to reproduce copyright material.

Example tasks on pages 4, 29 and 134 from Hamp-Lyons, L., & B. Heasley. (1987). *Study Writing*. Pages 23 and 52. Reprinted with the permission of Cambridge University Press.

Example tasks on page 10 from O'Keefe, J. (2000). *Invitation to reading and writing*. Pages 99 and 141. Reproduced with the permission of Pearson Education Inc, Upper Saddle River, NJ.

Diagrams on pages 15 and 135 from White, R., & Arndt, V. (1991). *Process writing*. Pages 32 and 63. Reprinted by permission of Pearson Education Ltd.

Example task on page 16 from Blass, L., & Pike-Baky, M. (1985). *Mosaic: a content-based writing book*. Page 121. Reprinted with the permission of McGraw-Hill Education.

Example task on page 30 from Bhatia, V.K. (1997). Applied genre analysis and ESP. In Miller, T. (ed) Functional approaches to written text. Reprinted with the permission of the author.

Diagram on page 39 from Ballard, B., & Clanchy, J. (1991). Assessment by misconception: cultural influences and intellectual traditions. In L. Hamp-Lyons (Ed.) *Assessing second language writing in academic contexts*. Page 22. Reproduced with the permission of Greenwood Publishing Group.

Diagrams on pages 56, 60, and 101 from Hutchison, T., & Waters, A. (1987). *English for Specific Purposes*: a learning-centred approach. Pages 62–3, 74 and 108–9. Reprinted with the permission of Cambridge University Press.

Example materials on page 67–8 from Holst, J. (1995) *Writ 101: Writing English*. page 48. Reprinted with the permission of the author.

Example task on page 87 from Jordan, R. (1990). *Academic Writing Course*. Page 39. Reproduced with the permission of Collins ELT.

Example task on page 88 from Swales, J., & Feak, C. (2000). *English in today's research world: a writing guide*. Page 17–18. Reproduced with the permission of The University of Michigan Press.

Example task on page 89 from Brown, K., & Hood, S. (1989). *Writing matters: writing skills and strategies for students of English*. Page 11. Reprinted with the permission of Cambridge University Press.

Example tasks on pages 91 and 134 from Grellet, F. (1996). *Writing for advanced learners of English*. pp. 58, 103, and 109. Reprinted with the permission of Cambridge University Press.

Diagram on page 102 from Jolly, D., & Bolitho, R. (1998). A framework for materials writing. In B. Tomlinson (Ed.), *Materials development in language teaching*

Series Editor's Preface

Learning how to write in a second language is one of the most challenging aspects of second language learning. Perhaps this is not surprising in view of the fact that even for those who speak English as a first language, the ability to write effectively is something that requires extensive and specialized instruction and which has consequently spawned a vast freshman composition industry in American colleges and universities. Within the field of second and foreign language teaching, the teaching of writing has come to assume a much more central position than it occupied twenty or thirty years ago. This is perhaps the result of two factors.

On the one hand, command of good writing skills is increasingly seen as vital to equip learners for success in the twenty-first century. The ability to communicate ideas and information effectively through the global digital network is crucially dependent on good writing skills. Writing has been identified as one of the essential process skills in a world that is more than ever driven by text and numerical data. A further strengthening of the status of writing within applied linguistics has come from the expanded knowledge base on the nature of written texts and writing processes that has been developed by scholars in such fields as composition studies, second language writing, genre theory, and contrastive rhetoric. As a result there is an active interest today in new theoretical approaches to the study of written texts as well as approaches to the teaching of second language writing that incorporate current theory and research findings.

This book is therefore quite timely. It provides a comprehensive and extremely readable overview of the field of second language writing, examining how theories of writing and the teaching of writing have evolved, the nature of good writing, the nature of texts and genres and how they reflect their use in particular discourse communities, the relationship between writing in the first and second language, how a curriculum can be developed for a writing course, the development of instructional materials for a writing class, the uses of the computer in writing instruction, and approaches to feedback and assessment. The book also examines approaches to research on second language writing and shows how teachers can investigate their students' writing problems and explore their own practices in the teaching of writing.

The book reflects Professor Hyland's dual role as a leading researcher in the field of second language writing and an experienced teacher of second language writing. Theory and research are hence used throughout to illuminate some of the pedagogical issues and decisions that are involved in teaching second language writing. The insights presented both through the text as well as through the tasks readers are invited to carry out will provide an invaluable source of ideas and principles to inform teachers' and student teachers' classroom decision making.

Preface

Writing is among the most important skills that second language students need to develop, and the ability to teach writing is central to the expertise of a well-trained language teacher. But while interest in second language writing and approaches to teaching it have increased dramatically over the last decade, teachers are often left to their own resources in the classroom as much of the relevant theory and research fails to reach them. This book addresses this problem by providing a synthesis of theory, research, and practice to help teachers of *language* become teachers of *writing*.

This book is written for practicing teachers and teachers in training who have little or no experience teaching writing to students from non–English-speaking backgrounds. More specifically, it attempts to meet the needs of those who are or will be teaching students who speak English as a second or foreign language in colleges, universities, workplaces, language institutes, and senior secondary schools. Those who teach children or teach basic literacy skills to adults will also find much of value. The book pulls together the theory and practice of teaching writing to present an accessible and practical introduction to the subject without assuming any prior theoretical knowledge or teaching experience.

This text is founded on the premise that an effective teacher is one who can make informed choices about the methods, materials, and procedures to use in the classroom based on a clear understanding of the current attitudes and practices in his or her profession. A strong teacher is a reflective teacher, and reflection requires the knowledge to relate classroom activities to relevant research and theory. The book's practical approach toward second language writing attempts to provide a basis for this kind of reflection and understanding. In the text the reader will find a clear stance toward teaching writing which emphasizes the view that writing involves composing skills and knowledge about texts, contexts, and readers. It helps to develop the idea that writers need realistic strategies for drafting and revising, but they also must have a clear understanding of genre to structure their writing experiences according to the demands and constraints of particular contexts. I incorporate this emphasis on strategy, language, and context throughout the book.

The book also recognizes that teachers work in a range of situations – in schools, colleges, universities, corporate training divisions, and language institutes – and with students of different motivations, proficiencies, language backgrounds, and needs. They also work in contexts where English is taught as a Second Language (*ESL*) or as a Foreign Language (*EFL*), a distinction based on the language spoken by the community in which English is being studied. An ESL situation exists when the local community is largely English speaking, such as Australia, the United States, or the United Kingdom, while EFL contexts are those in which English is not the host language. Like most polarizations, however, this distinction obscures more complicated realities. For instance, ESL contexts can be further distinguished between learners who are migrants and who may therefore need occupational and survival writing skills, and those who plan to return to their own countries once they complete their courses. EFL contexts may include those where an indigenized variety has emerged (Singapore, India) or where colonization has afforded English a prominent role in local life (Hong Kong, Philippines), and those where English is rarely encountered (Korea, Japan).

These differences will have an impact on the kind of language students need and their motivation to acquire it, the cultural and linguistic homogeneity of the students, and the resources available to teachers. There are, however, sufficient similarities between these diverse types of context to focus on issues that concern all those who teach writing to non-native English speakers. In recognition of these similarities I shall use the acronym *L2* as a generic form to refer to all users of English from non–English-speaking backgrounds and *ESL* as shorthand for all contexts in which such students are learning English. (Likewise, I use *L1* to refer to those for whom English is their primary language.) The text also treats these students and contexts as similar by systematically setting out the key issues of classroom teaching in both contexts, addressing topics such as assessing needs, designing syllabuses, writing materials, developing tasks, using technology, giving feedback, and evaluating writing. In this way I hope to provide teachers with the resources to plan, implement, and evaluate a program of writing instruction for any teaching situation in which they may find themselves.

The book provides opportunities for you to engage with the ideas presented. *Reflection tasks* occur regularly through the chapters, encouraging readers to think about their own views on a topic and their potential needs as writing teachers. Each chapter concludes with a series of *Discussion questions and activities* which ask readers to consider ideas, examples of lesson plans, questionnaires, tasks or materials and so on, or to devise those of their own.

Acknowledgments

Textbooks cannot be written in a vacuum and I am grateful to the students, colleagues, and friends who have encouraged me, discussed ideas, and provided insights which have contributed to this book. I am particularly indebted to friends in Hong Kong, Australia, Britain, and the United States, especially Sue Hood, Chris Candlin, Malcolm Coulthard, John Swales, and Ann Johns, whose conversations and texts over many years have stimulated and sustained my long interest in writing, in both first and second languages.

I also want to acknowledge the ESL teachers studying the Master of Arts in English for Specific Purposes course at City University of Hong Kong for their feedback on many of the ideas and approaches discussed in these pages, and to my research assistant, Polly Tse, for her good humor and help in tracking down elusive items on the reference list. I am also grateful to Jack Richards, the series editor, who gave me the encouragement to write this book.

My thanks, as ever, go to Fiona Hyland, not only for allowing me to make use of her data, her valuable feedback on draft chapters, and her stimulating ideas on teaching writing, but for her constant support and encouragement.

1 *Writing and teaching writing*

Aims: This chapter will explore some of the ways that writing is viewed and the implications this has for teaching. It outlines the kinds of knowledge and skills involved in writing and develops some general principles for L2 writing teaching through a critical analysis of the main classroom orientations.

As EFL/ESL writing teachers, our main activities involve conceptualizing, planning, and delivering courses. At first sight, this seems to be mainly an application of practical professional knowledge, gained through hands-on classroom experience. To some extent this is true of course, for like any craft, teaching improves with practice. But there is more to it than this. Experience can only be a part of the picture, as our classroom decisions are always informed by our theories and beliefs about what writing is and how people learn to write. Everything we do in the classroom, the methods and materials we adopt, the teaching styles we assume, the tasks we assign, are guided by both practical and theoretical knowledge, and our decisions can be more effective if that knowledge is explicit. A familiarity with what is known about writing, and about teaching writing, can therefore help us to reflect on our assumptions and enable us to approach current teaching methods with an informed and critical eye.

This chapter provides an overview of how different conceptions of writing and learning influence teaching practices in L2 classrooms. For clarity I will present these conceptions under different headings, but it would be wrong to understand them as core dichotomies. The approaches discussed represent available options which can be translated into classroom practices in many different ways and combinations. Together they offer a picture of current L2 writing instruction.

Reflection 1.1

Spend a few minutes to reflect on your own experiences as a writing teacher. (a) What are the most important things you want students to learn from your classes? (b) What kinds of activities do you use? (c) Do you think an understanding of different ideas about writing and teaching could help you to become a better teacher? (d) Why?

Guiding concepts in L2 writing teaching

A number of theories supporting teachers' efforts to understand L2 writing and learning have developed since EFL/ESL writing first emerged as a distinctive area of scholarship in the 1980s. In most cases each has been enthusiastically taken up, translated into appropriate methodologies, and put to work in classrooms. Yet each also has typically been seen as another piece in the jigsaw, an additional perspective to illuminate what learners need to learn and what teachers need to provide for effective writing instruction. So, while often treated as historically evolving movements (e.g., Raimes, 1991), it would be wrong to see each theory growing out of and replacing the last. They are more accurately seen as complementary and overlapping perspectives, representing potentially compatible means of understanding the complex reality of writing. It is helpful therefore to understand these theories as curriculum options, each organizing L2 writing teaching around a different focus:

- language structures
- text functions
- themes or topics
- creative expression
- composing processes
- content
- genre and contexts of writing

Few teachers adopt and strictly follow just one of these orientations in their classrooms. Instead, they tend to adopt an eclectic range of methods that represent several perspectives, accommodating their practices to the constraints of their teaching situations and their beliefs about how students learn to write. But although the "pure" application of a particular theory is quite rare, it is common for one to predominate in how teachers conceptualize their work and organize what they do in their classrooms (Cumming, 2003).

Teachers therefore tend to recognize and draw on a number of approaches but typically show a preference for one of them. So, even though they rarely constitute distinct classroom approaches, it is helpful to examine each conception separately to discover more clearly what each tells us about writing and how it can support our teaching.

Reflection 1.2

Which of the curriculum orientations previously listed are you most familiar with? Can you identify one that best fits your own experience of teaching or learning to write in a second language? Might some orientations be more appropriate for some teaching-learning situations than others?

Focus on language structures

One way to look at writing is to see it as marks on a page or a screen, a coherent arrangement of words, clauses, and sentences, structured according to a system of rules. Conceptualizing L2 writing in this way directs attention to writing as a product and encourages a focus on formal text units or grammatical features of texts. In this view, learning to write in a foreign or second language mainly involves linguistic knowledge and the vocabulary choices, syntactic patterns, and cohesive devices that comprise the essential building blocks of texts.

This orientation was born from the marriage of structural linguistics and the behaviorist learning theories of second language teaching that were dominant in the 1960s (Silva, 1990). Essentially, writing is seen as a product constructed from the writer's command of grammatical and lexical knowledge, and writing development is considered to be the result of imitating and manipulating models provided by the teacher. For many who adopt this view, writing is regarded as an extension of grammar – a means of reinforcing language patterns through habit formation and testing learners' ability to produce well-formed sentences. For others, writing is an intricate structure that can only be learned by developing the ability to manipulate lexis and grammar.

An emphasis on language structure as a basis for writing teaching is typically a four-stage process:

1. *Familiarization*: Learners are taught certain grammar and vocabulary, usually through a text.

Table 1.1: *A substitution table*

		types kinds classes categories		: A, B, and C. . These are A, B, and C. are A, B, and C.
There are The	Y		of X	
X	Consists of Can be divided into classes	Y	categories classes kinds types	. These are A, B, and C. : A, B, and C.
A, B, and C are	kinds types categories	of X.		

Source: Hamp-Lyons and Heasley, 1987: 23

2. ***Controlled writing***: Learners manipulate fixed patterns, often from substitution tables.
3. ***Guided writing***: Learners imitate model texts.
4. ***Free writing***: Learners use the patterns they have developed to write an essay, letter, and so forth.

Texts are often regarded as a series of appropriate grammatical structures, and so instruction may employ "slot and filler" frameworks in which sentences with different meanings can be generated by varying the words in the slots. Writing is rigidly controlled through guided compositions where learners are given short texts and asked to fill in gaps, complete sentences, transform tenses or personal pronouns, and complete other exercises that focus students on achieving accuracy and avoiding errors. A common application of this is the substitution table (Table 1.1) which provides models for students and allows them to generate risk-free sentences.

The structural orientation thus emphasizes writing as combinations of lexical and syntactic forms and good writing as the demonstration of knowledge of these forms and of the rules used to create texts. Accuracy and clear exposition are considered the main criteria of good writing, while the actual communicative content, the *meaning*, is left to be dealt with later. Teaching writing predominantly involves developing learners' skills in producing fixed patterns, and responding to writing means identifying and correcting problems in the student's control of the language system. Many of these techniques are widely used today in writing classes at lower levels of language proficiency for building vocabulary, scaffolding writing development, and increasing the confidence of novice writers.

Reflection 1.3

Consider your own writing teaching practices or your experiences of writing as a student. Do they include elements of approaches that emphasize language structures? Can such approaches be effective in developing writing? In what situations might they be a useful response to student needs?

Although many L2 students learn to write in this way, a structural orientation can create serious problems. One drawback is that formal patterns are often presented as short fragments which tend to be based on the intuitions of materials writers rather than the analyses of real texts. This not only hinders students from developing their writing beyond a few sentences, but can also mislead or confuse them when they have to write in other situations. Nor is it easy to see how a focus restricted to grammar can lead to better writing. Research has tried to measure students' writing improvement through their increased use of formal features such as relative clauses or the "syntactic complexity" of their texts (e.g., Hunt, 1983). Syntactic complexity and grammatical accuracy, however, are not the only features of writing improvement and may not even be the best measures of good writing. Most teachers are familiar with students who can construct accurate sentences and yet are unable to produce appropriate written texts, while fewer errors in an essay may simply reveal a reluctance to take risks, rather than indicate progress.

More seriously, the goal of writing instruction can never be just training in explicitness and accuracy because written texts are always a response to a particular communicative setting. No feature can be a universal marker of good writing because good writing is always contextually variable. Writers always draw on their knowledge of their readers and similar texts to decide both what to say and how to say it, aware that different forms express different relationships and meanings. Conversely, readers always draw on their linguistic and contextual assumptions to recover these meanings from texts, and this is confirmed in the large literature on knowledge-based inferencing in reading comprehension (e.g., Barnett, 1989).

For these reasons, few L2 writing teachers now see writing *only* as surface forms. But it is equally unhelpful to see language as irrelevant to learning to write. Control over surface features is crucial, and students need an understanding of how words, sentences, and larger discourse structures can shape and express the meanings they want to convey. Most teachers therefore include formal elements in their courses, but they also look beyond language structures to ensure that students don't just know how to write grammatically correct texts, but also how to apply this knowledge for particular purposes and contexts.

Reflection 1.4

Can you imagine any circumstances when you might focus on language structures in a writing class? Are there ways you might be able to adapt this focus to help students express their meanings?

Focus on text functions

While L2 students obviously need an understanding of appropriate grammar and vocabulary when learning to write in English, writing is obviously not *only* these things. If language structures are to be part of a writing course, then we need principled reasons for choosing which patterns to teach and how they can be used effectively. An important principle here is to relate structures to meanings, making language *use* a criteria for teaching materials. This introduces the idea that particular language *forms* perform certain communicative *functions* and that students can be taught the functions most relevant to their needs. Functions are the *means* for achieving the *ends* (or purposes) of writing. This orientation is sometimes labeled "current-traditional rhetoric" or simply a "functional approach" and is influential where L2 students are being prepared for academic writing at college or university.

One aim of this focus is to help students develop effective paragraphs through the creation of topic sentences, supporting sentences, and transitions, and to develop different types of paragraphs. Students are guided to produce connected sentences according to prescribed formulas and tasks which tend to focus on form to positively reinforce model writing patterns. As with sentence-level activities, composing tasks often include so-called free writing methods, which largely involve learners reordering sentences in scrambled paragraphs, selecting appropriate sentences to complete gapped paragraphs and write paragraphs from provided information.

Clearly, this orientation is heavily influenced by the structural model described above, as paragraphs are seen almost as syntactic units like sentences, in which writers can fit particular functional units into given slots. From this it is a short step to apply the same principles to entire essays. Texts can then be seen as composed of structural entities such as

Unit 1	Structure and cohesion
Unit 2	Description: Process and procedure
Unit 3	Description: Physical
Unit 4	Narrative
Unit 5	Definitions
Unit 6	Exemplification
Unit 7	Classification
Unit 8	Comparison and contrast
Unit 9	Cause and effect
Unit 10	Generalization, qualification, and certainty
Unit 11	Interpretation of data
Unit 12	Discussion
Unit 13	Drawing conclusions
Unit 14	Reports: studies and research
Unit 15	Surveys and questionnaires

Source: Adapted from Jordan, 1990.

Figure 1.1: A contents page from a functionally oriented textbook.

Introduction-Body-Conclusion, and particular organizational patterns such as narration, description, and exposition are described and taught. Typically, courses are organized according to common functions of written English, such as the example from a popular academic writing textbook shown in Figure 1.1.

Each unit typically contains comprehension checks on a model text. These are followed by exercises that draw attention to the language used to express the target function and that develop students' abilities to use them in their writing. Such tasks include developing an outline into an essay, or imitating the patterns of a parallel text in their own essay. Again, these offer good scaffolding for writing by supporting L2 learners' development. An example is shown in Figure 1.2.

While meaning is involved in these tasks and instructional strategies, they are essentially concerned with disembodied patterns rather than writing activities that have any meaning or purpose for students. An exclusive focus on form or function means that writing is detached from the practical purposes and personal experiences of the writer. Methods such as guided compositions are based on the assumption that texts are objects that can be taught independently of particular contexts, writers, or readers, and that by following certain rules, writers can fully represent their intended meanings. Writing, however, is more than a matter of arranging elements in the best order, and writing instruction is more than assisting learners to remember and execute these patterns. An awareness of this has led teachers to make efforts to introduce the writer into their models of writing and writing teaching,

There are basically two main ways to organise a cause and effect essay: "block" organization and "chain" organization. In *block organization*, you first discuss all of the causes as a block (in one, two, three or more paragraphs, depending on the number of causes). Then you discuss all of the effects together as a block. In *chain organization*, you discuss a first cause and its effect, a second cause and its effect, a third cause and its effect. Usually, each new cause is the result of the preceding effect. Discussion of each new cause and its effect begins with a new paragraph. All the paragraphs are linked in a "chain."

BLOCK	CHAIN
Introduction	Introduction
First cause	First cause
Second cause	Effect
Transition paragraph	Second Cause
First effect	Effect
Second effect	Third Cause
Third effect	Effect
Conclusion	Conclusion

Source: Adapted from Oshima and Hogue, 1999: 130–1.

Figure 1.2: A paragraph organization description.

and it is to orientations that highlight writers to which we turn in the next section.

Reflection 1.5
What arguments would persuade you to adopt a Functional orientation to your teaching?

Focus on creative expression

The third teaching orientation takes the writer, rather than form, as the point of departure. Following L1 composition theorists such as Elbow (1998) and Murray (1985), many writing teachers from liberal arts backgrounds see their classroom goals as fostering L2 students' expressive abilities, encouraging them to find their own voices to produce writing that is fresh and spontaneous. These classrooms are organized around students' personal experiences and opinions, and writing is considered a creative act of self-discovery. This can help generate self-awareness of the writer's social position and literate possibilities (Friere, 1974) as well as facilitate "clear thinking, effective relating, and satisfying self-expression" (Moffett,

1982: 235). A writing teacher in Japan characterized his approach like this:

I try to challenge the students to be creative in expressing themselves. Students learn to express their feelings and opinions so that others can understand what they think and like to do. I've heard that prospective employers sometimes ask students what they have learned at university, and that some students have showed them their poems. [quoted in Cumming, 2003]

Reflection 1.6
Can you recall an experience when you wrote a creative text, perhaps a poem or short story? Do you feel that this was helpful in developing your skills as a writer more generally? In what ways?

From this perspective, writing is learned, not taught, so writing instruction is nondirective and personal. Writing is a way of sharing personal meanings and writing courses emphasize the power of the individual to construct his or her own views on a topic. Teachers see their role as simply to provide students with the space to make their own meanings within a positive and cooperative environment. Because writing is a developmental process, they try to avoid imposing their views, offering models, or suggesting responses to topics beforehand. Instead, they seek to stimulate the writer's ideas through pre-writing tasks, such as journal writing and parallel texts. Because writing is an act of discovering meaning, a willingness to engage with students' assertions is crucial, and response is a central means to initiate and guide ideas (e.g., Straub, 2000). This orientation further urges teachers to respond to the ideas that learners produce, rather than dwell on formal errors (Murray, 1985). Students have considerable opportunities for writing and exercises may attend to features such as style, wordiness, clichés, active versus passive voice, and so on. In contrast to the rigid practice of a more form-oriented approach, writers are urged to be creative and to take chances through free writing.

Figure 1.3 shows typical writing rubrics in this approach. Both rubrics ask students to read personal writing extracts, respond to them as readers, and then to use them as a stimulus to write about their own experiences.

Expressivism is an important approach as it encourages writers to explore their beliefs, engage with the ideas of others, and connect with readers. Yet it leans heavily on an asocial view of the writer, and its ideology of individualism may disadvantage second language students from cultures that place a different value on self-expression (see Chapter 2). In addition,

In his article, Green tells us that Bob Love was saved because "some kind and caring people" helped him to get speech therapy. Is there any example of "kind and caring people" you have witnessed in your life or in the lives of those around you? Tell who these people are and exactly what they did that showed their kindness.

Violet's aunt died for her country even though she never wore a uniform or fired a bullet. Write about what values or people you would sacrifice your life for if you were pushed to do so.

Figure 1.3: Essay topics from an expressivist textbook.

it is difficult to extract from the approach any clear principles from which to teach and evaluate "good writing." It simply assumes that all writers have a similar innate creative potential and can learn to express themselves through writing if their originality and spontaneity are allowed to flourish. Writing is seen as springing from self-discovery guided by writing on topics of potential interest to writers and, as a result, the approach is likely to be most successful in the hands of teachers who themselves write creatively. Murray's (1985) *A writer teaches writing*, for instance, provides a good account of expressivist methods, but also suggests the importance of the teacher's own personal insights in the process.

So despite its influence in L1 writing classrooms, expressivism has been treated cautiously in L2 contexts. Although many L2 students have learned successfully through this approach, others may experience difficulties, as it tends to neglect the cultural backgrounds of learners, the social consequences of writing, and the purposes of communication in the real world, where writing matters.

Focus on the writing process

Like the expressive orientation, the process approach to writing teaching emphasizes the writer as an independent producer of texts, but it goes further to address the issue of what teachers should do to help learners perform a writing task. The numerous incarnations of this perspective are consistent in recognizing basic cognitive processes as central to writing activity and in stressing the need to develop students' abilities to plan, define a rhetorical problem, and propose and evaluate solutions.

Reflection 1.7
What cognitive skills might be involved in the writing process? What methods may help students to develop their abilities to carry out a writing task?

> **Selection** of topic: by teacher and/or students
> **Prewriting**: brainstorming, collecting data, note taking, outlining, etc.
> **Composing**: getting ideas down on paper
> **Response to draft:** teacher/peers respond to ideas, organization, and style
> **Revising:** reorganizing, style, adjusting to readers, refining ideas
> **Response to revisions:** teacher/peers respond to ideas, organization, and style
> **Proofreading and editing:** checking and correcting form, layout, evidence, etc.
> **Evaluation:** teacher evaluates progress over the process
> **Publishing:** by class circulation or presentation, noticeboards, Website, etc.
> **Follow-up tasks:** to address weaknesses

Figure 1.4: A process model of writing instruction.

Probably the model of writing processes most widely accepted by L2 writing teachers is the original planning-writing-reviewing framework established by Flower and Hayes (Flower, 1989; Flower and Hayes, 1981). This sees writing as a "non-linear, exploratory, and generative process whereby writers discover and reformulate their ideas as they attempt to approximate meaning" (Zamel, 1983: 165). As Figure 1.4 shows, planning, drafting, revising, and editing do not occur in a neat linear sequence, but are recursive, interactive, and potentially simultaneous, and all work can be reviewed, evaluated, and revised, even before any text has been produced at all. At any point the writer can jump backward or forward to any of these activities: returning to the library for more data, revising the plan to accommodate new ideas, or rewriting for readability after peer feedback.

Reflection 1.8
Consider the last longish piece of writing that you did. It may have been an assignment for a course, a report, or a piece of personal writing. Can you identify the stages you went through to get the text to "publishable" or public standard? Was the process similar to that sketched in Figure 1.4?

This basic model of writing has been elaborated to further describe what goes on at each stage of the process and to integrate cognitive with social factors more centrally (Flower, 1994). Building on this work, Bereiter and Scardamalia (1987) have argued that we need at least two process models to account for the differences in processing complexity of skilled and novice writers. They label these as knowledge-telling and knowledge-transforming models. The first addresses the fact that novice writers plan less than experts, revise less often and less extensively, have limited goals, and are mainly concerned with generating content. The latter shows how skilled writers use the writing task to analyze problems, reflect on the task, and set goals to actively rework thoughts to change both their text and ideas. For writing teachers the model helps explain the difficulties their L2 students sometimes experience because of task complexity and lack of topic knowledge. Its emphasis on reflective thought also stresses the need for students to participate in a variety of cognitively challenging writing tasks to develop their skills and the importance of feedback and revision in the process of transforming both content and expression.

A significant number of writing teachers adopt a process orientation as the main focus of their courses and the approach has had a major impact on writing research and teaching in North America. The teacher's role is to guide students through the writing process, avoiding an emphasis on form to help them develop strategies for generating, drafting, and refining ideas. This is achieved through setting pre-writing activities to generate ideas about content and structure, encouraging brainstorming and outlining, requiring multiple drafts, giving extensive feedback, seeking text level revisions, facilitating peer responses, and delaying surface corrections until the final editing (Raimes, 1992). The teaching strategies developed to facilitate process goals have extended to most teaching contexts and there are few who have not employed teacher-student conferences, problem-based assignments, journal writing, group discussions, or portfolio assessments in their classes.

A priority of teachers in this orientation therefore is to develop their students' metacognitive awareness of their processes, that is, their ability to reflect on the strategies they use to write. In addition to composing and revising strategies, such an orientation places great emphasis on responses to writing. A response is potentially one of the most influential texts in a process writing class, and the point at which the teacher's intervention is most obvious and perhaps most crucial. Not only does this individual attention play an important part in motivating learners, it is also the point at which overt correction and explicit language teaching are most likely to occur. Response is crucial in assisting learners to move through the stages of the writing process and various means of providing feedback are used, including teacher-student conferences, peer response, audiotaped feedback, and reformulation (see Chapter 7). Nevertheless, the effectiveness of error correction and grammar teaching in assisting learners to improve their writing remains controversial in this model (Ferris, 1997; Truscott, 1996).

Reflection 1.9

How might you persuade a process adherent of the potential advantages of providing students with grammatical and text information about the texts they are asked to write? Are you persuaded by these reasons? At what stages and in what ways might grammar best be introduced?

Despite considerable research into writing processes, however, we still do not have a comprehensive idea of how learners go about a writing task or how they learn to write. It is clear that cognition is a central element of the process, and researchers are now more aware of the complexity of planning and editing activities, the influence of task, and the value of examining what writers actually do when they write. But although these understandings can contribute to the ways we teach, process models are hampered by small-scale, often contradictory studies and the difficulties of getting inside writers' heads to report unconscious processing. They are currently unable to tell us why writers make certain choices or how they actually make the cognitive transition to a *knowledge-transforming* model, nor do they spell out what occurs in the intervening stages or whether the process is the same for all learners. While Berieter and Scardalamaia's idea of multiple processing models opens the door to a clearer understanding of the writing process, no complete model exists yet that allows us to predict the relative difficulty for students of particular writing tasks or topics or their likely progress given certain kinds of instruction (Grabbe, 2003).

It also remains unclear whether an exclusive emphasis on psychological factors in writing will provide the whole picture, either theoretically or pedagogically. Forces outside the individual that help guide the writer to define problems, frame solutions, and shape the text also need to be considered (Bizzell, 1992; Faigley, 1986). As I argued at the beginning of this chapter, each orientation illuminates just one aspect of writing; the process of writing is a rich amalgam of elements of which cognition is only one. Process approaches overemphasize "the cognitive relationship between the writer and the writer's internal world" (Swales, 1990: 220) and as a result they fail to offer any clear perspective on the social nature of writing or on the role of language and text structure in effective written communication. Encouraging students to make their own meanings and find their own text forms does not provide them with clear guidelines on how to construct the different kinds of texts they have to write.

I have devoted a great deal of attention to process teaching methods and the theories that underpin them as these represent the dominant approach in L2 writing teaching today. Once again, however, it is necessary to look beyond a single approach. Process theories alone cannot help us to confidently advise students on their writing, and this is perhaps one reason why there is little evidence to show that process methods alone lead to significantly better writing. Quite simply, equipping novice writers with the strategies of good writers does not necessarily lead to improvement (Polio, 2001). Students not only need help in learning how to write, but also in understanding how texts are shaped by topic, audience, purpose, and cultural norms (Hyland, 2002).

Reflection 1.10

How do you think the "social factors" that influence writing might be incorporated into a process orientation? Think of a writing task that might achieve this. *brainstorming?*

Focus on content

A fifth way of conceptualizing EFL/ESL writing teaching is in reference to substantive content what students are required to write *about*. Typically this involves a set of themes or topics of interest that establish a coherence and purpose for the course or that set out the sequence of key areas of subject matter that students will address (see Mohan, 1986). Students will have some personal knowledge of these themes and will be able to write meaningfully about them. This is a popular organizing principle for L2 writing courses and textbooks for students of all ages and abilities, and many teachers base their courses on topics students select themselves. In most cases such courses rarely focus exclusively on content and, in fact, represent interesting ways teachers can integrate and combine different conceptualizations of writing.

Reflection 1.11

teacher self-stories

Think of a set of topics or themes that might provide the basis of a writing course for a group of L2 students you are familiar with. What writing tasks and research issues do these topics suggest? What functions might students find useful to complete these writing activities?

research → *spider grams questions*

personal autobiography *self knowledge* *(thought provoking)*
stories/drama *based on*
journaling *photos topic*
poetry *(memories)*

family childhood love + relationships education school days hol days travel

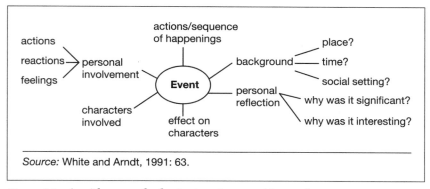

Source: White and Arndt, 1991: 63.

Figure 1.5: A spidergram for brainstorming a writing task.

Themes and topics frequently form the basis of process courses, where writing activities are often organized around social issues such as pollution, relationships, stress, juvenile crime, smoking, and so on. L2 students may be disadvantaged in such classrooms as they do not typically have a strong familiarity with either the topics or the types of texts they have to write. But these integrated writing activities may be useful to new migrants or students in academic preparation programs and can be important in encouraging learners to think about issues in new ways. Teachers may need to help learners acquire the appropriate cognitive *schema* (pl. *schemata*) or knowledge of topics and vocabulary they will need to create an effective text. Schema development exercises usually include reading for ideas in parallel texts, reacting to photographs, and various brainstorming tasks to generate ideas for writing and organizing texts. Figure 1.5 shows a spidergram or mind map used to stimulate ideas for an account of a personal experience. This kind of activity is useful for building a list of issues, and also for identifying relationships between them and prioritizing what it will be important to write about.

Clearly content-oriented courses can be tailored to students at different proficiency levels by varying the amount of information provided. At lower levels, much of the content can be supplied to reduce students' difficulties in generating and organizing material, while at more advanced levels students are often required to collaborate in collecting and sharing information as a basis for composing. Students may be asked to conduct research of some kind, either in the library, on the Internet, or through the use of interviews and questionnaires, so teachers may find themselves providing assistance with data collection techniques. Group work is frequently a key element of these classes and cooperation among students in generating ideas, collecting information, focusing priorities, and structuring the way they will organize their texts provides practical purposes for genuine communication.

A content orientation can also form the basis of courses that focus more on language structures and functions. Such courses help students to generate, develop, and organize their ideas on a given topic in ways similar to those discussed above for courses with process leanings. Students are then typically presented with language structures and vocabulary items directly relevant to the topic, which they then practice through a series of exercises. There may follow an introduction and explanation of the rhetorical patterns, which may be useful to students as a framework for expressing their ideas, developing learners' awareness of functions such as explanation and cause and effect described earlier. The two tasks shown in Figure 1.6 illustrate the different kinds of approaches to texts in the process and structural orientations to L2 writing instruction.

It should be clear that content-oriented methods tend to rely heavily on reading and exploit the close relationship between writing and reading in

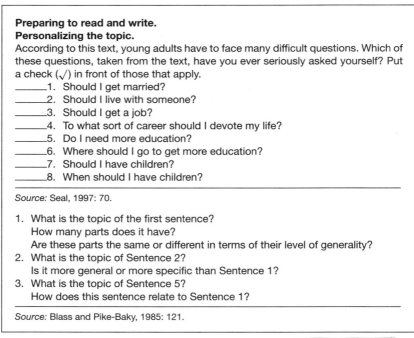

Preparing to read and write.
Personalizing the topic.
According to this text, young adults have to face many difficult questions. Which of these questions, taken from the text, have you ever seriously asked yourself? Put a check (√) in front of those that apply.
_____1. Should I get married?
_____2. Should I live with someone?
_____3. Should I get a job?
_____4. To what sort of career should I devote my life?
_____5. Do I need more education?
_____6. Where should I go to get more education?
_____7. Should I have children?
_____8. When should I have children?

Source: Seal, 1997: 70.

1. What is the topic of the first sentence?
   How many parts does it have?
   Are these parts the same or different in terms of their level of generality?
2. What is the topic of Sentence 2?
   Is it more general or more specific than Sentence 1?
3. What is the topic of Sentence 5?
   How does this sentence relate to Sentence 1?

Source: Blass and Pike-Baky, 1985: 121.

Figure 1.6: Exercises exploiting a reading text in topic-oriented process and structural materials.

L2 literacy development. Content-oriented courses aim to give students the skills and confidence to read texts efficiently as a basis for producing their own texts, but this relationship is not restricted to content alone. Reading provides input for both content and the appropriate means of its expression – a positive link that reflects the wider role of reading in developing composing skills.

Reflection 1.12

How might reading contribute to the development of L2 writing skills in the classroom setting? List some of the advantages that might accrue to readers.

gain vocab., structures, ideas

Research suggests that second language writing skills cannot be acquired successfully by practice in writing alone but also need to be supported with extensive reading (Krashen, 1993). Whether assigned or voluntary, reading has been shown to be a positive influence on composing skills at various stages of proficiency. This is because both processes involve the individual in constructing meaning though the application of complex cognitive and linguistic abilities that draw on problem-solving skills and the activation of existing knowledge of both structure and content (Carson and Leki, 1993; Grabe, 2001). Reading may yield for students new knowledge within a sub-ject area, but more importantly it provides them with the rhetorical and structural knowledge they need to develop, modify, and activate schemata which are invaluable when writing. In other words, extensive reading can fur-nish a great deal of tacit knowledge of conventional features of written texts, including, grammar, vocabulary, organizational patterns, interactional de-vices, and so on. Therefore, what students read – particularly the relevance of the specific genres to which they are exposed – are important elements.

This last point draws attention to the fact that literacy acquisition rarely occurs in a vacuum. Writing instruction typically is geared toward some end as students will employ their writing skills for various academic or professional purposes. In fact, although the different types of courses dis-cussed above all draw on content to some extent, "content-based" has come to mean an approach that focuses on the requirements of particular subject areas. In other words, such courses focus on the language, composing skills and specific text conventions associated with a particular domain and its "content" or subject matter. In this way writing instruction seeks to be motivating by focusing on contexts and content relevant and significant to learners.

Such courses may place considerable emphasis on preparing students to engage effectively in their target academic or professional communities, and most involve collaboration with students and/or subject teachers to draw on their specialist knowledge. In some cases this collaboration may entail the writing teacher loaning his or her expertise to a subject department to advise staff or instruct students in Writing Across the Curriculum (WAC) classes (Bazerman and Russell, 1994). In L2 contexts, collaboration more frequently involves a contribution by the subject specialists to the writing class, either through team teaching or advice on content (Dudley-Evans and St John, 1998). Perhaps most often there is a reciprocity between the two specialists in "linked courses" where a specialist writing course is integrated with the activities of a specialist content course by jointly planning tasks and coordinating instruction (Benesch, 2001). Once again, however, although content provides one orientation of the course, teachers typically draw on structural, functional, or process methods in its delivery, and frequently draw on a genre focus to highlighting the rhetorical structure of written texts.

Focus on genre

Teachers who take a genre orientation to writing instruction look beyond subject content, composing processes and textual forms to see writing as attempts to communicate with readers. They are concerned with teaching learners how to use language patterns to accomplish coherent, purposeful prose. The central belief here is that we don't just *write*, we write *something to achieve some purpose*: it is a way of getting something done. To get things done, to tell a story, request an overdraft, craft a love letter, describe a technical process and so on, we follow certain social conventions for organizing messages because we want our readers to recognize our purpose. These abstract, socially recognized ways of using language for particular purposes are called *genres*.

In the classroom, genre teachers focus on texts, but this is not the narrow focus of a disembodied grammar. Instead, linguistic patterns are seen as pointing to contexts beyond the page, implying a range of social constraints and choices that operate on writers in a particular context. The writer is seen as having certain goals and intentions, certain relationships to his or her readers, and certain information to convey, and the forms of a text are resources used to accomplish these. In sum, the importance of a genre orientation is that it incorporates discourse and contextual aspects of language use that may be neglected when attending to structures, functions, or processes alone. This means that it can not only address the needs of ESL writers to compose texts for particular readers, but it can also draw the teacher into considering how texts actually work as communication.

Reflection 1.13

Look at this list of genres, partly taken from Cook (1989: 95). Can you see any similarities and differences between them? Try to group them into categories in different ways, for example, spoken versus written, similar purposes, type of audience, main grammar patterns, key vocabulary, formality, and so on. You will find that genres often have things in common but are distinct in various ways.

sales letter	joke	anecdote	label	poem	memo
inventory	advertisement	report	note	chat	seminar
essay	manifesto	toast	argument	song	novel
notice	biography	sermon	consultation	jingle	article
warrant	ticket	lecture	manual	will	conversation
menu	prescription	telegram	editorial	sign	film review

Classroom perspectives on genre largely draw on the theory of systemic functional linguistics originally developed by Michael Halliday (e.g., Halliday, 1994; Halliday and Hasan, 1989). This theory addresses the relationship between language and its social functions and sets out to show how language is a system from which users make choices to express meanings. Halliday argues that we have developed very specific ways of using language to accomplish our goals, which means that texts are related to social contexts and to other texts. Broadly, when a set of texts share the same purpose, they will often share the same structure, and thus they belong to the same genre. So genres are resources for getting things done, and we all have a repertoire of appropriate responses we can call on for recurring situations, from shopping lists to job applications.

Most simply, Martin (1992) defines genre as a goal-oriented, staged social process. Genres are social processes because members of a culture interact to achieve them; they are goal-oriented because they have evolved to achieve things; and staged because meanings are made in steps and it usually takes writers more than one step to reach their goals. By setting out the stages, or moves, of valued genres, teachers can provide students with an explicit grammar of linguistic choices, both within and beyond the sentence, to produce texts that seem well-formed and appropriate to readers. All texts

Table 1.2: *Some Factual genres*

Genre	Purpose
• *recount*	to reconstruct past experiences by retelling events in original sequence
• *procedure*	to show how processes or events are accomplished – how something is done
• *description*	to give an account of imagined or factual events and phenomena
• *report*	to present factual information about a class of things, usually by classifying them and then describing their characteristics
• *explanation*	to give reasons for a state of affairs or a judgment

Source: Butt et al., 2000; Martin, 1989.

Stage	An Exposition Example	Stage	A Recount Example
Thesis	A good teacher needs to be understanding to all children.	**Orientation**	On Tuesday we went on a harbor cruise.
Argument	He or she must be fair and reasonable. The teacher must work at a sensible pace. The teacher also needs to speak with a clear voice so the children can Understand.	**Events in Chronological Order**	We went underneath the harbor bridge and then we went past some submarines. When we got to Clifton Gardens we had a picnic After we had finished we played on the climbings. Then Mr. Robinson came over and said Mr. Moses was giving out frozen oranges. Then after we finished that we went home.
Conclusion	That's what I think a good teacher should be like.	**Personal Comment (optional)**	It was a nice day out.

Source: Board of Studies, 1998b: 287.

Figure 1.7: Some factual genres.

can therefore be described in terms of both form and function, that is, how their elements are organized for making meanings and the purposes this serves. Some core "factual genres" are listed in Table 1.2.

Writing instruction begins with the purposes for communicating, then moves to the stages of a text which can express these purposes. Teachers can help students to distinguish between different genres and to write them more effectively by a careful study of their structures. Figure 1.7 shows how even primary school children can distinguish texts by their structure.

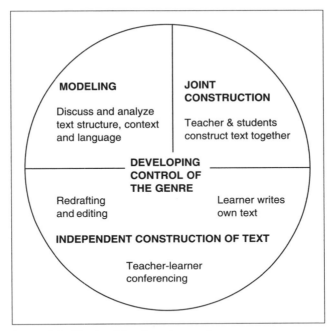

Figure 1.8: The teaching learning cycle.

In the writing classroom, teachers following a genre orientation draw on the work of the Russian psychologist Vygotsky (1978) and its interpretation by Bruner (1986). This stresses the view that learning occurs best when learners engage in tasks that are within their Zone of Proximal Development (ZPD), the area between what they can do independently and what they can do with assistance. Learning evolves from verbal interaction and task negotiation with a more knowledgeable person, and the teacher has a central role in "scaffolding" this development.

The method used to achieve this is a process of contextualizing-modeling-negotiating-constructing, which is usually presented as a cycle (Figure 1.8). At the beginning of this learning cycle direct instruction is crucial, as the learner gradually assimilates the task demands and procedures for constructing the genre effectively. The teacher here adopts a highly interventionist role, ensuring that students are able to understand and reproduce the typical rhetorical patterns they need to express their meanings. At later stages learners require more autonomy. Importantly, writing is the outcome of activity, rather than an activity itself. The classroom is characterized by talk, by many kinds of writing, and by the development of a linguistic *metalanguage* by which students can describe and control the structure and grammatical features of the texts they write. Grammar is important, but presented as a way of giving learners the language they need to construct central genres and to reflect on how language is used to accomplish this.

Genre pedagogy is underpinned by the belief that learning should be based on explicit awareness of language, rather than through experiment and exploration, so teachers provide students with opportunities to develop their writing through analyzing "expert" texts. Genres are both what students actively do with language and how they come to understand the ways it works; however, this "reproductive" element has been criticized as running the risk of a static, decontextualized pedagogy. This is, of course, a danger of all pedagogies, but untrained or unimaginative teachers may fail to acknowledge variation and choice in writing and so neglect the important step of contextualizing the language so that genre models are presented as rigid templates and forms represented as linguistic abstractions. When this happens, the explicit teaching of genres can impose restrictive formulae which can shackle creativity to prescribed structures (Sawyer and Watson, 1987). Students might then regard genres as sets of rules, a "how-to-do" list, or what Freadman (1994: 46) calls "a recipe theory of genre."

There is therefore a tension between expression and repression in genre teaching that is not fully resolved. It is clear, however, that learners must know how to employ conventional patterns and the circumstances where they can change them as much as they need ways of drafting and editing their work. For teachers it is important to foster creativity while acknowledging the ways language is conventionally used to express meaning.

Toward a synthesis: Process, purpose, and context

The different perspectives outlined above provide teachers with curriculum options, or complementary alternatives for designing courses that have implications for teaching and learning. These orientations are summarized in Table 1.3.

Reflection 1.14

Collect some L2 writing textbooks or in-house materials. Do they follow one of these orientations or do they combine several? Does one predominate in the overall approach or in individual tasks? Which approach currently has the most impact in your country or institution?

Table 1.3: *Summary of the principal orientations to L2 writing teaching*

Orientation	Emphasis	Goals	Main pedagogic techniques
Structure	Language form	• Grammatical accuracy • Vocabulary building • L2 proficiency	Controlled composition, gap-fill, substitution, error avoidance, indirect assessment, practice of rhetorical patterns
Function	Language use	Paragraph and text organization patterns	Free writing, reordering, gap-fill, imitation of parallel texts, writing from tables and graphs
Expressivist	Writer	• Individual creativity • Self-discovery	Reading, pre-writing, journal writing, multiple drafting, and peer critiques
Process	Writer	Control of technique	Brain-storming, planning, multiple drafting, peer collaboration, delayed editing, portfolio assessment
Content	Subject matter	Writing through relevant content and reading	Extensive and intensive reading, group research projects, process or structure emphasis
Genre	Text and context	Control of rhetorical structure of specific text-types	Modeling-negotiation-construction cycle • Rhetorical consciousness-raising

I have stressed that L2 writing classrooms are typically a mixture of more than one approach and that teachers frequently combine these orientations in imaginative and effective ways. Most commonly, however, these favor either a process or genre orientation and we should not gloss over the protracted – and often bitterly argued – debate on these two positions. This debate boils down to the relative merits of predominantly text-focused pedagogies, which emphasize the social nature of writing, and more writer-centered process methods, which stress its more cognitive aspects. By laying out the main attributes of these two orientations side-by-side, however, it can be seen how the strengths of one might complement the weaknesses of the other (Table 1.4).

Although this stark opposition of the two orientations oversimplifies far more complex classroom situations, it also helps to show how one might complement the other. The conflict between process and product can only be damaging to classroom practice, and the two are more usefully seen as supplementing and rounding each other out. Writing is a sociocognitive activity which involves skills in planning and drafting as well as knowledge of language, contexts, and audiences. An effective methodology for L2 writing teaching should therefore incorporate and extend the insights of the main orientations in the following ways:

• Broaden formal and functional orientations to include the social purposes behind forms

Table 1.4: *A comparison of genre and process orientations*

Attribute	Process	Genre
Main Idea	Writing is a thinking process	Writing is a social activity
	Concerned with the act of writing	Concerned with the final product
Teaching Focus	Emphasis on creative writer	Emphasis on reader expectations and product
	How to produce and link ideas	How to express social purposes effectively
Advantages	Makes processes of writing transparent	Makes textual conventions transparent
	Provides basis for teaching	Contextualizes writing for audience and purpose
Disadvantages	Assumes L1 and L2 writing similar	Requires rhetorical understanding of texts
	Overlooks L2 language difficulties	Can result in prescriptive teaching of texts
	Insufficient attention to product	Can lead to overattention to written products
	Assumes all writing uses same processes	Undervalue skills needed to produce texts

- Locate the process concepts of strategy, schema, and metacognition in social contexts
- Respect students' needs for relevant content through stimulating readings and source materials
- Support genre pedagogies with strategies for planning, drafting, and revising texts
- Situate writing in a conception of audience and link it to broader social structures

In practice this means a synthesis to ensure that learners have an adequate understanding of the *processes* of text creation; the *purposes* of writing and how to express these in effective ways through formal and rhetorical text choices; and the *contexts* within which texts are composed and read and which give them meaning. While I have discussed processes and purposes already, it is worth considering context in a little more detail as it is central to understanding and teaching writing.

The notion of context echoes the belief in genre that writing does not take place outside particular communities and that the genres we teach should be seen as responses to the purposes of those communities, whether professional, academic, or social (Bruffee, 1986). Skilled writers are able to create successful texts by accurately predicting readers' background knowledge and anticipating what they are likely to expect from a particular piece of writing. In our own domains – our homes, workplaces, or classrooms – we are comfortable with the genres we write because we are familiar with them and have a good idea how to create texts that will connect with our readers. We are able to draw on a shared community schema to structure our writing so that our audience can process it easily. But this knowledge of readers and their needs may be lacking when we try to communicate in an unfamiliar situation, such as a new profession, a new discipline, or a foreign language.

Reflection 1.15

We all belong to several "communities" or groups that share certain communicative purposes and common genres. Note one community to which you belong and list the genres that it uses. Why are these genres important to this community?

Teachers in process classrooms, as mentioned earlier, try to bridge this gap between writer and reader by using pre-writing tasks that develop an understanding of vocabulary and topics. But schema knowledge is far richer than this and includes considerable knowledge of contexts, interpersonal relations, the roles of readers and writers, and how all these influence texts. We don't only know what to write about and how to express ourselves, but what to include and leave out, how formal or informal we can be, and when it is appropriate to use the genre at all. Schemata, in other words, are culturally sensitive; they reflect the ways that members of different communities think. This means teachers should help learners develop these sociocultural schemata by extending their knowledge of form, process, and content to the discourse communities within which they serve particular purposes.

The notion of *discourse community* is not entirely precise and tends to mean different things to different theorists. However, it tries to capture the idea of like-mindedness among writers and readers, sometimes called *membership*, which is essential for understanding the specialist background knowledge we use to encode and decode texts appropriately (e.g., Swales, 1990). It is a powerful concept in joining writers, texts, and readers together and suggests that an understanding of target communities is useful to those wishing to become members, including L2 learners. By understanding these communities and their writing, students are better able to "interpret, produce and critique the texts they have to write" (Johns, 1997: 19).

Reflection 1.16

We have all had experiences where our attempts to communicate with someone from another discourse community has failed, perhaps when discussing music with your child's piano teacher, your frozen computer with a technician, or a vague interest of some kind with an enthusiast. Think of a recent occasion when you have had an experience like this. What happened and why did misunderstanding arise? Compare it with an experience where communication was effortless. What was different about the two situations?

The notion of context also incorporates ideas from New Literacy Studies that writing (and reading) only make sense within wider social and cultural practices (e.g., Barton and Hamilton, 1998). Context is more than the interactions of particular writers and readers, it refers to how institutions, societies, and cultures themselves influence writing. Such an extended notion of context has four main implications:

1. It recognizes that different communities use different genres, conventions, and even varieties of English, and that not all writing has the same standards of acceptability.
2. It takes account of the way English is used as an international language between nonnative speakers, and, in many countries, as an intranational language with local norms and models.
3. It highlights the fact that because socially powerful institutions, such as education and the professions, support certain genres and conventions, these become dominant and possess greater prestige.
4. It helps learners to guard against devaluing their own writing and to see so-called superior forms of writing simply as other practices that are open, like others, to scrutiny and challenge.

A synthesis of different writing orientations therefore means taking the best of existing approaches and using them to more fully understand writing and learning to write. It suggests that, in the classroom, teachers should focus on increasing students' experiences of texts and reader expectations, as well as providing them with an understanding of writing processes, language forms, and genres. Finally, it means that we need to be sensitive to the practices and perceptions of writing that students bring to the classroom, and build on these so that they come to see writing as relative to particular groups and contexts. In this way students can understand the discourses they have to write, while not devaluing those of their own cultures and communities.

Summary and conclusion

While every act of writing is in a sense both personal and individual, it is also interactional and social, expressing a culturally recognized purpose, reflecting a particular kind of relationship, and acknowledging an engagement in a given community. This means that writing cannot be distilled down to a set of cognitive or technical abilities or a system of rules, and that learning to write in a second language is not simply a matter of opportunities to compose and revise. This chapter has looked at the main orientations to teaching writing to L2 students and has argued that teachers should draw on the best of what these theories offer. It has stressed that L2 writers bring five kinds of knowledge to create effective texts and these should be acknowledged in teaching:

- Content knowledge – of the ideas and concepts in the topic area the text will address
- System knowledge – of the syntax, lexis, and appropriate formal conventions needed
- Process knowledge – of how to prepare and carry out a writing task
- Genre knowledge – of communicative purposes of the genre and its value in particular contexts
- Context knowledge – of readers' expectations, cultural preferences, and related texts

[handwritten margin note: 5 kinds of know.]

A number of conclusions for teaching can be drawn from the perspectives presented in this chapter:

- Composing is nonlinear and goal-driven. Therefore, students may benefit from having a range of planning, writing, and revising strategies to draw on.
- Writing seeks to achieve purposes through socially recognized ways of using language called genres. Therefore, teachers should provide learners with a metalanguage for identifying genres and their structures, through analysis of authentic texts and modeling genre stages.
- Writing is a purposeful and communicative activity that responds to other people and other texts. Therefore, writing tasks should not simply emphasize formal accuracy and discrete aspects of language, but be situated in meaningful contexts with authentic purposes.
- Writing is often structured according to the demands and expectations of target discourse communities. Therefore, teachers need to provide tasks that encourage students to consider the reader's perspective by incorporating a range of real and simulated audience sources.

- Writing is differently endowed with authority and prestige, which sustain inequalities. Therefore, instruction should build on students' own language abilities, backgrounds, and expectations of writing to help them see prestigious discourses simply as other ways of making meanings.

Discussion questions and activities

1 One definition of writing is "the process whereby a person selects, develops, arranges, and expresses ideas in units of discourse." Do you agree with this definition? Does it imply a particular orientation to teaching L2 writing? How would you define writing?

2 Look again at the sections on the Process and Genre approaches. How do you think each might answer these fundamental questions about teaching writing?
   - What is involved in the process of becoming a writer?
   - What are our criteria for good writing and how do we communicate these to learners?
   - How should teachers intervene in students' writing?

3 The process and genre approaches are often presented as polar extremes. Can you think of ways that they might be seen as complementary rather than as incompatible?

4 How important is the choice of textbook in influencing the orientation to teaching writing you might adopt in your classroom? Select a textbook and determine which orientation it favors. Could you successfully incorporate this textbook into a course guided by another orientation? Could you use it to support and supplement an orientation that you favor more?

5 Imagine you are designing a new writing course for Upper Intermediate level ESL students preparing for academic study in an English-speaking context. Would you choose one approach to guide your course or select elements from more than one? Which ones would you choose and why?

6 Look again at Reflection 1.13. Select one written genre from the list and find an authentic example of it to analyze. What are it's purposes, audience, formality, main vocabulary items, and grammar patterns? How far does your analysis match the intuitive comparisons that you made earlier? Which features are most useful for identifying the text as an example of the genre you chose? Which features would you choose to emphasize if you were teaching this genre?

7 Consider the following writing exercises. (a) Which orientation is foregrounded in each? (b) Are there elements of other orientations? (c) What

is the primary teaching objective of each one? (d) Could you adapt any of these exercises to suit a class of your own? How?

(i) In this exercise, you will read five topic sentences. For each of these, predict what you expect to read in the paragraph. Make notes about your predictions and then compare your notes with a partner's. *[handwritten: genre]* *[handwritten: culture shock/moving/ → 1 funny incident]*

1 Some very funny things happened to me during my first few days in the United States, but the most comical was our night in a Boston restaurant.

2 I am the product of two cultures, and I have adopted the desirable aspects of each culture without feeling guilt or conflict. *[handwritten: how can see 2 cultures in this person, traits]*

3 Moving to another culture is often a difficult step because you usually do not have family and friends around for emotional support. *[handwritten: explaining culture shock/reasons for]*

4 Although American informality is well known, many people interpret it as a lack of respect. *[handwritten: explaining American culture]*

5 One benefit of foreign travel is the realization that you have a great deal in common with people of other cultures. *[handwritten: how cultures act. are similar]*

(Blass and Pike-Baky, 1985: 20–1)

(ii) With a partner, look again at the text you wrote on the desirable and undesirable effects of scientific developments. Discuss how your text can be improved by using suitable grammar techniques and logical connectors to make the information clearer. Then rewrite your text individually. *[handwritten: process]*

(Hamp-Lyons and Heasley, 1987: 52)

(iii) Write a paragraph about your mother. *[handwritten: content]*

Before Writing
1. Divide the subject (your mother) into 4–6 "pieces" and list those topics.
2. Choose two of those topics and write a list of three even more specific topics.
3. Exchange your "even more specific topics" with your partner.
4. Read your partner's topics and choose two that you find most interesting.
5. Write two or three questions about each of those topics.

Writing	6. Choose one of the topics for which your partner has written questions.
	7. Write the paragraph, answering the questions (and any others that you can ask) with examples and specific details about your mother.
	8. Reread your paragraph, making any changes that will improve the paragraph.
	9. Rewrite the paragraph with the changes you made.
After Writing	10. Read three of your classmates' paragraphs about their mothers. Take notes.
	11. Choose the paragraph you liked best and be prepared to say why: "I like X's paragraph because . . ."

(Reid, 2000: 13)

(iv) Explanation

The writer of a promotional letter can use the Move ESTABLISHING CREDENTIALS not only by (1) referring to the needs of the business world in general or the needs of a customer in particular as in Mr. Huff's letter (not shown here) but by (2) referring to his own company's achievements/speciality as well. In the following example

C & E Hollidays, the name is synonymous with the very best in travel trade with 20 years of professional expertise, will present you with a variety of programs.

the writer ESTABLISHES CREDENTIALS by stating his company's past experiences and field of specialization. Either of these two strategies, or both, may realize this Move.

Instructions

Label the following text to indicate how many different strategies the author uses in ESTABLISHING CREDENTIALS of his company.

The next 12 months are going to be difficult ones for Singapore industries as a whole. We, at Marco Polo, are fully aware of the current market situation and are continuously upgrading our facilities and amenities to meet new competition.

(Bhatia, 1997: 143)

2 Second language writers

Aims: This chapter focuses on the key issues that distinguish second and first language writers and writing, highlighting the questions this distinction raises for ESL writing teachers.

The overview of writing instruction in the last chapter drew on theories principally developed from first language research. However, although there are important similarities between L1 and L2 writing, both teachers' intuitions and empirical studies suggest that there are also significant differences that teachers need to address to ensure their classroom expectations, teaching practices, and assessment procedures are fair and effective.

In a review of seventy-two studies comparing research into first and second language writing, Silva (1993: 669) noted that "L2 writing is strategically, rhetorically and linguistically different in important ways from L1 writing." Such differences may include the following writing and learning issues:

- Different linguistic proficiencies and intuitions about language
- Different learning experiences and classroom expectations
- Different sense of audience and writer
- Different preferences for ways of organizing texts
- Different writing processes
- Different understandings of text uses and the social value of different text types

Because an understanding of these various cognitive, social, cultural, and linguistic factors can help us to become better teachers, the following sections will explore their sources, nature, and effects and draw some implications for the L2 writing instruction.

31

Orientation

From your experiences as a teacher or student, what do you think are the main similarities and differences between writing in a first and in a second language? Brainstorm as many ideas as you can.

Potential L1 and L2 writer differences

In the last chapter we saw that a wide range of knowledge and experience is needed to write successfully in English. Borrowing Canale and Swain's (1980) framework, writers need, at least:

- *grammatical competence* – a knowledge of grammar, vocabulary, and the language system
- *discourse competence* – a knowledge of genre and the rhetorical patterns that create them
- *sociolinguistic competence* – the ability to use language appropriately in different contexts, understanding readers and adopting appropriate authorial attitudes
- *strategic competence* – the ability to use a variety of communicative strategies

When we add to this the fact that in the classroom writers may be asked for their opinions and ideas and to draft and edit their work, we begin to realize some of the challenges for students in achieving native-like proficiency.

Individual differences

Many adult second language writers never achieve target language proficiency, either because they reach a level of competence that allows them to communicate to their own satisfaction, or because they "fossilize" at a certain level. Individual learner differences are important reasons for this, with linguistic, social, and psychological factors all playing a role in a student's successful acquisition of a second language (e.g., Ellis, 1994; Skehan, 1989). No two learners are the same and their different learning backgrounds and personalities will influence how quickly, and how well, they learn to write in a second language. Students obviously bring to the L2 writing class different writing experiences, different aptitudes and levels of motivation; they have varying metacognitive knowledge of their L1 and experience of using it, particularly to write; and they have different characteristics in

Table 2.1: *Individual factors potentially influencing L2 acquisition*

Altman (1980)	Skehan (1989)	Larsen-Freeman and Long (1991)
Age	Language aptitude	Age
Motivation and attitude	Motivation	Motivation and attitude
Personality factors	Cognitive and affective factors	to learning
Previous language	a. extroversion	Personality factors
learning experience	b. willingness to take risks	a. self-esteem
Proficiency in the L1	c. intelligence	b. extroversion
Language aptitude	d. anxiety	c. anxiety
General intelligence (IQ)	e. analytic versus experiential	d. willingness to take risks
Gender	Language learning strategies	e. sensitivity to rejection
Learning style		f. empathy
preferences		g. inhibition
		h. tolerance of ambiguity
		Cognitive style
		a. Analytic/gestalt
		b. Reflexivity/impulsivity
		c. Aural/visual
		Gender
		Learning strategies

terms of age, sex, and socioeconomic status. Table 2.1 summarizes some of the dimensions of learner difference mentioned in three surveys (adapted from Ellis, 1994: 472).

Reflection 2.1 *mOti vatiUn + athtyde*
Which of these factors do you think is the most important in successfully developing proficiency in a second language? How do you think it might influence a student's L2 writing improvement?

Obviously a person's goals, attitudes, and abilities are likely to be crucial factors in their successful acquisition of writing skills in an L2 and, although little is known about the effects of many of these factors, our instructional strategies need to take account of them. But while understanding these learner differences is important, students should not be thought of as simply bundles of individual features. They are also members of social groups whose schemata, practices, and attitudes toward writing and learning may be very different from our own and also from those of L1 writers. The special status of our students as L2 writers has much to do with the fact that they draw on bicultural and bilingual understandings, and among the most important factors that distinguish them from L1 writers are the prior language and cultural experiences they bring with them to the classroom.

Language and strategy differences

Perhaps the most immediately obvious factor that distinguishes many second language writers is the difficulty they have in adequately expressing themselves in English. These writers typically have a different linguistic knowledge base than native English speakers. So while most of us have a vocabulary of several thousand words and an intuitive ability to handle the grammar of the language when we begin to write in our L1, L2 writers often carry the burden of learning to write and learning English at the same time. Largely because of this developmental aspect of language learning, research frequently finds texts written by L2 students to be less effective than those of their native English-speaking peers (Silva, 1997). Numerous studies suggest that tests produced by L2 writers are generally shorter, less cohesive, less fluent, and contain more errors (e.g., Purves, 1988).

Students themselves commonly identify language difficulties, particularly an inadequate grasp of vocabulary or grammar, as their main problems with writing and frequently express their frustrations at being unable to convey their ideas in appropriate and correct English. These quotes from students taking a writing course for pre-university and pre-graduate courses in New Zealand are representative of many students struggling to make meanings in English. They feel they have good ideas, but lack the linguistic resources to convey them in writing in a foreign language. Their goal is to approximate a native speaker's writing:

I have some ideas and I can't, I can make it in my language or in my opinions, sometimes it's English, but I can't write down correctly. Ah, my essay always don't be academic. It just tend to write personal writing always. Or my ideas don't stay one point always. Still quite unskilful and what I want to say isn't expressed, isn't explained in my essay. (Maho, Japanese student)

I will never reach the advanced stage because another language is not my own language . . . and it takes a long time to know when you describe something you have to choose another word, not just by some simple words. If I have a good idea but I cannot write down my idea and I cannot graduate. (Liang, Taiwanese student)

Right at first I tell you this is what I think in my language and I write in English and native speaker who use English fluently will not understand. But if I give this to my

Thai friends to read, they will understand and admire every time. . . . In my mind I can think more than I can write. I cannot find the suitable word. I just use simple words and not the ones that show the deep meaning. (Samorn, Thai student)

This is not to suggest a deficit orientation to what L2 writers can achieve. Many adult learners are successful writers in their first language and are able to bring sophisticated cognitive abilities and metacognitive strategies to the task of writing (Leki, 1992). But proficiency in first language oracy and literacy may not necessarily be an advantage. As the quotes above suggest, many intelligent and accomplished learners are unable to express themselves as they would like in English. Put simply, linguistic and rhetorical conventions do not always transfer successfully across languages, and may actually interfere with writing in the L2 (Connor, 1996). This comment from a successful Japanese student articulates some of the consequences of these language and strategy differences:

In the beginning I had a very difficult time making myself understood in writing. My sentences tended to be short and direct translation of Japanese sentences. I didn't know that I was supposed to be logical or linear in thinking and choose a position in writing an opinion paper. So I often contradicted myself within a paragraph because I was not sure myself if I would support one position or another. I was merely presenting the flow of my thoughts. The sentences I wrote that seemed very explicit to me were not explicit enough for professors. (Yoshiki Chikuma, in Silva and Reichelt, 2003)

The research on what aspects of literacy transfer from a learner's first language is conflicting and we should not directly attribute all aspects of L2 writing to L1 writing abilities. But while the impact of the first language on second language writing will obviously vary, it is a crucial feature distinguishing L1 and L2 writing. In some cases students will be able to draw on an L1 that is similar to the L2, with a common ancestry and a long history of contact, but in others the orthography of the writing system itself may pose a considerable barrier. There is also the question of the potentially positive influence of strategy transfer to the L2 context which can greatly facilitate the learner's development (Zamel, 1997). Much of the comparative research is limited by small samples and lack of reliable significance tests and the results are inconclusive and sometimes even contradictory. There do, however, seem to be a number of salient differences in the writing processes of L1 and L2 writers and in the fluency and accuracy of their writing. Table 2.2 summarizes this research by drawing on reviews by Silva (1993, 1997), Krapels (1990), and Leki (1992).

Table 2.2: *Findings of research into L1 and L2 writing*

- General composing process patterns seem to be largely similar in L1 and L2.
- Both L1 and L2 skilled writers compose differently from novices.
- Advanced L2 writers are handicapped more by a lack of composing competence than a lack of linguistic competence. The opposite is true for lower proficiency learners.
- L1 writing strategies may or may not be transferred to L2 contexts.
- L2 writers tend to plan less than L1 writers and produce shorter texts.
- L2 writers have more difficulty setting goals and generating material.
- L2 writers revise more but reflect less on their writing.
- L2 writers are less fluent, and produce less accurate and effective texts.
- L2 writers are less inhibited by teacher-editing and feedback.

Reflection 2.2

Do you agree that difficulties with grammar and vocabulary are likely to cause students the most problems when writing in English? What do you think writing teachers should do about this?

Cultural differences

Another important dimension of difference is culture. Cultural factors help shape students' background understandings, or schema knowledge, and are likely to have a considerable impact on how they write, their responses to classroom contexts, and their writing performance. Culture is generally understood as an historically transmitted and systematic network of meanings which allow us to understand, develop, and communicate our knowledge and beliefs about the world (Lantolf, 1999). This means that language and learning are inextricably bound with culture (Kramsch, 1993). This is partly because our cultural values are reflected in and carried through language, but also because cultures make available to us certain taken-for-granted ways of organizing our perceptions and expectations, including those we use to learn and communicate in writing.

Research shows that differences in expectations, strategies, and beliefs make intercultural contacts highly susceptible to the possibility of miscommunication, and this is why it is important for teachers to understand the potentially different ways that second language writers might respond to their teaching. However, the effects of the first culture on second and foreign language learning have not always been recognized in teaching methodologies, and teachers often mistakenly assume that learners have prior knowledge of text genres or share their cultural beliefs about writing.

Before considering these issues in more detail, however, it is important to remember that although linguistic and cultural factors may distinguish first and second language writers, L2 students cannot be lumped together as an undifferentiated group, nor should cultural norms be regarded as decisive. Seeing culture as static and homogeneous runs the risk of taking "a deterministic stance and a deficit orientation as to what students can accomplish in English and what their writing instruction should be" (Zamel, 1997: 341). Students have individual identities beyond the language and culture they were born into and we should avoid the tendency to stereotype individuals according to crude cultural dichotomies. Cultures are fluid, diverse, and nondetermining, and people may resist or ignore cultural patterns. But while we cannot simply read off a set of teaching approaches from students' cultures, neither should we ignore research that might help us understand the ways they may prefer to learn and write. To appreciate linguistic and cultural differences it is necessary to recognize that features in our students' essays may be evidence of alternative patterns and understandings, rather than of individual inability or poor study habits.

Reflection 2.3
In what ways are cultural factors likely to influence the ways students write and learn to write?

Cultural schemata and writing

One way in which different cultural schemata can influence L2 writers is through the conceptions of *learning* and *writing* that they make available. It is not always obvious that the ways we understand terms such as *learning* and *teaching* can vary across cultures, and neither teachers nor students may realize they are standing on different ground. Because teachers rarely think to spell out the basic ideas that underlie their expectations and judgments, these may remain inaccessible to students, with serious consequences for how they find their writing performance evaluated. It is important to bear in mind, then, that educational practices are shaped by the cultures in which they operate. The attitudes, approaches, and strategies we encourage and reward in our classes might therefore contrast and even conflict with those that are known and valued by our students.

This kind of hidden "cultural curriculum" can be found in the culturally divergent attitudes to knowledge that can seriously interfere in our assessment of L2 students' writing. Ballard and Clanchy (1991) point out that these attitudes spread along a continuum from respecting the conservation of knowledge to valuing its extension. Educational processes in Western contexts tend to reinforce an analytical, questioning, and evaluative stance to knowledge, encouraging students to criticize and recombine existing sources to dispute traditional wisdom and form their own points of view. In writing classes students are often asked to analyze problems, reflect on arguments, and rework their ideas through recursive redrafting. Thus, Bereiter and Scardamalia (1987) characterize mature writing as "knowledge transforming," where writers actively seek to elaborate and refine available knowledge.

Many Asian cultures, however, have a very different perspective that favors conserving and reproducing existing knowledge, establishing reverence for what is known through strategies such as memorization and imitation. Both these strategies demonstrate respect for knowledge, but may seem to the writing teacher like reproducing others' ideas. In Bereiter and Scardamalia's terms, it is "knowledge telling" which represents immature writing, where the writer's goal is simply to say what he or she can remember based on the assignment, the topic, or the genre. So by ignoring cultural considerations, teachers may see this as plagiarism or repetition, and be mislead into recasting such respect for knowledge as a developmental continuum from immaturity to maturity (Silva, Leki, and Carson, 1997). Figure 2.1 summarizes some of the implications of these distinctions.

Reflection 2.4

Look at the activities associated with the different approaches to learning listed in Figure 2.1. Think of a writing task that would require students to engage in an analytical and a speculative approach to learning. Devise the rubric you would give students for these two tasks.

Closely related to these culturally based attitudes to knowledge is the way that the writing classroom reflects conceptions of identity. In a review of cultural conceptions of self, Markus and Kitayama (1991) contrast Western *independent* views, which emphasize the separateness and uniqueness of persons, with many non-Western cultures, which insist on the *interdependence* of human beings to each other.

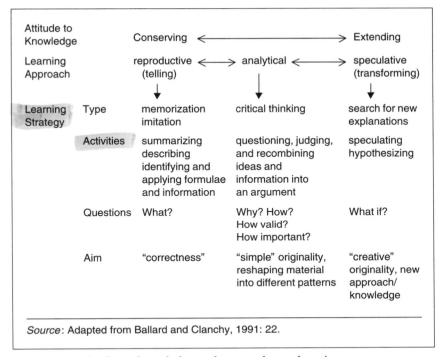

Attitude to Knowledge		Conserving ⟵⟶ Extending		
Learning Approach		reproductive ⟷ (telling)	analytical ⟷	speculative (transforming)
		↓	↓	↓
Learning Strategy	Type	memorization imitation	critical thinking	search for new explanations
	Activities	summarizing describing identifying and applying formulae and information	questioning, judging, and recombining ideas and information into an argument	speculating hypothesizing
	Questions	What?	Why? How? How valid? How important?	What if?
	Aim	"correctness"	"simple" originality, reshaping material into different patterns	"creative" originality, new approach/ knowledge

Source: Adapted from Ballard and Clanchy, 1991: 22.

Figure 2.1: Attitudes to knowledge and approaches to learning.

In the Western classroom, "good writing" is generally seen to involve the writer's individual creativity and critical thinking, and teachers frequently see their role as helping to develop these skills in their students. Teachers often expect writers to voice their judgments, display their knowledge, and give their opinions. Texts must display their author's individuality, and concepts such as *voice* and *textual ownership* are familiar in mainstream writing pedagogy. But such concepts can create problems for L2 writers from more collectivist or interdependently oriented cultures (Ramanathan and Atkinson, 1999). In these cultures, students are typically oriented by their education to group membership and to age and gender roles rather than to individual status (Heath, 1991), and writing is done less to express oneself than to pass on the knowledge one has received. The absence of a personal voice is largely irrelevant as the student does not presume to improve on acknowledged truths but to communicate what is socially shared.

So while the uncited inclusion of others' work allows Asian writers to display their knowledge, honor important thinkers, and show respect for the learning of their readers, excellence in the Western writing classroom requires the writer's unique signature and such borrowings are seen as mind-less regurgitation or as plagiarism. Pennycook (1996) offers an extensive discussion of cross-cultural differences on plagiarism, showing how students can be led into trouble through their different cultural and educational backgrounds.

Reflection 2.5

Have you ever observed plagiarism when teaching? In your opinion was it intentional or unintentional? What was your reaction and what did you do about it, if anything? Would you handle it differently now?

Such divergent cultural perspectives with regard to knowledge, texts, and the self are major factors to consider in learning and writing, yet we tend to take our own views for granted as self-evidently universal and can easily fail to recognize their cultural specificity. Teachers frequently see language problems as the main obstacle to effective writing, yet surface errors may actually be less serious than disjunctive perceptions of what "good writing" is. The fact that our students may be operating from fundamentally different positions about texts and authorship means that we should be aware of the effects these can have on their writing, be flexible in our judgments, and be explicit about our expectations and the reasons for our teaching methods.

Expectations about teaching and learning

Cultural variations in assumptions about the nature of knowledge, learn-ing, and writing are not the only differences between writing in a first and second language. Culture also intrudes into classrooms through the expecta-tions that students may have about instruction and the meanings they attach to the writing activities they are given. One currently influential theory of learning emphasizes the idea of "situated cognition" (Lave and Wenger, 1991), which holds that the setting and the activity of learning are insepara-ble from learning itself. In this sense L2 writing instruction should be seen as an expression of culture. Moreover, because of the diversity of educa-tional contexts, we should also anticipate that students' previous learning experiences may not have adequately prepared them for the kinds of tasks and assignments they encounter when learning to write in our classrooms.

Time, topic, and language may be important, as Leki and Carson's (1997) ESL students mentioned:

Time is the problem. Each time I write a paper in English I have to spend a lot of time to organize. So if you give me just a limited time, I cannot do very well.

There are sometimes subjects you never think to write about those. For example, they say write about a custom or an important value. I never thought about writing about them.

My principal objective in my English class is my grammar, not the idea, because sometimes the idea, . . . I made[up] the idea.

Perhaps the most obvious issue, however, is the fact that writing topics are potentially culture-sensitive and may be inappropriate for some groups. All cultures attribute different meanings to events and human relationships and these cultural frames influence what we find comfortable to write about. Religion, politics, status, death, and sex can be taboo topics, while the fact that "privacy" is not a universal concept means that writing about personal or family issues may seem intrusive to some learners. Similarly, not all writers will be happy to take a critical or combative stance toward an assigned topic or to commit themselves to a position. While questions of topic can be solved with a sensitive approach, teachers need to be aware that writers from other cultures may apply different standards to what is addressable in writing.

Reflection 2.6
Are there any topics that you might feel uncomfortable to write about in a classroom context? List some and consider why these are sensitive to you.

Teachers also need to be alert to the fact that some L1 teaching techniques may conflict with students' expectations. One potential problem area is that of feedback preferences. Many writing teachers, influenced by cognitivist and expressivist ideas in L1 classrooms, stress the expression of meaning in their teaching and tend to respond to the content of their L2 students' essays in their feedback. But the L1 and L2 literacy training of many ESL learners has involved traditional product-centered instruction, focusing on accuracy, so students often put a high premium on feedback that addresses the mechanics and grammar of their texts. In Hong Kong secondary schools, for example, students expect their English teachers to correct every grammatical error they make in their essays. These different experiences may create disparities between preferred teacher and student practices.

Another potential area of difficulty is that of peer review. A central feature of L1 process writing approaches, the practice of asking students to respond to the texts of their peers, is generally seen as beneficial in L2 writing instruction (e.g., Hedgcock and Lefkowitz, 1992). Group members are asked to comment on whether particular elements of an individual's essay are effective or not, supporting their views with examples from the essay (see Chapter 7). But while this may help some learners to develop better revision strategies and envisage their audience more effectively, peer response has been criticized as culturally inappropriate for learners from more collectivist cultures. Thus, in Carson and Nelson's (1996) study, the primary goal of Chinese students in such groups was social – to maintain group harmony – and this led them to avoid criticism of peers' work and to avoid engaging in a dialogue about the comments peers gave on their writing.

The following comments, from a Chinese and a Hong Kong learner, show similar concerns about peer feedback:

I want some comments and I asked ZC. Well, he said "it's all right." Nothing important, nothing useful. Maybe he didn't like to comment. Especially for Chinese, for Chinese people you know they seldom comment on some other people's work. I think it is not good.

The conference is not so useful because our group members just give good comments. We just say the essay is OK. Perhaps suggest a small change sometimes, especially grammar mistake. We don't usually make a criticism to our classmate.

Although such cultural strategies may encourage a positive group climate and avoid threatening the "face" of its members, they may be less effective in fostering a critical appreciation of texts or developing writing skills.

Reflection 2.7

Imagine you are using peer response methods with a group of students like Carson and Nelson's from a collectivist culture. How would you introduce the idea of peer response to them and how would you encourage them to share their writing and respond to their peers' work?

Teaching and learning styles

Awareness of differences in preferred learning and teaching styles is also potentially useful in L2 classrooms. Research suggests that students have their own learning styles or general approaches to learning and that these are at least partly shaped by their cultural backgrounds and prior experiences (e.g., Hyland, 1994). Learning styles are the "cognitive, affective and perceptual traits that indicate how learners perceive, interact with and respond to, their learning environment" (Reid, 1993: 56), and while some students have multiple learning styles that allow them to switch styles according to the context, most occupy points along a continuum between two opposing styles.

Research has focused largely on three broad types of style:

1. The **cognitive** dimension distinguishes *field-independent* learners who are mainly analytic and prefer instruction that emphasizes rules, from *field-dependent* students who flourish in cooperative, experiential classrooms with plenty of interaction and feedback on their writing.
2. The **affective** dimension differentiates students who depend on social and emotional factors from those who rely more on logic. It also separates out extroverts and introverts.
3. **Perceptual** learning styles are most relevant in the ESL/EFL class. *Visually* oriented students like to see information written down, while *auditory* learners prefer lectures and spoken input. *Tactile* or *kinaesthetic* students learn best if they are active and can work with tangible objects.

The difficulties in determining a single learning style for any particular student should not be underestimated. Very few learners are likely to display a single style in a uniform or exclusive way, and organizing a writing curriculum around these learner characteristics could be a largely frustrating experience. However, diagnosing students' preferred styles encourages teachers to consider the potential range of learning styles in their classes and to provide learners with the kinds of input and writing tasks that will help them learn best. This means raising students' awareness of productive strategies and adapting their own activities to the range of styles in their classes to avoid the "style wars" between their own and their students' styles, which can have a negative effect on both attitudes and learning (Bialystock, 1985).

Of particular interest to writing teachers in L2 classrooms is that although diversity in a culture is the norm, individuals within a culture tend to exhibit consistent patterns of learning when compared with those of other cultures (Oxford and Anderson, 1995). It is important to avoid stereotyping linguistic groups as having uniform preferences because factors such as age, gender, and learning experiences cross-cut cultures (Hyland, 1994), but, as Oxford, Holloway, and Horton-Murillo (1992: 441) point out, "although culture is not the single determinant, and although many other influences intervene, culture often does play a significant role in the learning styles

Table 2.3: *Results of Reid's study of learning style preferences*

Native language (number)	Very strong learning style preference	Strong learning style preference	Quite strong learning style preference	Minor learning style preference	Negative learning style preference
Arabic (193)	Kinesthetic Tactile	Auditory	Visual	Group	Individual
Spanish (205)	Kinesthetic	Tactile		Visual Auditory Individual	Group
Japanese (130)				Visual Auditory Kinesthetic Tactile Individual	Group
Chinese (90)	Kinesthetic Tactile	Auditory	Visual	Individual	Group
Korean (118)	Kinesthetic Tactile	Visual	Auditory	Individual	Group

Source: Reid, 1993: 58.

unconsciously adopted by many participants in the culture." The most well-known study linking learning styles and culture is Reid's (1987) self-report survey of the perceptual learning style preferences of 1,234 students from various cultures. Some of her findings are shown in Table 2.3.

Reflection 2.8

In the L2 writing class, teachers need to consider how the varied cultural and linguistics backgrounds of students might influence the ways they learn to write and to accommodate these in their teaching. Select one language group from Table 2.3 and consider if Reid's results accurately reflect what you know of this group's learning preferences. Can you recommend some writing tasks that might work successfully with this group?

In writing classes, students' perceptual style preferences can be accommodated in various ways:

- Students with an auditory preference work best on tasks like listening to lectures, conversations, or taped material as sources for writing and tasks that require interaction with others such as group or pair work involving information transfer, reasoning problems, and discussion.

- Predominantly visual learners may respond well to reading source texts, writing class journals, completing gapped texts, and transferring information from graphic, textual, or video material.
- Kinesthetic students like to participate actively and therefore suitable tasks include role-plays and simulations with writing elements, site visits, and projects involving data collection.
- Tactile students may work better with tasks that involve writing reports on building and testing models, developing and acting scripts for plays, and sequencing activities such as jigsaw texts.
- Students differ in whether they work best alone or collaboratively, and teachers should vary the emphasis they give to individual and peer writing to help students extend the ways they write.

So, while it may not be possible to discover a single learning style for each student, explicitly addressing the issue can be a good exercise for both teachers and learners. Reid's questionnaire (Appendix 2.1) is a useful means of gathering data, raising awareness, and explaining the purpose of different classroom activities. When this information is combined with an analysis of students' self-report data about their existing competencies as writers and their writing experiences (see Chapter 3), then teachers are able to devise instruction types, and writing activities which consider student variations and which capitalize on the strengths and address the weaknesses of them all.

Reflection 2.9
What do you think is your own preferred learning style? Have you always had the same preference or has it changed over time? How do you think this influences your preferred teaching style?

Cultural differences in written texts

Perhaps the most-examined aspect of culture in writing is the differing cultural expectations that people have about the ways texts are organized and the effects these may have on L2 literacy development. What is seen as logical, engaging, relevant, or well-organized in writing, what counts as proof, conciseness, and evidence, all differ across cultures. Although it is far from conclusive, research suggests that the schemata of L2 students differ from those of L1 writers in their preferred ways of organizing ideas, and these cultural preconceptions may hinder effective communication. This field is known as *contrastive rhetoric* (CR): "Contrastive rhetoric maintains that

Table 2.4: *Some differences between L1 and L2 student academic essays*

- different organizational preferences
- different approaches to argument (justification, persuasive appeals, credibility)
- different ways of incorporating material (use of quotes, paraphrase, allusion, unacknowledged borrowing, etc.)
- different ways and extent of getting readers' attention and orienting them to topic
- different estimates of reader knowledge
- different uses of cohesion and metadiscourse markers (see below)
- Differences in how overt linguistic features are used (generally less subordination, passives, modifiers, lexical variety, and specificity in L2 writing)
- Differences in objectivity (L2 texts often contain more generalizations and personal opinions)
- Differences in complexity of style

Sources: Connor, 1996; Grabe and Kaplan, 1996: 239; Hinkel, 1999.

language and writing are cultural phenomena. As a result, each language has rhetorical conventions unique to it. Furthermore the linguistic and rhetorical conventions of the first language interfere with the writing of the second language" (Connor, 1996: 5). The findings of contrastive rhetoric are inconclusive and show differences across L2 groups, but some of the results are summarized in Table 2.4.

The idea of cultural differences in rhetoric has been of interest to writing teachers since Kaplan's (1966) study of six hundred L2 student essays over thirty-five years ago. Kaplan found that students from different backgrounds systematically identified and developed their ideas in different ways. Compared with what he saw as the essentially linear pattern of English paragraphs, he suggested that Arabic speakers produced texts based on a series of parallel coordinate clauses; "Oriental" writers used an indirect approach and came to the point only at the end; and French, Spanish, and Russian speakers digressed and introduced extraneous material far more often than English writers. Because these culture-specific patterns were believed to negatively interfere with students' L2 writing, teachers were urged to provide students with explicit models of English expository paragraphs, concentrating on a "factual-inductive" organization with clear topic sentences. Exercises such as parallel writing, reconstructing jumbled sentences, and writing summaries (e.g., Kaplan and Shaw, 1983) were recommended to raise students' awareness of appropriate rhetorical structures.

Kaplan's original findings, however, have been widely criticized:

- for lumping different language groups together, for example, all Asians as "Oriental"
- for being too prescriptive in taking a rigid view of "correct" English rhetorical patterns

- for being too ethnocentric in privileging the writing of native English speakers as "linear"
- for being too simplistic in attempting to see L1 thought patterns in L2 essays
- for oversimplifying both L2 and L1 forms of writing

One problem has been in establishing equivalent writing tasks for comparisons as not all cultures share all genres. Kachru (1996), for instance, observes that the Indian genre of writing horoscopes has no parallel in the West and that the Anglo-American genre of written invitations is unknown in India. Thus, it may not be helpful to directly compare the argumentative essay, which seeks to prove one position correct and all others wrong, with its Indian counterpart, which puts forward several positions and allows the reader to decide.

CR has abandoned this strong view that writing reflects actual patterns of thinking, and now sees L1 rhetorical structures as learned cultural preferences (Kaplan, 1987). The different rhetorical modes discussed above are available to all writers and do not allow us to predict how students from different language backgrounds will write. Essentially L1 patterns represent tendencies which may intrude on writing in English, rather than inevitably interfere with it. However, research has continued to identify differing rhetorical patterns and conventions across a number of languages and to demonstrate the impact these may have on L2 students' writing in English at various proficiency levels.

Reflection 2.10
One criticism of contrastive rhetoric has been that it involves an idealized notion of what an English paragraph or composition is and ignores the genre variations that we find in real life. Should teachers encourage individual creativity when developing writing skills for academic genres? To what extent do you think L2 students might prefer to have models to follow?
→ guidelines but own ideas

Writer-responsible versus reader-responsible languages

Basically the L2 writer is writing from his or her own familiar culture and the L1 reader is reading from another context. One possible explanation for these difficulties therefore is that they are related to the amount of effort the writer expects the reader to invest in the text. Hinds (1987: 143) suggests that in languages such as English the "person primarily responsible for effective communication is the writer," but in Japanese (and perhaps Korean and classical Chinese too) it is the reader. Writers compliment their readers by not spelling everything out, while readers are said to savor hints and nuances. Similarly, Clyne (1987) argues that while English language cultures urge writers to produce clear, well-organized statements, German texts put the onus on the reader to dig out meaning, and this seems to apply to Spanish texts as well (Valero-Garces, 1996). Coherence, in other words, is in the eye of the beholder.

A good example of how skilled writers achieve this kind of clarity in English is their regular use of "signposts" to help readers through their arguments. It is the writer's task to provide appropriate transition statements when moving from one idea to the next and to regularly place signals in the text so the reader can see how the writer intends the text to hold together. These signals are called *metadiscourse markers*, and they serve to explicitly organize the text and comment on it by use of:

* sequencing points (*first, next, last*)
* connecting ideas (*however, therefore, on the other hand*)
* showing what the writer is doing (*to summarize, in conclusion, for example*)
* reviewing and previewing parts of the text (*in the last section we . . . , here we will address . . .*)
* commenting on content (*you may not agree that . . . , it is surprising that . . .*)

These features help the reader through a text (Hyland, 1999) but their significance may not always be obvious to L2 writers from more reader-responsible cultures. Americans, for instance, have been found to use far more of these features than Finnish writers, probably because Finnish schools teach students that metadiscourse is not only superfluous, but the sign of a poor writer (Mauranen, 1993).

Implications of contrastive rhetoric for teachers

One consequence of taking culture seriously in L2 writing teaching has been to broaden the concept of culture itself, and to identify the impact of professional, institutional, and disciplinary cultures on writing conventions. Such views of writing acknowledge that the schemata we use to produce and understand texts are sensitive to the ways of thinking of our discourse communities (Hyland, 2000). Most of the significant writing we do is in our communities – in school, in recreational groups, or in the workplace. Contrastive rhetoric shows us that writing is a cultural resource and that different genres and rhetorical conventions operate in different settings. Simply, good writers are people who are better able to imagine how their readers will respond to their texts because they are familiar with the conventions and expectations that operate in those settings. This helps to account for why many native English speakers find writing at university so difficult: it is not a failure to think logically or an inability to write, but the struggle is to acquire the literacy skills of a new culture.

One pedagogic response to the ideas and research of contrastive rhetoric has been to bend the ways of writing of nonnative speakers to those of Anglo-American conventions, a practice criticized in Phillipson's (1992) notion of "linguistic imperialism." However, it is obviously impossible to train the world's entire English-using population in the norms of one variety. Similarly, the majority of students learning English around the world is being taught by nonnative speakers of English and it is equally unrealistic to expect them to teach one set of writing conventions. Instead, contrastive rhetoric suggests that teachers need to become aware of different rhetorical conventions, to understand some of the issues L2 writers face, and to accept different conventions in the work of their learners. This tolerance, however, needs to be tempered with an understanding of the degree of variance that readers are likely to accept in the students' academic or work situations.

Teachers can therefore take a number of different insights from contrastive rhetoric. Principally, however, it serves to remind us to avoid stereotyping as it shows how different writing styles can be the result of culturally learned preferences, helping us to recognize that student difficulties in writing may be due to the disjunction of the writer's and reader's view of what is needed in a text. In short, CR encourages us to see the effects of different practices where we might otherwise only see individual inadequacies. Acknowledging the importance of prior experiences also has practical implications for what teachers do in their classrooms, suggesting that:

- Teachers should help students to become more aware of these variations so they can see that there are different cultural criteria for effective writing, and to recognize that both their own and the target practices are equally valid ways of accomplishing goals in different contexts.
- Teachers should explore ways of encouraging students to think about the needs, experiences, and expectations of their readers.
- Teachers should understand the patterns of the genres students will need to write in their target contexts and provide them with appropriate schemata for these.
- Students need to interrogate the tasks assigned to them to understand teacher expectations.

Summary and conclusion

This chapter has explored the main sources of differences between L1 and L2 writing. It has emphasized that while there are parallels in the composing processes of first and second language writers, the latter are distinguished by their bilingual and bicultural backgrounds and particularly their prior experiences as writers and learners. I have also emphasized that all writers are different and we should be cautious about jumping to conclusions about students based on cultural stereotypes. Learners have their own personalities and there are numerous individual variables that can intervene to influence their acquisition of L2 writing skills. However, culture is too intimately bound up with language, rhetorical styles, learning preferences, and understandings of knowledge, texts, and identity to simply ignore when considering writing instruction. The main points of the chapter can be summarized as follows:

- Individual differences influence how students learn, how they respond to instruction, and the progress they make to improve their writing.
- L2 writers are unique because of their bilingual, bicultural, and biliterate experiences, and these can facilitate or impede writing in various ways.
- L2 learners may have different conceptions of knowledge, self, and texts which conflict with teachers' instructional practices and judgments of writing quality.
- Both teachers and students have preferred learning styles which are partly shaped by cultural experiences and which may conflict with each other and hinder progress in learning to write.
- L2 learners' cultural schemata can impact on the ways they write and the writing they produce.
- Effective L2 writing instruction can make schemata differences explicit to students, encouraging consideration of audience and providing patterns of unfamiliar rhetorical forms.

Most important, cultural factors should be understood as a potential source of explanation for writing differences and used to recognize that there are numerous ways of making meanings. For inexperienced teachers or those without experience of other cultures, there is a danger of ethnocentrism about learning to write, of regarding L2 students as simply deficient writers. An appreciation of writing differences, however, can facilitate cross-cultural understandings and help us see that writing difficulties are not problems inherent in students themselves. Moreover, these understandings can support teaching practices that make such differences explicit to students. By openly addressing students' L1 writing experiences and rhetorical styles and by contrasting them with the expectations of target writing communities, teachers make both instruction and genres relative to context. Thus, we are not seeking to replace the ideas and practices students bring with them, but to add others to their repertoire so they can effectively participate in new situations.

Discussion questions and activities

1 This chapter is about L1 and L2 writing differences. What is the most interesting single difference for you? List the main issues associated with this factor for the writing teacher and describe how the teacher might successfully address them.

2 The following topics are taken from an L2 writing textbook widely used in the United States. Do you think all cultural groups are likely to be comfortable writing about these topics?

- In your country, how common is cohabitation, or consensual unions without marriage?
- In your culture, how do people view births outside of marriage?
- In your culture, do some people judge others by their manners at the table?
- What kind of role model do fathers in your country provide for their children?

From your own experience, do you think asking students to discuss their culture helps build on their personal experiences for writing or does it help draw boundaries which polarize cultural identities and prevent them responding as individuals?

3 The discussion of cultural differences in the use of language suggests that students would benefit from a clear understanding of how writing is used in their first language and culture. This would help them to develop an appreciation of the different relationships between writer and reader and how expression of purposes and meanings differ across cultures. How could students discover more about writing in their own culture? How might you as a teacher learn about the most frequent kinds of writing they do, who the audiences are, and the style of the writing?

4 Interview someone who has learned to write in a second language. What did he or she consider the main linguistic or cultural factors that affected this process? List the influences he or she identifies and note how these influences worked to assist or to hinder writing development.

5 In a small group, discuss what you see as the main features of contrastive rhetoric. How do you respond to the criticisms made of it? Describe how

contrastive rhetoric might influence:

a. the ways you understand your students
b. the ways you understand their writing
c. the ways you teach writing

6 Consider Hinds' distinction between "reader-responsible" and "writer-responsible" languages. How do you think a teacher might help a student from a "reader-responsible" culture write an effective essay in English? Suggest two or three teaching strategies or tasks to do this.

7 This text is the acknowledgment section of a report written by a Hong Kong undergraduate. While the writer has a good control of the language, it nevertheless seems "wrong." What aspects suggest the text was written by an L2 student and how does it reflect imperfect schema knowledge? Do you think cultural factors may have influenced the writer?

Having worked for more than half year in reading books and articles, collection of data in library and Internet, it was a tough job for me to go through words, find the appropriate framework and theories, and reduce plenty of stuff to complete this report. So I hereby use this golden opportunity to solicit special thanks to my excellent and compassionate supervisor Dr. Z. Ding because my report will surely not be completed without his constant encouragement and tremendous advice.

8 One aspect of potential cultural variation not mentioned in the chapter is that students may come to the writing class with a different view of the teacher's status, prestige, and role. How might different norms of deference and social distance influence students' experience of the class? How might you, as a teacher, address these different expectations of the way the teacher should conduct the class in your teaching?

9 Use Reid's questionnaire given in Appendix 2.1 to conduct a perceptual learning survey of your students or your classmates.
   • Were there different patterns of major learning style preferences for different cultural groups?
   • Can you explain your findings as cultural tendencies or are they best viewed as individual preferences?
   • What writing teaching strategies could you use to accommodate these preferences in a writing class?

Appendix 2.1: Perceptual learning style preference questionnaire

Name _____ Age_____ First Language _____ Sex _____
This questionnaire has been designed to help you identify the ways you learn best. Please respond to the statements below AS THEY APPLY TO YOUR STUDY OF ENGLISH. Decide whether you srongly agree (5), agree (4), are undecided (3), disagree (2), or strongly disagree (1). Circle the appropriate number. Please respond to each statement quickly and try not to change your responses.

1. When the teacher tells me the instructions, I understand better	5	4	3	2	1
2. I prefer to learn by doing something in class	5	4	3	2	1
3. I get more work done when I work with others	5	4	3	2	1
4. I learn more when I study with a group	5	4	3	2	1
5. In class, I learn more when I study with a group	5	4	3	2	1
6. I learn better by reading what the teacher writes on the board	5	4	3	2	1
7. When someone tells me how to do something, I learn better	5	4	3	2	1
8. When I do things in class, I learn better	5	4	3	2	1
9. I remember things I have heard in class better than things I have read	5	4	3	2	1
10. When I read instructions, I remember them better	5	4	3	2	1
11. I learn more when I can make a model of something	5	4	3	2	1
12. I understand better when I can read instructions	5	4	3	2	1
13. When I study alone, I remember things better	5	4	3	2	1
14. I learn more when I make something for a class project	5	4	3	2	1
15. I enjoy learning in class by doing experiments	5	4	3	2	1
16. I learn better when I make drawings as I study	5	4	3	2	1
17. I learn better in class when the teacher gives me a lecture	5	4	3	2	1
18. When I work alone, I learn better	5	4	3	2	1
19. I understand things better in class when role playing	5	4	3	2	1
20. I learn better in class when I listen to someone	5	4	3	2	1
21. I enjoy working on an assignment with two or three classmates	5	4	3	2	1
22. When I build something, I remember what I have learned better	5	4	3	2	1
23. I prefer to study with others	5	4	3	2	1
24. I learn better by reading than by listening to someone	5	4	3	2	1
25. I enjoy making something for a class project	5	4	3	2	1
26. I learn best in class when I can participate in related activities	5	4	3	2	1
27. In class, I work better when I am alone	5	4	3	2	1
28. I prefer working on projects by myself	5	4	3	2	1
29. I learn more by reading textbooks than by listening to lectures	5	4	3	2	1
30. I prefer to work by myself	5	4	3	2	1

Scoring: There are five questions for each category, grouped in the following way:
Visual: 6, 10, 12, 24, 29   Auditory: 1, 7, 9, 17, 20   Kinesthetic: 2, 8, 15, 19, 26
Tactile: 11, 14, 16, 22, 25   Group: 3, 4, 5, 21, 23   Individual: 13, 18, 27, 28, 30

Add the scores for each category and multiply by 2. Results can be understood as:
Major learning style preference   38–50
Minor learning style preference   25–37
Negligible   0–24

Source: J. Reid, personal communication.

3 Syllabus design and lesson planning

Aims: This chapter examines basic principles and techniques of syllabus design and identifies the central components of an integrated writing course. It focuses on practical aspects of the teacher's planning tasks: conducting needs analyses, constructing a syllabus, and designing units of work and lessons.

Students cannot acquire everything they need to improve their writing skills at once, nor can they learn effectively from a random collection of exercises and assignments. Teachers therefore have to develop a systematic plan of what needs to be learned, selecting and sequencing the content and tasks that will lead to the desired learning outcomes. This requires teachers to devise a syllabus and plan lessons based on it. A syllabus is a coherent plan for a course of study, providing a map for both teachers and learners which specifies the work to be accomplished by students based on explicit objectives. Teachers may not always have complete freedom to choose what their courses will include, and may find their syllabus handed down to them by administrators or prescribed in set texts. But there is usually some flexibility, and it is always good practice to plan teaching with reference to syllabus goals.

The fact that L2 writing is taught in a huge variety of settings all over the world, each with its own institutional constraints, teacher preferences, and learner goals, means that writing courses can differ enormously. Any of the orientations discussed in Chapter 1 can form the basis of a writing syllabus and these can be combined in many different ways (Ur, 1996). Despite this variety, however, designing any kind of writing syllabus requires teachers to:

- Analyze learner needs
- Select what is to be learned based on these needs
- Sequence the elements for effective learning
- Provide opportunities for writing
- Monitor learner progress and provide effective intervention

54

Orientation

Are writing courses like other courses in English language teaching in the ways they are designed and organized? In what ways might planning a writing syllabus be similar or different to designing other types of language syllabus? Is devising a syllabus always useful in course planning?

Elements of a writing syllabus

Some central questions a teacher should address when designing a syllabus are:

> Which aspect of writing should be the main organizing principle for the course?
> How much time should be given to writing as opposed to discussion, feedback, language work, and so on?
> What kinds of writing will students do?
> How can the development of writing skills and target genres be integrated?
> What role should grammar play?
> What will constitute progress?

While these questions can be answered in numerous ways, our own syllabi will respond to the characteristics of the students, the teaching context, and our own stance concerning effective learning. In other words, the design of a syllabus is influenced by three factors:

1. It should begin with the needs of the learner and incorporate these.
2. It should take account of wider curricular goals, both within and outside language learning.
3. It will reflect the teacher's philosophy of writing, including a view of language and learning.

More explicitly, learning to write needs to be seen in the context in which it occurs, so that what we know about writing and learning are linked to the particular students and environment we are going to face. This process starts with a fact-finding stage to discover the current proficiencies and wants of the students and the constraints of the learning situation in terms of time, resources, and so on. It then identifies, as far as possible, the competencies and tasks that will be required of students in target contexts. The teacher then uses this information to decide on course objectives and writes the syllabus

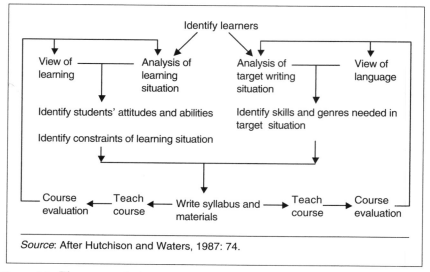

Source: After Hutchison and Waters, 1987: 74.

Figure 3.1: The course design process.

so that they can be achieved. This involves drawing on his or her experience and beliefs to select and sequence what is to be learned and the methods, materials, and activities to support this. An ongoing evaluation ensures a continuous review, encouraging reflection on each stage of planning by assessing the effectiveness of the tasks, the appropriateness of the content, and the adequacy of the resources in light of the course objectives. Figure 3.1 shows diagrammatically how these elements interact.

These ideas are not new, nor did they originate in the field of language teaching. Modern views of syllabus design largely began with Tyler (1949), who observed that teachers seemed unable to explain the goals of their teaching and how these might be achieved. He argued that educational objectives should describe learner behavior rather than teacher behaviors and should identify the outcomes of teaching. While there has been criticism of this rather rationalist view, the idea that instruction begins with an informed judgment of the skills and knowledge required by learners and proceeds through development of methods, materials, and assessment which then feed back into the model has been widely adopted in education. Richards (2001) and Yalden (1987) provide overviews of these developments.

In English language teaching, several models of syllabus design have been proposed (e.g., Brown, 1995; Hedge, 2000), but the elements of Figure 3.1 provide the basis for the following practical step-by-step process, bearing in mind the necessity of constant evaluation and possible modification of the course at each step. The following sections and chapters will address these steps:

Consideration of the students (personal goals, proficiency levels, interests, etc.)

↓

Consideration of the learning context (duration, resources, relationships to other courses)

↓

Consideration of the target context (future roles of learners and the texts and tasks they need)

↓

✗Establishment of course goals and objectives (projected outcomes of the course)

↓

Planning the syllabus (personal beliefs about writing applied to data on learners and context)

↓

Devising units of work and lessons (division of syllabus into manageable chunks of work)

↓

Creation or evaluation and selection of materials (Chapter 4)

↓

Teaching the course (Chapters 5, 6, and 7)

↓

Evaluation of learners (Chapters 7 and 8)

Reflection 3.1

The following advantages for having a syllabus are often cited. Do you agree with each of them? Would you add any others? What do *you* use a syllabus for? Prioritize the list from most important to least important for your own particular circumstances.

3   ✓ 1. Provides a basis for assessment
     2. Gives moral support to teachers and learners by making learning seem manageable
     3. Reassures administrators that thought and planning have gone into the course
ℓ   ✓ 4. Establishes goals for learning
2   ✓ 5. Helps teachers plan and organize their teaching

6. Makes teachers accountable for what they do in their classrooms
7. Gives learners a sense of direction and a way of previewing and revising
8. Provides a statement of what writing is and what is important in learning to write
4 ✓ 9. Provides a set of criteria for selecting materials and evaluating textbooks
10. Helps achieve standardization of learning across different classes (and years and schools)

Analyzing student needs

Designing an L2 writing syllabus starts with the question "Why are these students learning to write?" When preparing a course for adolescents in schools or for adults in English for General Purposes (EGP) contexts, it may be difficult to identify the eventual needs of learners, but gathering what information we can about students is essential to making a course as effective as possible. The term *needs analysis* is used to refer to the techniques for collecting and assessing this kind of information: the means of establishing the *how* and *what* of a course. It is a continuous process since we modify our teaching to better accommodate our students as we come to learn more about them. In this way needs analysis actually shades into *evaluation* – the means of establishing course effectiveness.

What are needs?

Needs is actually an umbrella term that embraces many aspects: What are learners' goals, backgrounds, and abilities? What are their language proficiencies? Why are they taking this course? What kinds of teaching do they prefer? What situations will they need to write in? How are writing knowledge and skills used in these situations? Needs can be perceived objectively by teachers or subjectively by learners, can involve what learners know, don't know, or want to know, and can be analyzed in a variety of ways (e.g., Brown, 1995).

Once again, needs analysis is not unique to language teaching. It is used widely in corporate training and aid development programs worldwide as a basis for securing funding and credibility by linking proposals to genuine needs (e.g., Pratt, 1980). In education contexts, needs analysis emerged in the 1960s through the ESP movement as the demand for specialized language programs expanded and, in North America, as the "behavioral objectives" movement sought to measure all goals with convincing precision and accountability (Berwick, 1989). Today, needs analysis is a form of educational technology represented in a range of research methodologies which can be applied before, during, or after a language course.

Despite this apparently straightforward description, needs are not always easy to determine and can refer to students' immediate language skills or future goals, the requirements of employers, institutions, or exam bodies, or the visions of government organizations acting for the wider society. While needs are often seen as the gap between current and target needs (often called "lacks"), this gives a misleading objectivity to the process, suggesting that teachers simply need to identify and address an existing situation. In reality, needs reflect judgments and values and as a result are likely to be defined differently by different stakeholders with school administrators, government departments, parents, employers, teachers, and learners themselves having different views (Richards, 2001: 54). Teachers construct a picture of what learners need from a course through their *analyses*, bringing to bear their values, beliefs, and philosophies of teaching and learning.

To simplify this, we can distinguish between *present situation* analysis and *target situation* analysis (cf. Dudley-Evans and St John, 1998):

- *Present situation analysis* refers to information about learners' current abilities, familiarity with writing processes and written genres, their skills and perceptions; what they are able to do and what they want at the beginning of the course. Data can therefore be both objective (age, proficiency, prior learning experiences) and subjective (self-perceived needs, strengths, and weaknesses).
- *Target situation analysis* concerns the learner's future roles and the linguistic skills and knowledge required to perform competently in writing in a target context. This involves mainly objective and product-oriented data: identifying the contexts of language use, observing the language events in these contexts, listing the genres employed, collecting and analyzing target genres.

Reflection 3.2

What information do you think it is most important to collect about learners at the beginning of a writing course? What do you think might be the best ways to collect this information? How could this information help you in designing your writing syllabus?

---

info. to gather →

Present Situation Analysis	Target Situation Analysis
Why are learners taking the writing course? compulsory or optional whether obvious need exists personal/professional goals motivation and attitude what they want to learn from the course	**Why does the learner need to write?** study, work, exam, promotion, etc.
	What genres will be used? lab reports, essays, memos, letters, etc.
How do learners learn? learning background & experiences concept of teaching & learning methodological & materials preferences preferred learning styles & strategies	**What is the typical structure of these genres?**
	What will the content areas be? academic subject, professional area, personal interest, secondary school, craftsman, managerial
Who are the learners? age / sex / nationality / L1 subject knowledge interests sociocultural background attitudes to target culture	**Who will the learner use the language with?** native or nonnative speakers reader's knowledge – expert, layman, etc. relationship – colleague, client, teacher, subordinate, superior
What do learners know about writing? L1 and L2 literacy abilities proficiency in English writing experiences and genre familiarity orthography	**Where will the learner use the language?** physical setting: office, school, hotel linguistic context: overseas, home country human context: known/unknown readers

Source: After Hutchison and Waters, 1987: 62–3.

Figure 3.2: A framework for needs analysis.

Figure 3.2 summarizes the information that the syllabus designer needs to gather about both the present and target situations in the form of general questions.

Reflection 3.3

Do you think target or present needs should be given priority in designing an L2 writing syllabus? How could a syllabus actually be designed to take account of students' current wants?

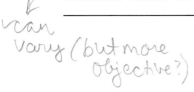
can vary (but more objective?)

Table 3.1: *Some common needs data collection methods*

Personal goals and priorities	brainstorming, group discussions, individual interviews, student diaries
Learning preferences	interviews, group discussions, questionnaires, observations diaries
Background information (age, gender, prior learning, immigration status, L1, L1 literacy, occupation, years in country)	enrollment documents, individual interviews, questionnaires, observations
Current L2 proficiency (English literacy and writing experiences)	placement or diagnostic tests, individual interviews, classroom observations
Target behaviors	interviews with learners, interviews with "experts," literature reviews, genre analyses, examinations of tasks, observations of target sites, questionnaires, case studies

Collecting needs data

In order to collect data on the various needs described above, the teacher may have to draw on a range of different sources and techniques. Brown (1995: 45) lists twenty-four different procedures for collecting needs data, grouping them into six main categories: existing information, tests, observations, interviews, meetings, and questionnaires. The list might be extended to target situations by also including literature reviews and text analyses. Table 3.1 lists some of the main methods used to collect different types of information in needs analysis.

It is rarely necessary to employ all these procedures, and the choice will obviously depend on the time and resources available. It should be remembered, however, that different methods address different areas and it is always a good idea to triangulate approaches to data collection (i.e., collect information from several sources) to achieve a more reliable and comprehensive picture.

Reflection 3.4

Select one of the methods listed in Table 3.1 and consider how it might be useful when designing a syllabus. What are its strengths, what information could it provide, and how could you use this data in syllabus planning? Can you foresee any problems in using this method? How might you overcome these?

Writing tests. One of the most widely used sources of information about learners is writing tests. Students are normally tested upon entering a course or institution and the results can also be useful to course designers, both for sorting students into levels of writing proficiency and revealing areas of weakness that can be addressed in the course.

Writing assessment will be discussed in detail in Chapter 8, but it is important to note the limitations of placement tests for measuring students' writing skills as part of a needs analysis. Indirect measures of writing such as multiple choice tests are widely used for their convenience, but are unreliable indicators of learners' abilities. Unfortunately the main alternative, a single timed essay, provides little information about students' abilities to produce a sustained piece of writing for different audiences or purposes. Moreover, the holistic scoring procedures generally used to mark such essays often fail to distinguish students with mid-range scores who may have different writing strengths and weaknesses (e.g., Hamp-Lyons, 1991). A response to two different writing tasks, such as an imaginative writing and an information transfer essay, increases the chances of accurately placing students and providing reliable information about their writing abilities.

Text analyses. Perhaps the most important source of target situation data in devising an L2 writing syllabus is the analysis of authentic texts. Examples of the texts that learners are expected to produce in their target contexts provide invaluable information about relevant content, format, and language for teaching and may also be used as classroom materials. Analyzing texts may seem a daunting prospect for many teachers, but it is important to identify the main features of the kinds of writing to be taught. The regularities in texts of the same kind allow commonly occurring patterns to be described and taught. One pattern found in a range of academic, business, and social genres is the *problem-solution* pattern discussed by Hoey (1983). This has four basic moves:

Situation: Last week we announced our annual sale of high-quality computer equipment.

Problem: This proved so popular that all stock was sold within a few days and many customers were unable to buy the goods they needed.

Response: We have placed an order for more stock with our suppliers, which will arrive tomorrow.

Evaluation of response: Customers can now find everything they need in our shop.

Other familiar patterns in English texts are *claim-justification, general-particular*, and *hypothetical-real*. Because these are common patterns across many genres they are highly productive teaching items, and the fact that they can be expressed at different levels of complexity means that they can be taught to students at different proficiency levels.

As noted in Chapter 1, texts may be described in terms of the ways they are structured, or staged, to achieve different purposes in writing, and a large research literature has developed which describes many school and professional genres. This research is a good place to start to understand how particular genres work and the clusters of register, style, lexis, and other features that distinguish them. Teachers can find descriptions of sales letters (Bhatia, 1993), research article introductions (Swales, 1990), application letters (Henry and Roseberry, 2001), business faxes (Akar and Louhiala-Salminen, 1999), and many other professional genres that students may have to write. Macro-genres such as *narrative, recount, argument*, and *report*, which routinely occur in the kinds of writing required in school and university contexts, have also been described (e.g., Butt et al., 2000; Lock and Lockhart, 1999).

Reflection 3.5
Choose a text suitable for a particular group of students you are familiar with. Can you recognize its genre? Are there any particular features of the text that suggest this? Can you identify any stages in the text? Compare your responses with those of a classmate.

Questionnaires, interviews, and observations are important methods of collecting needs analysis data (see Chapter 9). *Questionnaires* are perhaps the most widely used means of collecting needs data and are useful for eliciting information on students' personal goals, attitudes, and backgrounds, although careful thought is needed in constructing questions to avoid ambiguity and to achieve a balance between gathering sufficient data and not overburdening L2 respondents. Structured *interviews*, drawing on prepared questions, are more time-consuming, but help build rapport with students and allow follow-up questions to better understand their needs. Finally, *observing* students actually writing can be useful in discovering students' difficulties with writing tasks and, like interviews and questionnaires, can also provide information about the behaviors, expectations, and perceptions of those in target contexts.

Reflection 3.6
Look again at the learning styles questionnaire in Appendix 2.1. Do you think this would be useful as part of a needs analysis exercise? What other questions would you want to include to make it broader in scope? Could you adapt this for a class for lower proficiency students?

Finally, a caution. I have considered needs largely in terms of language needs and the behaviors students need to acquire to perform successfully in particular domains of writing. But all decisions about what to teach and how to teach it are not simply neutral professional questions but involve issues of power with possibly important consequences for learners. In devising writing syllabi we need to reflect on whether students' needs are best served by adopting exclusively pragmatic and instrumental goals, or whether this simply accommodates them uncritically to the authority of existing institutions. A writing course for adult migrants, for example, might not only help participants to access resources through completing social services documents, but also to express and defend their interests in other areas. Similarly, courses preparing learners for academic study in English might help learners to articulate their reservations about their subject courses, providing them with the means to negotiate their roles and to help them "participate more democratically as members of an academic community and in the larger society" (Benesch, 2001: 61).

Reflection 3.7
Benesch (2001) refers to *rights analysis* as a way of highlighting power relations and seeing teaching as more than initiating students unquestioningly into particular discourse communities. What kind of methods could you use to identify the implicit and explicit regulation in a particular setting? How might you go about including this information in a writing course to facilitate students' access to greater cooperation and decision making in their target communities?

Analyzing the learning context

In addition to learner issues, teachers need to ensure that their writing syllabi will operate successfully in the local context, acknowledging the opportunities and constraints presented by the situation in which the course will run. By analogy with needs analysis, this is sometimes referred to as *means analysis* (Holliday and Cook, 1982) and involves consideration of the teachers, methods, available materials, facilities, and the relationship of the writing course to its immediate environment. Obviously, some of these elements are predetermined by circumstances while others permit teacher intervention.

Reflection 3.8

Consider a language teaching context you are familiar with and list some of the most important factors that are likely to influence the effectiveness of the course. Now rank them in order of importance. Are the most influential factors on your list always likely to be the most significant in syllabus design?

The first step in examining the local teaching context is to determine whether available resources will support the proposed course. Teachers are a key factor in the success of a teaching program and consideration needs to be given to their training, experience, attitudes, and expertise. Teachers already burdened with heavy workloads, for instance, may lack any enthusiasm to teach a new course, while those familiar with process orientations may lack the experience and commitment to implement a writing syllabus that emphasizes text genres and language outcomes. Local conditions must also be sufficient to ensure that adequate materials are available or can be developed. Are copies of a set text easily obtainable? Is there a teaching resource room? Can teachers develop resources with computers and photocopiers? Will library facilities support proposed assignments?

The syllabus designer must also carefully consider course constraints and what objectives can be realistically achieved within them. Intensive courses, for example, may be suitable for concentrating learners on a particular skill, such as report writing, but they may lack opportunities for reflection on texts or writing. The relationship of the course to other courses and to the wider curriculum is also important. In schools and universities students' needs are typically immediate as they will have to cope with the demands of an external exam or with writing in other subjects. Sometimes this will be in adjunct classes where the writing course runs parallel with a subject course and shares assignments with it (e.g., Benesch, 2001). In contrast, other courses prepare learners for writing in their future professional worlds. In these circumstances the kinds of writing students do and the topics they write about may be more negotiable depending on the predictability of these needs.

Institutional factors may also need to be taken into account as part of the learning context. Writing courses are typically delivered in institutions such as schools, language institutes, training centers, and so on, each of which will differ considerably in their aims and the priority they give to writing in the curriculum. Individual institutions also vary in terms of their "culture" or patterns of interaction, relationships, and decision making, influencing such issues as morale, teacher cooperation, attitudes toward innovation, and independent decision making among teachers. Each of these factors can affect how the syllabus is received and implemented in a particular institution.

More broadly, teachers should be sensitive to local sociocultural attitudes and practices when designing a writing syllabus. In Chapter 2 I discussed the importance of recognizing students' prior learning experiences and views toward classroom instruction. Means analysis considers similar factors at a societal level, stressing the fact that cultures differ in the status they afford English, the ways it is taught, and the uses to which writing is put. Canagarajah (1999: 5), for instance, describes how university students in the Jaffna peninsula of Sri Lanka expressed subtle forms of opposition to the ideologies embedded in their English syllabus. He suggests that teachers need to develop "a thinking on language, culture, and pedagogy that is motivated by the lived reality and everyday experience of periphery subjects." Similarly, Holliday (1994), discussing Egypt, cautions against the imposition of alien pedagogic models in non-Anglo EFL writing contexts.

Reflection 3.9

Imagine that your institution, or one you are familiar with, is installing a new media lab and has decided that all L2 writing instruction will be taught using computers and other technological aids. What factors might affect the reception of this idea and how could negative factors be addressed?

Some of the main dimensions and issues of context analysis are listed in Table 3.2.

It is important to bear in mind that a characteristic of most L2 writing courses is limited time and that this will almost certainly be insufficient to meet all students' needs. It is also true that the time available for collecting and analyzing needs data is also constrained, and in practice teachers may have to make syllabus decisions with incomplete information. What is crucial, however, is that writing syllabi are planned in advance and that as much data as possible are gathered to shape a relevant and interesting

Table 3.2: *Some features of the teaching context that can affect syllabus design*

● The society	Whether it is a Foreign or Second Language context EFL/ESL
	Attitudes toward English in the society (imperialistic, pragmatic, indifferent, etc.)
	The kinds of teaching methods and materials that are culturally appropriate
	The kinds of roles normally associated with teachers and learners
● The institution	Influence of "stakeholders" (school, employer, sponsor, government, etc.)
	The "culture" of the institution (attitudes to innovation, teacher autonomy, etc.)
	Morale of staff and students within the institution
● The resources	The number, background, and professional competence of teachers involved
	Teachers' knowledge and attitude to the syllabus, materials, and methods
	Availability of materials, aids, library facilities, etc.
	Technological and reprographic resources (computers, photocopiers, etc.)
	Physical classroom conditions (pleasant, noisy, cold, etc.)
● The course	The length of the course and what it can reasonably hope to achieve
	Whether the course is intensive or extensive and frequency of sessions
	Whether the course is linked to other courses in the curriculum
	Whether the course focuses on students' current or future needs
	Whether there is an external examination
● The class	Whether the group has been selected on the basis of language proficiency
	Whether the group is homogenous in terms of goals, age, interests, etc.

writing course. We should also note that needs analysis is not a "done-once-then-forgotten activity." Behind every successful writing course there is a continuous process of questioning and revision to check the original results, evaluate the effectiveness of the course, and revise objectives. Teacher-led classroom research, monitoring of student writing, and ethnographic observation can play useful roles in developing appropriate practices throughout the course (see Chapter 9). Needs analysis, then, is always dynamic and ongoing.

Setting course goals and objectives

Once collected and analyzed, needs analysis data are used to formulate course goals (or aims) and objectives. Goals are rather general statements about what the course hopes to accomplish (Brown, 1995). They are the global target outcomes around which the syllabus is organized given the students' purposes and abilities, their target needs, and institutional requirements. The following are the goals for a process-oriented university academic writing course (Holst, 1993).

The course has been designed to help students:

- Realize the power of writing to assist learning in clarifying thinking and understanding;

- Develop efficient and effective techniques for generating, organizing, drafting, and editing written texts;
- Master the conventions and techniques of academic writing in the university;
- Develop grammatical competence and awareness in their written expression.

Goals can vary in their emphasis on affective, learning, language, and cognitive outcomes, but they should seek to reflect skills that can be described, practiced, and assessed in the course. It is also worth bearing in mind that goal statements do not directly and objectively relate to needs. Once again, judgments are involved as the teacher brings his or her beliefs and views about language and learning to syllabus planning. It is the teacher, not the analysis, that determines which skills and abilities are worth pursuing and achieving.

While goals tend to be broad statements of purpose, instructional objectives are more specific, describing "the particular knowledge, behaviours, and/or skills that the learner will be expected to know or perform at the end of the course" (Brown, 1995: 73). Objectives thus break down goals into smaller, achievable units of learning which can provide the basic framework of the course and a coherent learning program for students. The goals listed above for an academic writing course, for example, translate into the following objectives (Holst, 1993: 4).

By the end of the course, a student will be able to:

- Specify a purpose, audience, and format for a given writing task;
- Generate questions and ideas using a variety of brainstorming, free writing, and analytical techniques;
- Draft a paper rapidly;
- Edit a draft for sense, organization, audience, and style;
- Evaluate and edit others' writing;
- Analyze a specialist text for its structure and characteristic stylistic features;
- Write an essay with a thesis, supporting argument, introduction, and conclusion;
- Write an essay using multiple sources and appropriate citation techniques.

Some planners (e.g., Mager, 1975) advocate that objectives should specify three essential dimensions:

- *Performance*: what learners will be able to do
- *Conditions*: the parameters within which they can do it
- *Criteria*: the level of competence expected

So, for example, an objective from an elementary writing course might be: *By the end of the course students will be able to complete gapped sales letters from the textbook with 80 percent accuracy.* This kind of precision allows objectives to be finely graded for different proficiency levels by modifying the conditions and criteria. It is likely, however, that most teachers would find such behavioral objectives too unwieldy – as the system generates more objectives than they could possibly teach, and too constraining – forcing them to focus only on a narrow band of skills and products. More realistically, Richards (2001: 122–4) suggests that four features provide sufficient guidance for syllabus planning, teaching, and assessment. Objectives should:

- describe a learning outcome – objectives should be phrased in terms of what learners will be able to do at the end of the course rather than what they will do during it.
- be consistent with goals – all objectives should contribute to the overall purpose of the course.
- be feasible – objectives should be possible to achieve in the time frame of the course.
- be precise – vague and ambiguous objectives are unhelpful.

Reflection 3.10

Which of the following objectives violate Richards' criteria? Which points do they fail to meet for a writing course?

1. Learners will learn about note taking from different sources.
2. Students will be able to take detailed notes on familiar topics.
3. Students will know how to use useful English expressions in personal letters.
4. Learners will brainstorm essay ideas in groups.
5. Course participants will be able to publish their writing in international journals.
6. Students will be able to recognize and use greetings, feedback, and closures in casual conversation.

Objectives thus provide information for teachers and learners about what will be accomplished and act as reference points for selecting and sequencing content and activities into units of work and lessons. While teachers may see the planning role of objectives as more important, the value of providing learners with detailed information about goals and objectives is crucial. If

Table 3.3: *Syllabus information for students*

- ✔ Course name, number, and any prerequisites
- ✔ Instructors' names and contact details
- ✔ Course goals and objectives
- ✔ Materials – titles of set texts or handouts, where to get them, and details of any reading assignments
- ✔ Instructional methods – time devoted to input, workshops, discussions, etc., and expectations about participation and attendance
- ✔ Course schedule – class-by-class calendar of topic coverage and assignments
- ✔ Course requirements – assignments with weightings and deadlines and full assessment criteria

---

they know what the course will offer them, how it is relevant to their needs, and what they have to do to meet course requirements, then students are more likely to be involved in the course and to appreciate and accept the learning experience in which they will engage. It can be useful therefore to provide learners with a handout with the information in Table 3.3.

Developing the syllabus

The next stage of designing an ESL writing syllabus is to determine the content, tasks, and assignments which will meet the objectives that have been established for the course. An effective writing syllabus will include a balance of writing skills and text knowledge and a variety of topics, task types, genres, and input, with discussions, talk, and data gathering as input for writing. As I have noted, these decisions do not automatically flow from needs data or instructional objectives but involve making judgments. A syllabus publicly announces what the teacher regards as important to the course and to good writing and so reflects his or her philosophy of writing, including beliefs about language and learning.

Reflection 3.11

Can you think of ways by which our beliefs about language, learning, and writing might influence our decisions about how to select and sequence items for a syllabus?

We saw in Chapter 1 that a writing course can be organized around one or more of a number of guiding orientations depending on the teacher's views. I want to take a broad perspective here and suggest that language is a resource for making meanings to achieve particular purposes in social contexts and that learning involves gaining control of these resources. This view does not commit the teacher to any single course orientation but ensures that he or she makes provision for each of the five kinds of knowledge and skills listed at the end of Chapter 1:

- *Process* – making provision for students to develop their composing skills with different types of writing practice (journals, timed essays, out-of-class assignments, etc.)
- *Genre* – ensuring relevant genres are included and deciding how these will be modeled/introduced
- *Context* – familiarizing learners with the contexts in which the genres are used and the roles and relationships they imply
- *System* – teaching the elements of the language system students need to understand the genre and complete the writing tasks
- *Content* – selecting and sequencing the topics and content domains students will learn "through"

Clearly there are a number of ways a syllabus can be organized to include these elements, but all approaches begin by selecting one as the core element, then organizing the others to form a coherent sequence which ensures that students can progress smoothly from one developmental step to the next. In a content-based syllabus, for instance, topics are selected according to their relevance or interest to learners and sequenced by learner need or difficulty. Process writing syllabi generally focus on students gradually learning to create texts by mastering writing strategies. As a result they are organized around a series of assignments (Ferris and Hedgcock, 1998) sequenced to facilitate multi-drafting, polishing, and evaluating written work. In a genre writing syllabus, on the other hand, the basic element is text-types, selected according to learner need and sequenced according to their use in a real-life situation or increasing levels of technicality, abstractness, or rhetorical complexity (Paltridge, 2001).

Reflection 3.12

In many target contexts one genre often relates to or interacts with others. They form part of "genre sets." Think of a situation where one genre normally follows another. For example, what written genres usually precede a research essay or a job interview? Could these connections be useful in designing a writing course? Consider how you might make use of this idea in syllabus design.

Table 3.4: *Planning a writing course*

- Write course objectives based on overall goals and established by needs analysis.
- Organize the objectives so they can be achieved through manageable chunks of writing elements (i.e., units of work based on content, genres, processes, etc.).
- Link and sequence these units of work.
- Organize each unit to achieve its objectives.
  1. Select element for the starting point of the unit (topic, genre, process strategy, language point).
  2. Select texts, contexts, audience, content, and so on for the unit.
  3. Identify text features that are required to complete the writing tasks.
  4. Select methodology – procedures, input sources (reading/film/visit/etc.) and resources to support progress toward the objectives of the unit.
- Select teaching and learning activities and sequence them to move from teacher-supported to independent tasks with learners gaining increasing control of an aspect of writing.
- Integrate diagnostic and achievement assessment into the units to measure learner progress.
- Integrate course monitoring for the ongoing evaluation and revision of the course.

Whatever a teacher's preference, syllabus planning always takes time. Although objectives provide a framework for structuring learning, these have to be transformed into units of work and individual lessons. The scope of the course needs to be determined, or the range and extent to which content will be covered, given the proficiency of the students, the time, and resources available and so on, must be planned. Then ideas for units of work have to be generated through brainstorming and refining possible themes or topics, finding suitable texts, understanding how these texts work, and devising appropriate activities.

Of critical importance at this stage is determining the linguistic and strategic resources that students will need in order to complete writing tasks. This will involve deciding on the techniques learners require to generate material, gather data, structure ideas, and express meanings in constructing specific genres. Teachers therefore have to look carefully at texts to understand the distinct ways meanings are coded, both at the level of the whole text in relation to its purpose, audience, and message, and how paragraphs and sentences are structured (Knapp and Watkins, 1994). This information then has to be related to the learners' current abilities and the tasks and activities selected to help guide them to construct effective texts (see Chapter 4). Table 3.4 sets out the steps in this process.

Teachers also need to consider the content areas through which students will learn to write. Macken-Horarik (1996) has suggested a framework for planning topic areas based on a series of experiential domains which make increasing demands on learners in terms of the knowledge on which they

	Everyday	⇨ Applied	⇨ Theoretical	⇨ Critical
Type of knowledge	Common sense	Practical	Formal education	Informed
Identity and Roles	Familiar	Practitioner	Impersonal	Complex
Topics and language	Home, family, community	Work skills	Technical and professional	Interpretative
		Domestic		Persuasive
		Hobbies		

Source: After Macken-Horarik, 1996.

Figure 3.3: Experiential content domains.

draw to provide content for writing and what this involves for the types of texts they write. As can be seen from the summary in Figure 3.3, L2 learners with little formal education can begin their writing instruction with topics associated with the everyday domain, while those who bring specific skills to the classroom are introduced to genres and varieties of language through those skills. Students with higher levels of education in their L1 and with clear needs usually begin with the applied or theoretical domains. Clearly, however, many topics can be considered from any of the four domains, allowing students to move from one domain to another within a single topic or for a disparate group of students to work on the same topic in different domains.

Reflection 3.13
Consider how you might use the information in Figure 3.3 to plan for a group of learners with diverse educational backgrounds and experiences. Select one topic that all the students could work on in different domains. How would group work help you to organize learning in the class?

Sample approaches to syllabus organization

It may be helpful at this point to briefly consider how all of this fits together into the final syllabus. I have noted that process and genre orientations are

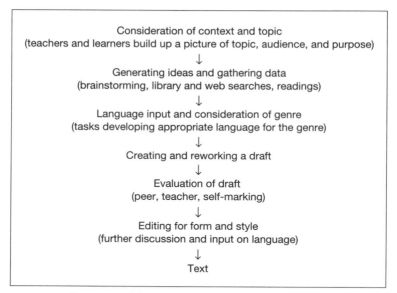

Consideration of context and topic
(teachers and learners build up a picture of topic, audience, and purpose)
↓
Generating ideas and gathering data
(brainstorming, library and web searches, readings)
↓
Language input and consideration of genre
(tasks developing appropriate language for the genre)
↓
Creating and reworking a draft
↓
Evaluation of draft
(peer, teacher, self-marking)
↓
Editing for form and style
(further discussion and input on language)
↓
Text

Figure 3.4: A process-driven syllabus model.

the dominant approaches to L2 writing teaching, but we have also seen the need to combine and sequence other elements within these syllabuses. Whatever the approach, it is important to recognize that learning to write requires knowledge about language, knowledge of the context and purpose for the writing, and the skills in crafting texts.

A *process-driven* writing course will give priority to techniques for generating, drafting, reshaping, and evaluating texts, with each unit of work perhaps emphasizing a particular element of the process and assisting learners to see its recursive nature. It will recognize, however, that all writing is embedded in a particular context and written to achieve a particular purpose, and that these contexts have to be made explicit and linked to relevant content areas. Topics may be negotiated with learners or generated by the priorities of a needs analysis, with selected readings used to enhance topic knowledge and raise genre and rhetorical awareness. Although each unit of work will move through the process cycle, the learners' needs for explicit linguistic knowledge will be acknowledged with input provided in various ways to ensure they have the resources to create the texts they are asked to write. Each unit of work will therefore incorporate opportunities for learners to develop their writing strategies together with explicit teaching of the structures and realization features of target genres. Figure 3.4 shows this diagrammatically.

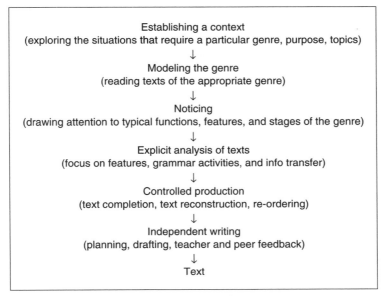

Establishing a context
(exploring the situations that require a particular genre, purpose, topics)
↓
Modeling the genre
(reading texts of the appropriate genre)
↓
Noticing
(drawing attention to typical functions, features, and stages of the genre)
↓
Explicit analysis of texts
(focus on features, grammar activities, and info transfer)
↓
Controlled production
(text completion, text reconstruction, re-ordering)
↓
Independent writing
(planning, drafting, teacher and peer feedback)
↓
Text

Figure 3.5: A genre-driven syllabus model.

Genre-driven courses, on the other hand, will take texts as the starting point but provide opportunities for learners to develop text-generating strategies. The guiding principle is that literacy development requires an explicit focus on the ways texts are organized and the language choices that users must make to achieve their purposes in particular contexts. Genres offer a focus for understanding the types of texts students will need in a given situation and also act as vehicles for relevant topics. Beginning with contexts, students gradually acquire an understanding of how texts and sentences are structured so that they are meaningful, clear, and accurate and a means of discussing the relationship between a text and its context and how it changes in different situations. The syllabus aims to move the learner through various tasks related to the genre being taught and the kinds of process skills required to produce it, gradually withdrawing support as confidence and abilities are developed. Figure 3.5 outlines this model.

In sum, all syllabus design should acknowledge that the skills involved in learning to write include the ability to draft, revise, conference, edit, proofread, and publish, and to form well-structured, effective texts. Whether the teacher starts from contexts, processes, genres, topics, or structures, each aspect should be included and related to the others in ways that gradually develop students' abilities to write and to understand the effects of the available choices. Various sources of input and activities are essential, with opportunities for learning through readings, discussions, and controlled exercises as well as independent writing.

Reflection 3.14

How can a syllabus and course outline help us in planning writing instruction? List the advantages to students of a planned writing course. Which of the two models sketched in Figures 3.4 and 3.5 do you think offers the most to L2 writing students?

Planning units of work

Teachers do not generally develop lessons directly from their syllabus, but break the syllabus down into units of work which are instructional blocks of several lessons planned around a single instructional focus or theme. Richards (2001: 166) lists five factors that account for a successful unit of work:

1. Length – sufficient material but not overly long to create boredom
2. Development – one activity leads smoothly to the next in a logical way
3. Coherence – the unit has an overall sense of coherence
4. Pacing – each activity moves along and no activity is markedly longer than the others
5. Outcome – at the end of the unit, students know how to do a related series of things

 Once again, objectives are important to ensure that appropriate learning is achieved. Just as syllabus objectives specify the knowledge and skills students will acquire at the end of a course, lesson and unit objectives describe the observable behaviors learners will display at the end of the unit. The way that units relate directly to the course objectives can be seen in this example from a school context:

Syllabus objective:

Students will be able to produce a range of well-structured and well-presented factual texts for a wide variety of purposes and audiences.

Unit objectives:

Students will collect information on a series of events by completing a worksheet.

Students will write a recount in the form of a diary.

Students will use these sources to jointly compose a factual recount of a
class excursion.

Individual students will develop the recount by adding in words/phrases
to describe people, events, locations, time, in more detail.

The proposed outcome is clearly stated in terms of student behaviors
that can be observed and evaluated, using action verbs such as *collect*,
write, and *compose*. While not all teachers write detailed objectives for
units and lessons, they do have clear outcomes in mind, ensuring that
each activity can be justified in terms of what the syllabus is seeking to
achieve.

It is a good idea for novice teachers to include their objectives in plans
to ensure a successful connection is made with syllabus aims and to provide a principled means of integrating and sequencing tasks and content.
These two teachers mention two ways of using the syllabus objectives for
planning:

The syllabus is set by the Ministry in my school, but I find it useful in planning
classes. We use a textbook for writing classes in my school but it's mainly a grammar
book and not very interesting, so I have to organize the classes myself or it would
just be grammar drills. When I prepare a class or series of classes I check to see
what is on the syllabus and what is appropriate to teach next. I use this to plan and
schedule the activities I want the students to do and the kinds of text analyses we
will do. The objectives help me go in the right direction. Then I go to the resource
room and use materials as I need them.

I usually start with a topic for a unit and we normally work this out in class, what
the students are interested in. Then I collect texts for readings around the topic. The
syllabus is a kind of checklist for what I need to do with the topic. So it tells me
whether students have to write a report or argument or whatever and what levels of
competency are required. My job is to put the syllabus into practice in as interesting
and effective a way as I can with lots of writing for the students.

To organize a series of lessons into a unit of work requires a theme.
Unit themes are best seen as real-life activities or situations in which people do specific things through writing rather than grammatical structures,
functions, or text-types. Common starting points for units are situations or
topics, as these provide potentially relevant and motivating ways to get into
writing while unifying a set of contexts and activities. The choice of situation or topic evokes a set of social contexts that can be organized according
to the experiential domains listed in Figure 3.3. Clearly, the situations and
topics selected for the units will depend on the proficiency of the students
and the objectives of the course, although many themes can be explored
within several domains.

Table 3.5: *Possible themes for organizing units of work*

Possible situations for writing	Possible topics for writing
• Responding to customer inquiries	• Impact of science
• Applying for a job	• Work and leisure
• Researching an argument essay	• Crime and punishment
• Writing a feasibility report	• Love and marriage
• Enrolling at university	• Terrorism

Each context suggests the key genres which tend to occur in that context and these provide a basis for selecting appropriate readings, text models, and discussion themes. In turn, these lead to decisions about the content material and the language input needed for particular learners, working from the target situation analysis or topic for the content and the text type for language. From here the tasks, language activities, and writing skills that students will need to practice can be developed. Situations for writing may be based on the students' target professional or academic contexts, and so involve an event sequence of relevant genres. The situation "applying for a job," for instance, is likely to involve scanning newspapers, writing applications and resumes, writing to referees, being interviewed, and follow-up letters. Topics can stimulate writing projects and serve to develop the different process skills for various kinds of writing. The topic "technology," for example, suggests a factual description (explaining how something works), a narrative of personal experience (an encounter with phone banking), an argumentative essay (pros and cons of the Internet), and so on. Some common situations and topics for units of work are given in Table 3.5.

Grabe and Kaplan (1996: 266–376) provide a range of excellent ideas for learning and assessment that can be drawn upon in this regard. In three chapters they offer seventy-five instructional themes or topics appropriate for teaching writing at beginning, intermediate, and advanced levels of proficiency organized into five general principles which can be useful for writing teachers:

1. Preparing students for writing through awareness, confidence building, development tasks, and so on
2. Assisting and guiding writing through ideas for organizing, adding information, and responding
3. Working with writing through different topic ideas and multi-drafting
4. Writing for different purposes through different genres
5. Extending the writing curriculum through independent opportunities for writing and awareness of styles.

When one or more topics have been selected, these then have to be organized and sequenced. Organizing provides an overall coherence to the course for students and is crucial in devising materials and activities. This involves deciding on the theme of each unit, how many lessons each unit will comprise, and how they will be sequenced. Themes can be sequenced in a number of ways and this will depend on the course and the learners. However, it is common to use one of the following principles:

- Begin with topics or situations that are concrete and relate to learners' prior experiences and everyday life and move on to more applied or theoretical topics later.
- Begin with topics that are relatively simple and that progress to more advanced activities.
- Begin with topics that meet the most urgent needs of learners. This is particularly relevant to new migrants and ESP learners.
- Begin with topics or situations that are less controversial or that generate simple polar opinions to allow students to develop the confidence to handle and express more varied views.

Planning lessons

Just as a unit of work is made up of a series of lessons that contribute to its coherence, lessons themselves should also be internally consistent so that students can recognize what is being learned and work toward an expected outcome. Lesson planning is one way of ensuring that this happens. Plans, however, should not be seen as commandments set in stone to be rigidly respected; some activities may not work as expected and not everything that is likely to occur in a class can be anticipated.

But this does not mean that lesson planning is wasted effort. It both familiarizes teachers with the lesson content and helps them to anticipate what may go wrong and so prepare for the unexpected. Equally importantly, planning lessons prompts us to think of our learners, their needs, interests, and difficulties, as well as encouraging reflection on our teaching by providing a framework for evaluating both successes and failures (Richards and Lockhart, 1994). So although lesson plans are useful, they are proposals for action rather than scripts to follow: a means to identify aims, consider learning, and predict problems. While there is no "right format" in constructing lesson plans, most consist of certain core components, written out in more or less detail depending on the teacher and the class, as shown in Table 3.6. An example lesson plan is shown in Appendix 3.1.

Table 3.6: *Elements for a lesson plan format*

✔ Lesson objectives – concrete aim, e.g., to design and draft a crime prevention leaflet; to build vocabulary for describing places for "my country" essay and practice structure of a short description
✔ Previous learning – reminder of work completed in previous units and class
✔ Materials and aids – textbook, handouts, any audiovisual materials needed
✔ Housekeeping – announcements, assignments to be collected or given, and so on
✔ Sequence of activities – time given to each activity, the tasks (discussion, input, reading, writing), the interaction types (individual, pair-work, groups) and instruction for transitions between tasks
✔ Contingency task – additional activity to fill out time or to substitute if one falls flat

Table 3.7: *Organization of a lesson*

1. Having a clear purpose	Know why you are giving the lesson – what it is leading to. It is often helpful if students know this too.
2. Selecting syllabus elements	The syllabus outline provides the basis of what is chosen. It is important that each lesson follows the last so learners experience a sense of progression through the syllabus.
3. Fitting activities to available time	Anticipate how long each activity will take and match activities to the time available. Appropriate pacing and variation of activities is vital. Open-ended activities (pair work, discussions of texts, feedback sessions) always take longer than expected.
4. Giving the lesson a clear structure	Each lesson needs an introduction to activate prior learning, linking it with previous lessons and stating objectives. Each activity is introduced to ensure students know what is expected of them and transitions are clearly signaled and organized. Having a variety of activities helps maintain students' interest and energy. Closure is achieved through a review of what has been done, the purpose that has been achieved, or a link with the next lesson.

Organization is the key to a successful lesson and this means careful time management, clearly setting out what both the teacher and learners will be doing at each phase of the class. For Feez (1998: 129), lesson organization involves the four main steps outlined in Table 3.7.

Reflection 3.15

In your view, what makes a good lesson in a writing class? What input should the learners receive? What kinds of tasks should be included and how should they be organized? Should students do a lot of writing in class or should this mainly be a homework activity?

Two remaining considerations in planning lessons concern setting the tasks and managing class interaction. The choice of writing tasks partly depends on the proficiency of the students and their familiarity with the genre being studied, but when students are working with a new genre it may be necessary to invest considerable time on activities that focus on the purpose, structure, and language features of the text as well as the most effective ways of planning and drafting it.

Teachers also need to be sensitive to the importance of different interaction patterns and seek to maintain motivation and concentration through a variety of patterns: teacher-fronted, class discussion, group and pairwork. It might also be useful to consider the advantages of varying the tempo of the lesson through a mix of difficult and easy activities or the extent to which tasks "stir or settle" learners, either enlivening them with controversial discussion, or calming them with reading tasks (Ur, 1996: 217). This variety needs to be carefully planned, however, with particular thought given to transitions between tasks and to pulling the class together at the beginning and end to ensure that students have a sense of structure and progression.

Finally, there is the issue of evaluating the effectiveness of the class and drawing lessons from this. It is important to reflect after a lesson and consider whether it was successful in achieving its aims, motivating learners, and facilitating learning. Reflection needs to go beyond impressions of whether the students seemed to be enjoying the class or whether the planned material was covered. The crucial issue is whether the students learned the material well or progressed with the writing tasks they were given. Periodic checks on learner performance or questionnaires asking students to evaluate the course are helpful, but reflection is the most immediate and effective technique. Brown (1995) and Richards and Lockhart (1994) suggest a number of systematic self-assessment tools, but most teachers simply can consider the students' responses to the activities and ask whether they would make changes next time: to the timing, the instructions, the kinds of writing done, the support provided, the sequence of learning, or the activity itself. Learning from what we have done is the best way to improve our practices, and reflection can offer a starting point for planning the next class.

Summary and conclusion

Designing a syllabus and the units of work and lessons that realize it in the classroom can be challenging tasks for writing teachers. This chapter has therefore offered principles and approaches to make these tasks more manageable. The main points were:

- Course design is based on a clear understanding of learners' backgrounds, interests, expectations, and abilities, and on knowledge of the texts and contexts of their target situations.
- All writing courses should take account of the realities of the institutional and cultural constraints and requirements within which they are taught.
- All syllabuses are shaped by our views on writing, including how we see language and learning. There is no such thing as "theory-free" teaching.
- Successful syllabi, units of work, and lesson plans are based on clearly formulated and achievable course goals and instructional objectives derived from pre-course and ongoing needs analysis.
- Planning needs to consider the processes, genres, contexts, language features, and content that will be addressed in the course.
- Effective lessons and units of work need a balance of tasks, interactional patterns, and opportunities for writing, but they also need to provide sufficient scaffolding for learners in terms of language input, content, contextual data, and process skills at early stages of learning to write a genre.
- Flexibility is an essential element of all planning and delivery.

Discussion questions and activities

1 Some teachers prefer not to use a syllabus, arguing that learning is too complex, personal, and multifaceted to be organized by a formal syllabus and no syllabus can adequately cater for the needs of individual learners. How do you respond to this argument?

2 Given constraints of time and other resources, it is often impossible to gather as much information about learners and their needs as we would like. Given such constraints, what kind of information do you consider it is most important to collect for a needs analysis? Justify your answer and suggest how you would use this information.

3 Look again at the framework for needs analysis in Figure 3.2 and use it to devise a needs analysis questionnaire for a group of new students you are about to teach. You might want to include questions which address the following areas:

- The situation in which students need to write in English
- The types of writing they will have to do
- What students hope to learn from the course
- Self-assessment of current writing abilities in English
- Views on textbooks or methods of learning

- Learning style preferences
- Views on English as an international language of communication

4 The following goals are taken from the school English writing syllabus for years 7 to 10 in New South Wales, Australia (Board of Studies, 1998a: 27). While the extract is incomplete, can you identify the main orientation of this writing syllabus? Select some of these general statements to write more specific instructional objectives.

The course will involve students in developing:

- A sense of the appropriate register for the situation.
- An ability to write to a purpose: to describe, narrate, reflect, inform, persuade, argue, make an exposition.
- An ability to write to an audience: the class, the teacher, other person, imagined persons or groups, the general reader, oneself.
- An ability to write in various forms: personal records, stories, novels, poems, plays, articles, letters, news items, items for use in various media.
- An ability to assess one's own writing and from this grow in confidence and competence as a writer.
- An awareness in their writing of the conventions which promote clarity of meaning.

5 What would be a suitable theme for writing class for a group of learners you know? Consider how you might use this theme to sketch out a unit of work. In particular, think about the following questions:

What situational contexts, content, and genres does the theme suggest?
Do the genres form a natural sequence?
What kinds of readings could exploit the themes?
What are some of the main language forms that students would need to write these genres?
What would be a suitable writing assignment for this theme?

6 What are the advantages of writing lesson plans and reflecting on their effectiveness? Using the format outlined in Table 3.6, create a lesson plan for a writing course you are familiar with or for a textbook unit that you would like to use. Evaluate its strengths and weaknesses for a particular group of learners.

7 Look at the lesson plan in Appendix 3.1 for a 90-minute intermediate EFL class. Using the criteria and principles discussed in this chapter, consider its strengths and weaknesses. Are the objectives clear and achievable? Do the activities address the instructional objectives? Is there a balance of tasks and sufficient scaffolding? How would you follow up this lesson to develop narrative writing further in the next class?

Appendix 3.1

Lesson plan for a writing class

Goal		Learners will write a short accident report	
Objectives		1. To develop questions for describing an incident	
		2. To make notes on a short newspaper report	
		3. To discuss, compare, and combine information from notes in pairs	
		4. To draft a report of an accident from their notes	
Previous work		Taking notes from short texts. Model of report structure	
Materials		2 newspaper articles on same event (10 copies), OHT of model, OHT of Categories for questions	
Housekeeping		Record attendance. Give assignment date.	
Activities	T -> SS	Remind students of report.	5 min.
		Elicit purpose and structure. Put up OHT of structure	
	T -> SS	Introduce activity. Elicit questions students would ask if reporting an accident for a newspaper	5 min.
	T -> SS	Write up categories of information on board	5 min.
		What sort of incident? When did it happen?	
		Where did it happen? Who was involved?	
		What happened to each person?	
		What was the result? How did they feel?	
	T -> SS	Distribute articles – one to each student	
	S,S,S	Students, make notes on article using above categories	15 min.
	T -> SS	Put students in pairs – one with article A and one with Article B	
	S ↔ S	Students compare notes and add extra details from Partner	10 min.
	S,S,S	Students individually write up report from notes	30 min.
	S - -S -S - S	In groups students share each other's work	10 min.
	T -> SS	Discuss how the questions might be useful in other types of reports	10 min.
Extra activity		Groups select a headline for the text	

4 Texts and materials in the writing class

Aims: This chapter builds on the previous one by discussing the role of instructional materials in the writing class, elaborating the steps in selecting and supplementing published materials, in finding and using texts, and in designing and evaluating writing materials.

Teaching materials are central to writing instruction and are widely used to stimulate, model, and support writing. They tend to be mainly paper-based, but also include audio and visual aids, computer-mediated resources, and real objects. These materials provide most of the input and exposure to written language that learners receive in the classroom, and as a result our decisions about texts, coursebooks, and practice media are no less important than those we make when planning syllabuses and lessons. Because course outcomes significantly depend on them, teachers need to ensure that their classroom materials relate as closely as possible to the profiles of their learners, to program goals, and to their own beliefs as teachers. This means they have to be able to develop clear principles and procedures to make the best use of existing resources and create their own.

This chapter will consider the major issues and steps in these processes. Focusing mainly on print resources, it will explore the role of materials in L2 writing instruction, the value of authentic materials, textbook assessment, and procedures for modifying and developing materials.

Orientation

What different kinds of teaching materials – print, audio, visual, digital – are you familiar with? Why might writing teachers decide to supplement or modify a textbook with their own texts or activities? Write a list of potential sources of materials you might use to supplement a writing textbook.

Table 4.1: *The roles of materials in writing instruction*

1. *Language scaffolding*: Sources of language examples for discussion, analysis, exercises.
2. *Models*: Sample texts provide exemplars of rhetorical forms and structures of target genres.
3. *Reference*: Typically text or Web-based information, explanations, and examples of relevant grammatical, rhetorical, or stylistic forms.
4. *Stimulus*: Sources of ideas and content to stimulate discussions and writing and to support project work. Generally texts, but can include video, graphic, or audio material, items of realia, Internet material, or lectures.

The roles of materials in the writing class

Materials are generally used to provide a stimulus to writing or discussion, as a starting point for language input and analysis, and as ideas for organizing lesson activities. In EFL contexts, moreover, materials play a particularly important role as they may be the only contact that learners have with English and offer the only opportunities for them to study target texts. Table 4.1 lists the main roles materials play in writing instruction.

Reflection 4.1
Where would you go to find materials to fulfill each of these four roles? Can some materials perform more than one role? Which are likely to be the most important of these roles when teaching inexperienced writers? Are there any other purposes for using materials in L2 writing instruction?

Language scaffolding

An important role of instructional materials is to provide the foundation for learners' understandings of writing and language use. They are often used to present a focus for language, for example, to "scaffold" learners' evolving control of different texts as a preliminary to guided writing, or their understanding of salient text structures and vocabulary through sentence-level reinforcement exercises (e.g., Macken-Horarik, 2002; Rothery, 1986).

Materials that assist learners toward producing clear and accurate sentences and cohesive texts are obviously very important when learning to write, and will be discussed in more detail in Chapter 5. It is important to note here, however, that the most effective language exercises are not

a. Read the passage again and draw a box around all the words which have the same meaning as the word example. Notice how they are used and the punctuation that is used with them.

b. Now draw a line under all the examples. E.g., For example, many birds utter warning calls at the approach of danger.

c. The following sentences are based upon the information contained in the passage above. Complete the sentences making use of each of the following words (use each only once).

Illustration for example   a case in point   an example   for instance   such as

1. At the approach of danger many birds utter warning calls: this is _____ of animals communicating with each other.
2. Cries, _____ those of anger, fear, and pleasure, are uttered by apes.
3. There are important differences between human language and animal communication: _____, animals' cries are not articulate.
4. Animals' cries lack, _____, the kind of structure that enables us to divide a human utterance into words.
5. A good _____ of changing an utterance by substituting one word for another is a soldier who can say "tanks approaching from the north" or "tanks approaching from the west."
6. The number of signals that an animal can make is very limited: the great tit is _____ .

Source: Jordan, 1990: 39.

Figure 4.1: Materials illustrating some features of general descriptive texts. *Source:* Jordan, 1990: 39.

presented in isolation from the ways they are used in specific kinds of texts and domains, but relate closely to these to help students create meanings for particular readers and contexts. An example is shown in Figure 4.1, which highlights typical features of exemplification texts.

Models

Models are used to illustrate particular features of the text under study. Representative samples of the target discourse can be analyzed, compared, and manipulated in order to sensitize students to the fact that writing differs across genres and that they may need to draw on the particular structures and language features under study to achieve their writing goals. This approach is known as *consciousness raising* (e.g., Swales and Feak, 2000), a process that assists students both to create text and reflect on writing by helping them to focus on how a text works as discourse rather than on its content.

Informal elements in academic style

Table 1.2 Occurrences of six informal elements in thirty research articles

Element	No. of occurrences	Avg. per paper	No. of authors using element
Imperatives	639	21.3	30
I/my/me	1020	34.0	23
Initial *but*	349	11.6	23
Initial *and*	137	4.6	17
Direct questions	224	7.5	17
Verb contractions	92	3.1	11

Take a photocopy of what you consider to be a good but typical paper from your own specialized area, and with a highlighter, highlight all occurrences of the six informal elements that you find. Count and tabulate your findings. Then list and count the number of each different verb you found in the imperative (if any). If you are in a class, email your instructor your findings.

In general, how does your field compare to those in Table 1.2? What explanations for any differences occur to you? Which of these elements would you feel comfortable using yourself?

Have you come across or been told other prescriptive rules such as "never start a sentence with *however* as the first word," or "never use *which* to introduce a defining or restrictive relative clause"? Do you think such rules have validity?

Source: Swales and Feak, 2000: 17–18.

Figure 4.2: Model-based materials for consciousness raising in an advanced-level textbook.

It encourages and guides learners to explore the key lexical, grammatical, and rhetorical features of a text and to use this knowledge to construct their own examples of the genre. Two very different ways of using models for consciousness raising are shown in Figure 4.2, a task for post-graduate students, and Figure 4.3, an intermediate EFL exercise.

Typically students examine several examples of a particular genre to identify its structure and the ways meanings are expressed, and to explore the variations that are possible. Materials used as models thus help teachers to increase students' awareness of how texts are organized and how purposes are realized as they work toward the independent creation of the genre. As far as possible the texts selected should be both *relevant* to the students, representing the genres they will have to write in their target contexts, and *authentic,* created to be used in real-world contexts rather than in classrooms. So chemistry students, for example, would need to study reports of actual lab experiments rather than articles in the *New Scientist* if they wanted to eventually produce this genre successfully. An effective way of making models relevant to learners is to distribute and analyze exemplary

Models or examples can help you with what to write and how to write it.
- Look for models of the kind of writing you want to do.
- Keep a file of these so you will have them when you need them.
- Think about the content (the information included, the questions asked, the ideas mentioned).
- Look closely at the language used. Underline or make notes on any useful expressions.
- Look closely at the organization of ideas.
The model on the left was useful in writing the advertisement on the right.

BABYSITTER required to mind 8-year-old boy before and after school, 3 days/wk. Preferably with other school-aged children. Lewisham area. Phone Jim after 6pm, 71 3029.	*Tutor required to help with English after 5 p.m., 2 nights/wk. Preferably in my home. Summer Hill area. Phone Ming after 4.30 p.m. 798-2014*

Source: Brown and Hood, 1989: 11.

Figure 4.3: Model-based materials for writing in a lower intermediate textbook.

samples of student writing, collected from either the present or previous courses.

Reflection 4.2
What kinds of models might you use with a group of students you are familiar with? What features would you concentrate on when using these texts?

Reference materials

Unlike materials for modeling and scaffolding, which focus on practice, reference works concern knowledge. This category includes grammars, dictionaries, rhetorics, reference manuals, and style guides, but they all function to support the learner's understanding of writing through explanations, examples, and advice. Many students welcome this type of textual support, and reference works are particularly useful to learners engaged in self-study with little class contact. Some teachers recommend reference texts as resources when students come to edit their texts as they typically provide a great deal of well-organized and self-explanatory information. Some caution needs to be exercised in assigning reference books, however, as many tend to be highly idiosyncratic in their selections, subjective in their analyses, and prescriptive in their advice. Few are actually based on an analysis of real texts and more often simply represent their authors' intuitions about good writing rather than their research into it (Hyland, 1998).

Many students rely heavily on bilingual dictionaries or electronic translators and on the thesaurus, grammar checker, and dictionary components of their word processor. There is nothing wrong with this, of course, particularly in early stages of learning, as they may well provide what the student is looking for. Yet these resources are unable to show how words are actually used in the foreign language and fail to give sufficient information about grammatical context, appropriacy, and connotation. In the longer term, students are likely to find a good monolingual dictionary, either paper or electronic, more useful. This is particularly true if learners are trained to use it effectively and are able to combine the information it gives with that provided by computer-generated concordances (Chapter 6). Advice and practice in how to use these tools can have enormous benefits for L2 learners. Useful suggestions on dictionary activities can be found in Nation (1990) and concordance tasks in Tribble and Jones (1997).

Reflection 4.3

Do you ever use a reference source when you write? What kinds of information do you use it for? Would you ask your L2 students to refer to this source? Why or why not?

Stimulus materials

Materials are also commonly employed to initiate pre-writing and postwriting reflections and tasks. The purpose of these materials is to involve learners in thinking about and using language by stimulating ideas, encouraging connections with particular experiences, and developing topics in ways that articulate their ideas and engage readers. They provide content schemata and stimulate creativity, planning, and editing with a sense of audience, purpose, and direction. Stimulus materials include:

- Readings: poems, short stories, journalistic texts, autobiographies, professional texts
- Audio materials: songs, rap lyrics, music, lectures, recorded conversations, radio plays

Pages on canvas

Look at the paintings on the next page [Magritte: *The submissive reader* and Mul-
ready: *The Sonnet*] and decide what each of the two women is reading (e.g., a
letter? A message? A poem?) and why she is reacting so strongly.
Write the texts they are reading.
Then exchange and compare the texts written by members of your group.

Poems about paintings

Choose one of the paintings reproduced below and write a poem about it. Remember that you can:

- Describe the whole painting or only one of its details.
- Describe the theme or the technique of the painter.
- Describe the painting factually or describe the feelings it evokes.
- Describe what you see or what one of the characters in the picture sees.
- Ask yourself questions about what is "outside the frame": what is unsaid or
  mysterious in the painting.
- Reflect on the painter as much as the painting: why was such a theme chosen?
  Why was it treated in such a way?

Source: Grellet, 1996: 103, 109.

Figure 4.4: Materials using visual materials as stimuli.

- Visual materials: video documentaries, movies, TV programs, pho-
  tographs, pictures, cartoons
- Electronic materials: Web pages, bulletin board discussions, chat rooms
- Realia: household objects, Lego bricks, cuisenaire rods, kit-form models

Each type of stimulus has its own particular characteristics which lend
it to different uses. Generally, the more detailed and explicit the material
is, the greater support it offers learners, so that a picture sequence, a letter of complaint, or a love song can provide relatively unambiguous and
structured ways of generating writing. On the other hand, material that is
open to numerous interpretations allows room for students to exercise their
creativity and imagination in their responses. Thus, a single picture, a poem,
or Lego bricks used to symbolize real objects can encourage divergent and
original writing. Two examples of materials that use paintings as sources
for writing are shown in Figure 4.4.

The main sources of stimulus for writing are texts themselves. Readings
are useful in developing students' extensive reading skills, encouraging
them to think critically about their own and others' work, and promoting
the habit of reading for pleasure. In addition, they also have the more instrumental purposes of stimulating interest in a writing topic and activating

students' prior content knowledge and experiences as a basis for writing. Teachers often select short stories, magazine articles, agony letters, and so on as a way of introducing a topic for discussion and brainstorming ideas for an essay on a similar theme. Many teachers make use of commercially produced literary anthologies designed for L1 students and containing personal essays, short fiction, humor, journalistic texts, poems, and other published writings. These anthologies sometimes include writing prompts and, occasionally, examples of student writing and so offer the teacher additional instructional options. These can, for instance, be used to illustrate good writing and elements of effective style, but generally the features of the texts provided are not explicitly dissected and analyzed as writing models.

Reflection 4.4

What kinds of materials do you think are likely to be most useful to you as a teacher? Does the answer to this question depend on the learners and the teaching context? Why might this be?

Materials and authenticity

An important consideration when selecting or designing materials is that of authenticity. This is the question of how far teachers should seek to use unedited real-world language materials or texts which are simplified, modified, or otherwise written or spoken to exemplify particular features for teaching purposes. While many textbooks contain invented examples and teachers often draw on their intuitions about the language used in texts, there are serious problems with this.

Clarke (1989: 73) observes that authentic materials have come to represent almost a "moral imperative" for language teachers. Clearly there are important reasons for selecting authentic texts as genre models. Careful needs analyses will have led to the genres students must learn to identify and create in their target contexts, and these cannot be easily imitated for pedagogic purposes (e.g., Kramsch, 1993; McDonough and Shaw, 1993). Simplifying a text involves altering its syntax and lexis to improve readability or to highlight a given feature, and this also alters the fundamental nature of the genre. There are considerable difficulties in maintaining cohesion, coherence, and rhetorical structure when rewriting, and texts that are created artificially as teaching materials to emphasize one particular element are only likely to distort others. Students may then fail to see how the elements of a text work together to form text structure. It also needs to be borne in mind that authentic texts carry considerable information about those who write them, their relationship to their audience, the culture of the community in which they are written, and the general contexts in which the genre is used. Much of this is lost with simulated texts.

On the other hand, authentic texts are not always good models and teachers should be careful to weed out those that are poorly structured and incoherent. Nor is it always easy to obtain genuine examples of target texts, particularly in professional workplaces, where access may be restricted for security or privacy reasons. Even where authentic texts are available, exploiting these creatively and effectively to engage learners and maximize the potential of the material can be an enormous burden on teachers.

Finding authentic texts of the right length, the right level of comprehensibility, and with an accessible degree of cultural reference can be extremely time consuming, especially when teachers need to develop relevant and interesting activities that will make the most effective use of them (Bell and Gower, 1998). This may lead teachers to compromise. The problem is to control the difficulty of the material while maintaining authenticity. So although we need to ensure that students have good writing models, we should also take care that the level of the materials is not so far beyond them that they become disheartened and narrow their focus to the single words or phrases that they don't understand, rather than looking at the text as a whole.

Reflection 4.5

To what extent should the materials used in L2 writing classes always be authentic? Does an authentic text guarantee relevance and interest? Is authenticity or relevance the more important criterion? In what circumstances do you think it might be suitable to use commercial or teacher-written materials?

The issue of what students are asked to do with these authentic materials raises the problem of authentic use, as selecting real texts does not guarantee that they are used in ways that reflect their original communicative purpose. Once we begin to study and use them for writing tasks, letters, poems, memos, reports, essays, and so on become artefacts of the classroom rather than communicative resources. Nor is it always easy to clearly distinguish authentic from pedagogic materials, as many published materials include

Table 4.2: *Advantages and disadvantages of authentic materials*

Advantages	Disadvantages
Expose learners to real language	Language may be beyond learner competence
Encourage learners to process real texts	
Provide models relevant to learners' target needs	Not graded or sequenced for learning
	Places high demands on teacher expertise and time
Provide information about target culture	
Increase learner motivation and strategies	May be difficult to obtain a range of texts
Facilitate creative teaching to exploit texts	Can be bland, boring, and de-motivating
Maintains natural coherence and cohesion of text	May be poorly written
	Class use does not reflect original purpose

real texts within them, providing examples of writing from real communicative contexts. As a result, Day and Bamford (1998) criticize the "cult of authenticity" and advocate simplified readings, while Ellis (1999: 68) has recently argued for "enriched input," or texts flooded with exemplars of target features in meaningful texts. Table 4.2 summarizes the main pros and cons of authentic materials.

So, for these and other reasons, many teachers feel there is nothing intrinsically wrong with using created materials, especially at lower levels of language proficiency where students need the guidance and support of controlled input. In fact, many writing programs employ a mixture of authentic and created materials. The question of whether to use created materials largely depends on the pedagogic purpose the materials are to serve. What will students do with the materials? What do we want them to learn? When we move away from texts as genre models, for instance, the need for authenticity is less pressing and it might be preferable to use an adapted text or a specially written one. Materials created specifically to stimulate writing, practice language items, introduce content, and highlight features of target texts may actually be more effective than real texts. The bottom line is that students should not be misled about the nature of writing.

Reflection 4.6

Look again at the pros and cons of using authentic materials summarized in Table 4.2. Which of these points do you agree and disagree with? How would you respond to those you disagree with? Which argument do you find most convincing? How important is it to achieve authenticity?

Selecting and assessing textbooks

Commercial textbooks probably represent the most commonly used materials in the writing class and there are few teachers who do not make some use of them. Novice teachers can gain considerable support from having a textbook to work through, acquiring from it the confidence that they are covering all the important aspects of writing in a logical sequence and following tried and trusted principles of teaching. Many experienced teachers also rely heavily on them as a source of ideas for course structure, practice activities, and language models – dipping into them even when they are not used as set texts. In fact, owing to the constraints of inexperience, institutional pressures, or inadequate preparation time, published texts sometimes become not just a resource, but the entire writing course.

Reflection 4.7
Based on your experience as a student, what features of textbooks have you found most helpful to your learning? What do you think are the main advantages of a textbook to an L2 writing teacher? What dangers are there of depending too much on a textbook?

While there are obvious advantages for teachers and institutions in using textbooks, they also need to be treated with some caution. Sheldon, a long-time critic of published materials, argues that "The whole business of the management of language learning is far too complex to be satisfactorily catered for by a pre-packaged set of decisions embodied in teaching materials. Quite simply, even with the best intentions no single textbook can possibly work in all situations" (1987: 1).

Scrutiny of a dozen widely used writing textbooks on my desk reveals a number of common deficiencies: cultural biases in the readings, ad hoc grammar explanations poorly related to particular genres, vagueness about users' current proficiencies or backgrounds, lack of specificity about target needs, an over-reliance on personal experience themes, over-reliance on a single composing process, and invented and misleading text models. Most disturbingly, there is often little recognition given to the teaching implications of current linguistic research in these texts and so they ignore key features of writing and fail to reflect the ways writers actually use language to communicate in real situations. Table 4.3 summarizes these points. The staggering volume of commercial resources that teachers have to choose

Table 4.3: *The advantages and disadvantages of textbooks to the writing teacher*

Advantages	Disadvantages
Framework – gives course a sense of structure	Inadequacy – fails to address individual needs
Syllabus – guide to content to be covered	Irrelevance – content may not relate to needs
Resource – ready-made and tested texts and tasks	Restrictive – inhibits teachers' creativity
Reference – source of language information	Homogeneity – fails to address in-class variety
Economy – cheaper than in-house materials	De-skilling – teachers just mediate materials
Convenience – easy to use, store, and carry	Inauthentic – texts and readings often invented
Guidance – support and ideas for novice teachers	Intuitive – models based on author's intuitions
Autonomy – facilitates out-of-class work	Cultural inappropriacy – unsuitable content
Face validity – students see course as credible	Cost – may be a financial burden to students

from simply adds to the difficulties of selecting a textbook that corresponds with their own views of writing and most effectively meets the objectives of a course.

Teachers can consult colleagues for recommendations and views, and there are also numerous evaluation checklists that can be used for selecting textbooks (e.g., Cunningsworth, 1995; Harmer, 2001; Reid, 1993), but these tend to be very subjective and no set of criteria fits all situations (Johnson and Johnson, 1999). Textbook criteria are essentially local and selection involves more than simply matching needs to available resources. It is important that teachers feel they can work with the book to achieve their goals with a particular group of learners, and this means that they cannot just accept what others believe is appropriate. First, we need to be clear about the role we want the book to perform, then establish and check it against our own assessment criteria, and finally adopt a systematic and principled post-course evaluation of the book to determine how successful it was.

Before examining any textbook, it is helpful to consider some general issues:

- What is the general orientation of the course? Is it driven by genre, writing processes, topics?
- What role is the textbook required to play? A source of readings, models, information, content, or exercises? All of these? Will it be core to the program or will it supplement other materials?

- Who are the learners? What are their proficiency levels, their expectations of textbooks, their budgets?
- What are the learners' goals? Their immediate and target writing needs?
- What are the institutional constraints? Do financial, cultural, or educational factors restrict the choice?
- Who are the teachers? What training, skills, and experience do they have?

This consideration of the teaching context will provide a basis for determining the type of book needed, its orientation, role, proficiency level, and its suitability for teachers and the institution.

Following this initial reflection on the context, particular texts can then be screened according to a number of general requirements. For example, does the textbook:

1. Represent a coherent view of writing and learning?
2. Include interesting and appropriate readings that provide relevant content schemata?
3. Cover topics that are culturally appropriate and are included in the syllabus?
4. Present clear models of the genres we want our learners to recognize and reproduce?
5. Stimulate learning and writing by engaging students' interest, building their confidence, and encouraging them to use their existing knowledge and skills?
6. Contain varied, interesting, and relevant activities to help students develop appropriate pre-writing, composing, and editing skills?
7. Include helpful explanations and clear examples of relevant language use?
8. Provide strategies, suggestions, and supplementary materials for presenting and practicing writing?

Some of these requirements may be more important that others, but they do help to narrow the field. It is, in any case, easier to begin with a few key criteria than an unwieldy list, then go on to examine the shortlisted texts in more detail. A suggested basis for such criteria, which can be expressed as statements and then rated on a three-point scale, are outlined in Table 4.4.

Reflection 4.8
What do you consider to be the most important criteria for selecting a writing textbook? Do you have any to add to those listed in Table 4.4? What can the writing teacher learn from evaluating materials?

Table 4.4: *Some criteria for writing textbook assessment*

Aims and Approach	Degree of correspondence to students' needs and expectations, relevance to course goals and instructors' teaching philosophies and preferences, degree of cultural appropriacy.
Bibliographic Features	Quality and availability of the package (teacher's book, software, tapes); author's qualifications; degree of value for money and cost effectiveness.
Design	Attractiveness of layout, degree of visual appeal, readability of fonts, tables, etc., ease of navigation through the book, clarity of instructions, durability.
Organization	Extent to which sequencing and progression of exercises is suitable and coherent, how far sequencing and progression of units is suitable, appropriacy of proficiency level, smoothness of skill integration, extent of scaffolding at early stages, degree of recycling, and recursion of skills and content.
Content	Degree of authenticity, relevance, and appropriacy of the text genres, extent to which purposes, audiences, and contexts are addressed, interest level of readings and topics, sufficiency, accuracy, and reliability of language explanations, variety of tasks and models, proportion of time given to different types of knowledge, provision of evaluation tools, appropriacy and currency of topics and subject-matter areas.
Methodology	Extent to which tasks, exercises, and methods are appropriate to learners' proficiencies and goals, correspondence to teachers' preferred methods, how far independent writing is developed, degree of educational validity. Degree of likely learner involvement.
Usability	Flexibility of pathways through the book, degree of student-friendliness, and of teacher friendliness, completeness as a course, feasibility of completing book in available time, degree of usefulness of supporting materials and aids.
Overall	General quality of the text and its suitability for the purpose it is selected to perform.

Modifying writing textbooks

It is important to be realistic in our expectations about what a textbook can offer. The fact that publishers must target a mass audience to make a profit is likely to reduce the value of the book in any local context, but a textbook should not be rejected simply because it does not meet all instructional needs. Preparing new materials from scratch for every course is an impractical ideal and it is far more time- and cost-effective to be creative with what is available. Often a book may be useful if we supplement omissions or adapt activities to suit our particular circumstances. The eight points listed above to screen books for classroom use can be helpful in identifying where there are gaps between what students need and what the textbook offers. This will provide some principles to guide the modification process.

There are five ways of adapting materials, although in practice they actually shade into each other:

- *Adding*: supplementing or extending what the textbook offers with extra readings, tasks, or exercises.
- *Deleting*: omitting repetitive, irrelevant, potentially unhelpful or difficult items.
- *Modifying*: rewriting rubrics, examples, activities, or explanations to improve relevance, impact, or clarity.
- *Simplifying*: rewriting to reduce the difficulty of tasks, explanations, or instructions.
- *Reordering*: changing the sequence of units or activities to fit more coherently with course goals.

Reflection 4.9
Consider what action you would take to address each of these common textbook problems.

1. Text models are inauthentic and misleading. *add*
2. Exercises based on the texts are difficult, mechanical, or repetitive. *modify or delete*
3. Readings are unmotivating and difficult to exploit. *add*
4. Textbook fails to adequately situate the texts in terms of purpose, audience, and contexts. *modify*
5. Textbook addresses narrative writing only. *add*
6. There are too many activities on each reading. *delete*
7. Language explanations are linguistically flawed and unreliable. *simplify*
8. Course is too short to cover the book, but there are good texts and activities scattered through it. *reordering*

Clearly the problems listed in Reflection 4.9 require a variety of responses and make different demands on the teacher, but for most existing resources can be augmented with the other materials. Locating an authentic text that more accurately reflects the way language is used in that genre would be an appropriate response to 1, for instance, while additional readings or exercises would also address 2, 3, 4, and 5. Supplementing the dull readings with more motivating nontext materials might be a better solution to the third problem, however, and a film, photograph or taped interview might help resolve the lack of contextualization difficulty in 4. Nor is it always necessary to seek out new materials or engage in lengthy rewriting. Instead of replacing the exercises in 2, for instance, it might be possible to simply modify the rubrics to change the focus of the activities by attending to meanings and not just isolated forms, for instance. With 6 the central questions can be identified and the others deleted, and 7 may offer teaching opportunities with advanced learners who may be able to identify the errors. Question 8 suggests a more creative approach to the textbook, reordering the sequence of activities to ensure that the objectives of the course are met.

Modifying textbooks is an important skill for all writing teachers as it not only improves the resources available to students but also acts as a form of professional development. Teaching is largely a process of transforming content knowledge into pedagogically effective forms, and this is most in evidence when teachers are considering both their learners and their profession in modifying and creating materials.

Designing materials for the writing class

Designing new writing materials can be an extremely satisfying activity, demonstrating a professional competence and perhaps fulfilling a creative need in addition to offering students a more tailored learning experience. It is, however, also typically an intensive and time-consuming process. Dudley-Evans and St John (1998) estimate that to produce just one hour of good learning materials from authentic texts consumes at least fifteen hours of a teacher's time in locating sources and developing accompanying activities and exercises. There are good reasons therefore to lean heavily on existing materials as a source of ideas and for organizing materials writing teams, with two or three teachers sharing responsibilities for all aspects of the project. Team writing can involve individuals in creating separate units of work or in collaborating on finding texts, developing language and content exercises, and writing tasks. The advantages of working in teams can be considerable, not only in terms of the greater potential for a more diverse and higher quality final product as a result of combining interests and expertise, but also because collaboration can reduce the amount of effort, time, and frustration invested in the process.

The processes of creating new materials and modifying existing ones are very similar, and Hutchison and Waters (1987) suggest a framework

Table 4.5: *A model of materials design*

- **Input**: Typically a text in the writing class, although it may be a dialogue, video, picture, or any communication data. This provides
  - A stimulus for thought, discussion, and writing
  - New language items or the re-presentation of earlier items
  - A context and a purpose for writing
  - Genre models and exemplars of target texts
  - Spur to the use of writing process skills such as pre-writing, drafting, editing
  - Opportunities for information processing
  - Opportunities for learners to use and build on prior knowledge
- **Content Focus:** topics, situations, information, and other nonlinguistic content to generate meaningful communication
- **Language Focus:** Should involve opportunities for analyses of texts and for students to integrate new knowledge into the writing task.
- **Task:** Materials should lead toward a communicative task, in which learners use the content and language of the unit, and ultimately to a writing assignment.

Source: Adapted from Hutchison and Waters, 1987: 108–9.

for materials design that includes both adaptation and creation in a model which incorporates input, content, language, and a task. Table 4.5 shows what the model looks like when considering writing materials.

Reflection 4.10

Take a unit from any writing textbook and identify the four components of materials in Table 4.5. Consider how you would need to adapt it for the needs of a particular group of learners that you know. Can you think of an additional writing task that could be developed from it?

The model in Table 4.5 reflects the particular instructional roles of materials discussed earlier in this chapter, but emphasizes the integration of key elements in materials design. Materials lead to a task, and the resources of language and content that students need to successfully complete this task are supplied by the input. The teacher's aim should be to enable learners to communicate effectively in writing, and they cannot do this if they are simply given a topic and asked to write. They need to have something to write about, they need to know how to generate and draft ideas, and they need to have sufficient language and genre knowledge to perform the task. The materials students are given must facilitate this, and as a result materials development, whether this means creating new materials or

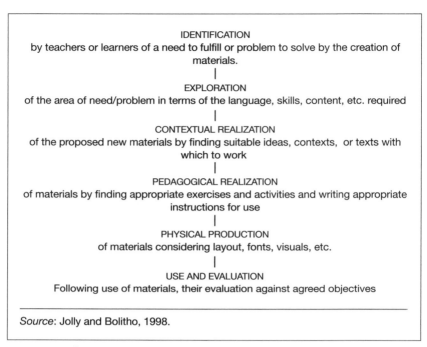

IDENTIFICATION
by teachers or learners of a need to fulfill or problem to solve by the creation of materials.

|

EXPLORATION
of the area of need/problem in terms of the language, skills, content, etc. required

|

CONTEXTUAL REALIZATION
of the proposed new materials by finding suitable ideas, contexts, or texts with which to work

|

PEDAGOGICAL REALIZATION
of materials by finding appropriate exercises and activities and writing appropriate instructions for use

|

PHYSICAL PRODUCTION
of materials considering layout, fonts, visuals, etc.

|

USE AND EVALUATION
Following use of materials, their evaluation against agreed objectives

Source: Jolly and Bolitho, 1998.

Figure 4.5: The process of materials writing.

adapting existing resources, is likely to begin by noticing the absence of one or more of these elements. A clear step-by-step outline of the materials writing process is suggested by Jolly and Bolitho (1998: 97) and shown in Figure 4.5.

Many materials writers use most or all of these steps, although the order is flexible and the process is often recursive. It typically begins by identifying a gap, a need for materials because the existing coursebook fails to meet a course objective or because the students need further practice or information in a particular area. The teacher may then need to explore this area to gain a better understanding of the particular skill or feature involved, perhaps consulting a grammar, a rhetoric, colleagues, specialist informants, online bulletin boards, or other sources. Next, he or she will need a suitable input source. In the writing class this is usually a text, and it will have to develop a culturally appropriate and relevant cognitive and linguistic schema for the writing skills to be targeted in the unit. The next step involves developing tasks to exploit the input in a meaningful way, ensuring that the activities are realistic, that they work well with the text, that they relate to target needs and learner interests, and that tasks are clearly explained.

The materials then need to be produced for student use. The importance of the physical appearance of materials should not be underestimated as attractively presented materials are likely to possess greater face validity and impact, arousing interest and encouraging students to engage with the activities. In addition, a clear layout, consistent rubrics, and careful proof-reading demonstrate to students the interest the teacher has invested in the materials and focus the student on learning rather than working out what they have to do with them. Tomlinson (1998: 8) also suggests that the way materials are presented can reduce learner anxiety. So if materials contain lots of white space, include illustrations that relate to students' own culture, and are supportive rather than examining in their tone, they can potentially improve student learning.

Reflection 4.11

Find some materials currently used to teach writing. What do you think of their presentation? Are they attractively laid out, clear and motivating to work with? How might you improve the design?

Following production, materials are then used in class and finally evaluated for their success in meeting the identified need. *Materials evaluation* refers to attempts to measure the effectiveness of materials, and although this may be a vague and subjective exercise, it is worth conducting a systematic ongoing and post-course appraisal of the materials we use. Some teachers do this by keeping a journal of how successful different lessons and activities were as part of an ongoing course evaluation (see Chapter 3). Others simply jot notes in the margins of their own copy of the materials. It is also a good idea to involve students in the process as the main stakeholders in learning and get their impressions and responses via a brief questionnaire. Using the materials in class and revising them in the light of this experience recycles the design and development process and encourages reflection.

Once the course is finished, time should be allocated for revisions. If several teachers have been using the materials, then they should meet to pool impressions and compare experiences of how the materials might be improved. Teachers can then use their notes and general responses to grade different activities in terms of their effectiveness, or complete a post-course evaluation such as that given in Table 4.6.

Table 4.6: *A post-course materials evaluation guide*

1.	Did the materials meet the needs of the students? Why/Why not?
2.	Did they help you to meet the syllabus objectives? Why/Why not?
3.	Were they easy to use? Why/Why not?
4.	What were the most successful units or lessons? Why were these successful?
5.	What were the least successful? Why?
6.	How did the students react to the materials?
7.	What is your overall evaluation of the materials?
8.	What changes would you recommend for the next time they are used?

Reflection 4.12

Which steps in Jolly and Bolitho's procedures for materials creation in Figure 4.5 are likely to cause the writing teacher most difficulties? Consider how you might overcome these problems.

Selecting and locating texts

One of the main steps in Jolly and Bolitho's materials design schema is what they call "Contextual realization." Having identified a need and explored the nature of that need, the teacher begins the hunt for materials that will link with topics and activities that have real-world relevance for learners. This ensures that the materials students study will be contextualized with the topics that have been identified in the initial needs analysis.

Text selection is therefore an important first consideration as materials need to assist learners toward control of the rhetorical and grammatical features of relevant texts. We also need to consider how texts are related to other texts in order to plan a learning sequence of text types which scaffold learner progress, ensuring that novice writers will move from what is easy to what is difficult and from what is known to what is unknown. One way to proceed here is to determine the broad family of text-types that students should work with, as this enables us to establish the kinds of language and skills that students require to complete different assignments. So, for example, because they have different purposes for writers, Descriptions and Recounts generally have different structures and language characteristics. Descriptions, for instance, tend to contain action verbs and make use of the present tense, while Recounts are often told in the past tense. Knowledge of these kinds of differences allows teachers to see what students are able to do and what they need to learn.

Table 4.7: *Families of text-types*

Text families	Main feature	Sample written text-types
Exchanges	Joint construction	emails, Internet chat, letters
Forms	Printed, with respondent spaces	simple and complex formatted texts
Procedures	Steps to achieve a goal	instructions, procedures, protocols
Information texts	Provide news or data	descriptions, explanations, reports
Story texts	Retell events and respond to them	recounts, narratives
Persuasive texts	Argue for/against a thesis	expositions, discussions, opinion texts

The six broad families of text-types in Table 4.7, taken from the Australian *Certificate in Spoken and Written English* ESL curriculum, can help us to identify the kinds of texts needed as input. Examples of these text-types can be found in various genres. Appliance manuals and documents with self-assembly furniture provide good examples of instructions and procedures, for example, while recounts and narratives may be found in short stories, biographies, newspaper and magazines articles, and literary sources. Journalistic materials are also good sources for exposition and argument texts.

Where students' writing needs are related to particular genres used in specific target contexts, teachers need access to such texts as authentic models. Students typically do not have to write newspaper articles, magazine features, or textbook chapters and, while these genres may offer excellent sources of stimulus and content, they provide poor target models. In fact, second language writers who are only familiar with published texts, whether literary, journalistic, or academic, are ill-equipped to create workplace or academic genres. Some learners, of course, need to acquire a familiarity with book reviews or press releases to develop the skills to write them in target situations, and these can be easily obtained from published sources. For students in academic writing classes linked to, or preparing for, disciplinary study, examples of good essays can usually be obtained from the department concerned. More problematic are professional and workplace texts which may be closely guarded and require some ingenuity and persistence to obtain, although students themselves can sometimes acquire these.

Forms of journalism and print media are also fruitful sources of readings and subject content to stimulate ideas and encourage writing. Current events, social issues, and personal experiential accounts all provide topics to exploit in the writing class and these can be found in a range of newspapers and other published texts, while more specialist content is available in subject textbooks, popular science journals such as *New Scientist* and *The Economist*, and from specialist Websites. The audiovisual mass media can also be exploited for writing materials, and films, TV, radio and music recordings all provide a rich source of content for writing. Nor need teachers search for this material alone, as students can locate appropriate materials to be used as input for discussions or writing assignments.

Having chosen a suitable input text, the teacher needs to decide how to best use it. In Jolly and Bolitho's terms this involves developing pedagogical realizations for the material. Tasks will be discussed in more detail in Chapter 5, but typical exploitation activities might pursue a number of objectives. If a naturally occurring piece of data from a real situation has been selected, for instance, it might be presented as a model text to highlight certain features of grammar, vocabulary, or text structure, encouraging students to notice what they may have previously ignored. For example:

- How is the text laid out? Are there headings, diagrams, and the like?
- How does the text open or close?
- What tense is it mainly written in?
- Does the writer refer to him- or herself? How?
- What are the typical thematic patterns?

Alternatively, the teacher might want students to explore the context of the text:

- Who is the text written for?
- Why was it written?
- What is the tone? (e.g., formal or informal? personal or impersonal?)
- What is the relationship between the writer and the intended reader?
- What other texts does it assume you have a knowledge of?

On the other hand, we may have a stimulating piece which might be better suited to building content schemata and initiating writing through extensive reading and group discussion. Here the teacher is more likely to develop questions to aid comprehension of the passage and reflection on its personal or professional meaning to the students. The objective is to encourage reflection and engagement so that students might see the texts as relevant to their own lives and to unlock the desire to express this. Some initial questions might focus on the following aspects of the text:

- What is the text about?
- Who can write such a text? To whom?
- What knowledge does it assume?
- Have you had a personal experience similar to this?
- Have you seen a text like this before? Where? Have you written such a text?
- What shared understandings are implied in the text?

Reflection 4.13

Find an authentic text that has been written for a genuine communicative purpose. It could be a letter, a memo, a newspaper article, and so on. Decide how you might use this in a writing class.

Finding and selecting practice materials

While locating appropriate texts is important, these are not the only type of materials that might be needed. In addition to providing text models and content input, teachers may decide they need materials to create language exercises or that will give their students more information about a language point or more data for a research project. So, while a text can often be exploited pedagogically in a number of ways, teachers usually have a particular broad purpose in mind which is likely to influence where they search for materials.

Ideas for exercises, assignments, and discussions might be easily drawn from published textbooks, while language examples and reference information may be taken from grammars, rhetorics, and other learning resources. Although some of these may be found in an institution's teaching resources library, the Internet is also an excellent source of information and exercises that target writing skills. Much of this material is of variable quality and designed for L1 writers, but sites such as Dave's Internet Café (http://www.eslcafe.com) has discussion groups and writing exercises for L2 students, and there are many On-Line Writing Labs (OWLs) to which students can be directed for out-of-class activities. The Internet is also a source of authentic text data and of a growing number of free, searchable online corpora which can be used for exploring authentic uses of language. These resources are discussed further in Chapter 6.

Reflection 4.14

Where might you look for resources to meet the following materials needs?

1. Materials for basic handwriting practice for beginner writers from China.
2. Information on the use of qualification and uncertainty devices in academic research articles.
3. The basic framework of an argumentative essay for upper secondary school writers.

4. Out-of-class practice activities to develop undergraduates' summarizing skills.
5. Input for a writing project on environmental air pollution.
6. A model of a claim rejection letter for clerks in an insurance office.
7. A text recounting an intense personal experience as input for a term essay assignment.
8. Practice activities to develop independent pre-writing skills.

A final invaluable source of materials, ideas, and advice on language and teaching matters is other teachers. More experienced colleagues generally have a bank of reliable materials which they may be willing to share or, if not, they can usually be relied upon to guide new teachers toward other sources. Beyond immediate colleagues, however, Internet discussion lists allow teachers to access the wisdom of teachers around the world through their email. Discussion lists are free topic-specific informal discussion groups where teachers (or students) can exchange ideas, get information, or discuss problems with others by simply registering and posting a message. All messages are delivered to every member of the group, and a specific question can generate dozens of responses (see Chapter 6). Figure 4.6 summarizes the main sources of materials for writing teachers and the principal roles these resources can play in the classroom.

Source	Content stimulus	Language Input	Text models	Language Reference	Exercises or activities
Writing textbooks	✓	✓	?	✓	✓
Literary texts	✓	✓	✗	✗	✗
Journalistic texts	✓	✓	✗	✗	✗
Video/audio libraries	✓	?	✗	✗	✗
Internet writing sites	?	✓	?	✓	✓
Internet discussion lists	✗	✓	✗	✓	?
Students	?	✓	?	✗	✗
Workplaces	✓	✓	✓	✓	✗
Subject teachers	✓	✓	✓	✓	✗
Specialist textbooks/ publications	✓	✓	✓	✗	✗
Corpus data	✗	✓	✓	✓	✗

Figure 4.6: Some common sources of writing materials and main roles these typically offer.

Reflection 4.15
Select one source of materials listed in Figure 4.6. How useful do you think this source might be to you as a teacher in providing writing materials? In what circumstance might you access it?

The process of locating, selecting, and re-creating materials as something teachers can use for their own purposes involves constant checking and rechecking, both of the syllabus – to ensure that the activities being devised will benefit learners, and of the input text – to ensure it is being exploited effectively. Materials should contribute toward students' understanding of a target genre (its purpose, context, structure, and main features) or provide opportunities to practice one or more aspects of the writing process (pre-writing, drafting, revising, and editing). In other words, the activities that are devised from a selected text should be carefully planned to lead to the syllabus goals.

Summary and conclusion

This chapter has provided a practical introduction to materials design, outlining the roles that materials play in the writing class, exploring the principles of textbook selection and evaluation, and offering suggestions for locating and devising texts and other materials. I have emphasized the importance of matching materials to the proficiency and target needs of learners and the value of providing students with varied material from a range of sources. The main points can be summarized as follows:

- Like syllabus design and lesson planning, the selection and design of materials should be carefully based on students' target needs and current abilities as well as our own perspectives on how learners can best understand texts and develop their writing skills.
- Teachers need to be aware of the different roles that materials play in writing instruction in order to make the best choice and use of them.
- Authentic materials are important when used as models of target texts, but teachers should not be tyrannized by the "authenticity imperative" when selecting materials to scaffold writing.
- General principles of context, learning, orientation, and student characteristics can help us assess textbooks, with more specific criteria coming into play when examining and using specific books.

- It is almost always necessary to supplement or modify textbooks and this involves balancing work on process and product to enhance an understanding of language, content, and skills.
- The choice of input texts needs to take into consideration both the language demands it will make on learners and the opportunities it provides for developing content and rhetorical schemata.
- Flexibility should, once again, always be an important component of both planning and delivery.

Discussion questions and activities

1 Drawing on the criteria in Table 4.4, devise an assessment checklist for a writing textbook currently in use in an institution you are familiar with. Support your evaluation with a two-page commentary discussing its strengths and weaknesses for the learners, course, and institution in which it is used.

2 How would you evaluate a teacher's manual accompanying a writing textbook? What features do you consider most important in a manual? Devise a checklist of these features and use it to assess a teacher's manual.

3 Find a text that might be appropriate for a particular group of learners. Why did you select this text and what role could it play in the writing class? What are some of its main language structures and functions? Does it have interesting or relevant content? How might you exploit it as an item of instructional material?

4 This task is borrowed from Penny Ur (1996: 189). Imagine you are to be given a grant to buy a package of supplementary materials for your writing course. Each package costs about the same and you will be given a similar grant every six months, so eventually you will be able to buy them all. In what order would you buy them and how will you decide? Work out an order of priority and justify your decisions. Then compare your answer with another student. The packages are:

- A set of computers and writing development software
- A set of teachers' reference books and journals
- Audiovisual equipment including overhead and slide projectors and tape recorders
- Video/digital camera and playback equipment
- Computers and printers for teachers use with word processing software
- A large and varied library of reading material including literary and academic texts

5 Collect some reference materials such as style guides, rhetorics, student writing manuals, grammar books (either print or electronic). Select one

topic or entry and read the information they give for that entry. Are the texts consistent in the information and degree of importance they give to it? How far does the information or advice agree with your own knowledge or ideas on the issue? Consider how you might make best use of this information in a writing class.

6 Visit one of the OWLs listed in the Appendix to Chapter 6 or on the National Writing Centres Association Website. Evaluate its usefulness to you as a writing teacher or its suitability for a particular group of students you know. Consider both technical aspects (layout, links, use of graphics, speed, etc.) and pedagogic aspects (accuracy of information, interest, usefulness of tasks, etc.) in your assessment.

7 Tomlinson (1998) has attempted to apply some general principles of Second Language Acquisition theory to the development of materials for teaching languages. Some of these are given below. What do you consider to be the most important of these principles in designing materials for L2 writing classes? Select five and justify your decisions.

   a. Materials should achieve impact (through novelty, variety, presentation, content, etc.).
   b. Materials should help learners feel at ease (through presentation, personal "voice," etc.).
   c. Materials should help learners to develop confidence (pushing them beyond current ability).
   d. Materials should be seen as relevant and useful by learners.
   e. Materials should require and facilitate learner self-investment (through gaining interest, etc.).
   f. Materials should expose learners to language in authentic use.
   g. Materials should draw learners' attention to linguistic features of the input.
   h. Materials should provide learners with opportunities to use the language communicatively.
   i. Materials should recognize that the positive effects of instruction are usually delayed.
   j. Materials should recognize that learners have different learning styles.
   k. Materials should recognize that learners differ in affective attitudes.
   l. Materials should maximize learning potential by encouraging emotional, intellectual, and aesthetic involvement.
   m. Materials should provide opportunities for feedback on effectiveness, not just accuracy.
   n. Materials should not rely too much on controlled practice.

8 Take the five principles you have selected from the above list and briefly explain how you might ensure that your materials met each of them.

5 Tasks in the L2 writing class

Aims: This chapter will examine the role and construction of tasks for the writing class and explore related issues, including language support for writing and the sequencing of tasks in a teaching-writing cycle.

Tasks are fundamental in learning to write and represent a central aspect of the teacher's planning and delivery of a writing course. The tasks we assign help determine students' learning experiences and their success in developing an understanding of texts and a control of writing skills. So, while the text is the core of writing materials – providing models, contextual background, language information, content schemata, and stimulation to write, it is the task – what learners are actually required to *do* with the materials, that is at the heart of a teaching unit.

The notion of task has attracted considerable attention in language teaching and has come to be regarded as a central concept in curriculum design (e.g., Crookes and Gass, 1993; Nunan, 1989). Essentially, the term *language task* refers to any activity with meaning as its main focus and which is accomplished using language. Tasks are the routes learners take to solve problems in the classroom, and their importance results from the fact that learning to write involves engaging in activities rather than learning discrete items. Tasks assist teachers to provide a learning environment that both encourages writing and develops an understanding of how language is used for communicative purposes. This chapter will explore the following:

- The different types of writing tasks and their components
- The role of grammar and the provision of language assistance for novice writers
- The importance of composing heuristics and extended writing tasks
- The sequencing of tasks to support and develop student writing

Orientation

What do you understand by a writing task? Is task design simply a matter of setting an appropriate essay title or are their other factors we need to consider? What skills and knowledge do you think tasks should seek to develop in the L2 writing class?

Types of writing tasks

Tasks in the L2 writing class are either *real-world tasks*, which are based directly on the learners' target communicative goals, or *pedagogic tasks*, designed to develop their genre knowledge and composing skills. An initial needs analysis will provide an inventory of the target tasks for which the students are preparing, and these real-world tasks can be grouped into pedagogic task-types to bridge students' current and target competences.

Many pedagogical tasks aim to promote discrete skills, such as improving punctuation, developing pre-writing abilities, or increasing an understanding of rhetorical forms. These tasks are selected on the basis of *metacommunicative criteria*, in other words, what the students need to know in order to build the competence required to accomplish real-world objectives at a later stage. Such tasks should not be selected in isolation but devised with students' ultimate communicative goals in mind to ensure that they contribute toward relevant target writing. Moreover, not only should the tasks be based on the texts students need to write, but learners should as far as possible be able to see this link.

Figure 5.1 sets out some writing tasks commonly used in L2 writing classes. While not exhaustive, the list represents a range of activities compiled from a variety of writing textbooks and classified according to the types of competence to which they most contribute. As I have noted in earlier chapters, writers need to gain control of five areas of writing knowledge to create effective texts: knowledge of the ideas and topics to be addressed (content), knowledge of the appropriate language forms to create the text (system), knowledge of drafting and revising (process), knowledge of communicative purpose and rhetorical structure (genre), and knowledge of readers' expectations and beliefs (context). The tasks are listed in order of broadly increasing difficulty.

Task type	Content	System	Process	Genre	Context
Extract information from a written text	✔				
Generate word lists for writing	✔		✔		
Brainstorm/speedwrite to generate ideas	✔		✔		
Create spidergrams/mind maps for pre-writing	✔		✔		
Combine sentences provided in materials		✔	✔		
Identify purpose and use of a text				✔	✔
Practice construction of simple and complex sentences		✔			
Reorganize jigsaw texts or scrambled sentences		✔		✔	
Complete gapped paragraphs with target structures/lexis		✔			
Complete unfinished texts		✔		✔	
Analyze an authentic text for patterns and features				✔	
Practice use of metalanguage to identify parts of texts (e.g., topic sentence, thesis, introduction, transition)				✔	
Practice identifying genre stages and presentation				✔	
Compare texts with different purposes/ structure/ audience				✔	✔
Create a parallel text following a given model		✔		✔	
Create a text using visual information		✔		✔	✔
Negotiate an information gap/ opinion gap to construct a text	✔	✔			
Draft a text based on the outcome of pre-writing activities	✔		✔		
Participate in a dialogue journal exchange	✔		✔		✔
Practice specific rhetorical patterns (narrative, description, argument, process, etc.)			✔	✔	

Figure 5.1: Commonly used types of writing task and their pedagogic functions.

Task type	Content	System	Process	Genre	Context
Practice various text-types (letters, summaries, criticisms)			✔	✔	
Rewrite a text for another purpose (i.e., change the genre)				✔	✔
Revise a draft in response to others' comments	✔	✔	✔	✔	✔
Proofread and edit a draft for grammar and rhetorical structure		✔	✔	✔	
Write a multidraft, essay-length text	✔	✔	✔	✔	✔
Read and respond to the ideas/ language of another's draft	✔	✔	✔	✔	✔
Research, write, and revise essay-length text for specific audience and purpose	✔	✔	✔	✔	✔
Research, write, and revise a workplace/ disciplinary text	✔	✔	✔	✔	✔

Figure 5.1: (continued)

Reflection 5.1

Consider the following rubrics adapted from a number of writing textbooks and identify which task-types in Figure 5.1 they represent. What kinds of knowledge do they develop? Which are *real-world* and which are *pedagogic* tasks?

1. In the following article on nuclear hazards the linking words and phrases are missing. Choose the most appropriate word or phrase from those given, then compare your answers. *ped.*
2. Write a paragraph describing the information in the table. Use quantity qualifications instead of percentage figures. Begin "Last year all overseas students completed university registration forms." *ped.*
3. The following sentences are either formal of informal. Write F or I after each one. *ped.*
4. The following sentences can be put together to form a newspaper report but they are in the wrong order. Work with a partner to put them in the right order and decide how the underlined words help to link the text together.

5. The advertisement states a problem and offers a solution to it. Imagine that you are a journalist and write a short report in which you evaluate the appliance and the solution it offers.   *real world*

6. Write the first rough draft of your essay from your outline. Revise the draft for content and organization and write a second draft. Proofread the second draft for grammar, sentence structure, and mechanics. Write a final copy.   *real w-*

7. Read the following letter of complaint about nondelivery of a shipment from your company. Now look at the other documents relating to the order extracted from the customer file and draft a polite response setting out the reasons for the delay and promising redress.   *real w*

Task components

It can be seen from Figure 5.1 that writing tasks vary enormously in their focus, in the demands they make on students, in the support they offer writers, and in their distance from the actual real-world target tasks learners wish to perform. All tasks, however, also have features in common which are useful to consider when designing and evaluating writing tasks. Nunan (1989) suggests that all language tasks have five core components (Table 5.1). Understanding these components can help teachers design tasks that offer students a balance of knowledge and skills practice as well as a variety of learning experiences, writing activities, and sources of stimulation.

An example of a simple writing task might have the following components:

- **Input**: A short biographical text (used as a model and to formulate questions)
- **Goal**: Gathering personal information and writing a brief biography

Table 5.1: *Components of a language task*

- **Input**: a text, film, dialogue, graphic, lyrics, etc. provided by materials for students to work on
- **Goal**: learning objective of the task, the immediate payoff of the activity related to overall goals
- **Setting**: the classroom arrangements implied in the task
- **Roles**: the parts teachers and learners play in task execution and the relationships between them
- **Activity**: what the learners do with the input to accomplish the task

Source: Nunan, 1989.

- **Setting**: Whole class discussion / Pairs / Individual work in class
- **Roles**: Student: Conversational partner and individual writer
   Teacher: Controller, monitor, and facilitator
- **Activity**: 1. Read and discuss a short biographical text.
   2. Devise interview questions.
   3. With a partner ask and answer questions about family, country, school, etc.
   4. Write a one-page biography of each other.

Reflection 5.2
Select a writing task from a textbook or elsewhere and identify its five task components.

Task *input* is the textual, visual, aural, electronic, or multimedia data students work on to complete the task. We noted in the previous chapter that input can be derived from a range of diverse sources and virtually anything that presents or informs about writing or language can serve as input materials (Tomlinson, 1998). The *goal* of a task is the general intention that lies behind it, relating the task to the objectives of the unit and beyond these to those of the syllabus (Richards, 2001). While task goals are not necessarily explicitly stated, teachers always need to consider what they want students to achieve when designing tasks so that they can effectively prepare them for authentic writing situations. Task goals should therefore provide a link between classroom activities and real-world objectives through the needs analysis conducted at the beginning of the course.

Setting, where and how the learning will take place, is a further important consideration of task design. One dimension of setting is the actual site where learning occurs, whether it is in the classroom, the library, the multimedia laboratory, at home, or in the community. Providing a range of environments, and particularly a balance of in-class and out-of-class writing assignments, not only offers students different kinds of practice, but is also an important way of avoiding repetition and adding variety to a writing course. Most writing teachers assign at least one homework writing task during a course, particularly if this is a major assignment involving multidrafting, but writing classes may also benefit from varying the way students gather material for writing, collecting input data from trips to museums, cinemas, or relevant sites and by directly using the target discourse community or wider community as a resource for learning.

In addition to the physical setting, the social setting has important implications for task design. This concerns how learners are asked to engage with the task and with other students, particularly whether they will work individually, as pairs, in small groups, or as a whole class. Much writing, whether in or out of class, is done by students working on their own and this has clear advantages in helping learners to develop their decision-making and reflective skills while providing opportunities for self-paced writing practice. However, while writing is often seen as a private, isolated act, a great deal of professional and workplace writing is actually done cooperatively. This is generally to draw on a range of expertise, to ensure that documents are completed within tight deadlines, or to persuade a diverse audience from a variety of perspectives (Bargiela-Chiappini and Nickerson, 1999).

Although teachers need to carefully consider the effects of group dynamics on learning (Hadfield, 1992), grouping does not only have advantages in providing real-life rehearsal in negotiation and collaborative writing skills. It can also have considerable pedagogic payoffs. Both pair and group work encourage the sharing of ideas and so dramatically increase the amount of interaction in planning, researching, and editing, with different opinions and contributions brought to the writing task. In addition, task collaboration also contributes to the development of learner autonomy as students are able to make their own decisions without direct teacher involvement (Harmer, 2001). Not all students are comfortable working in groups, however, and others may dislike individualized learning. Many teachers try to accommodate different learning styles by varying the patterns of interaction they use for writing and scaffolding tasks. Writing workshop environments, where students are able to choose whether to work on their own, in pairs, or in groups and where they have opportunities to consult the teacher while working on tasks, provide a solution to the limitations of the lockstep classroom where all students work in the same way.

Reflection 5.3

Look again at the task you selected for Reflection 5.2 or select another task. Decide what interactional patterns it involves. Could these patterns be changed to create greater interaction between students?

Closely related to settings are the teacher and learner *roles* implied in writing tasks. In contrast to earlier teacher-fronted "chalk and talk" methodologies, the variety of tasks in modern writing classes creates more roles and responsibilities for both students and teachers (Wright, 1987). Students are no longer the passive recipients of teacher-provided stimuli, simply responding to writing prompts as best they can. They are now often required to take a more active part in their learning by interacting with others, interrogating materials, and using their initiative to take greater responsibility for learning. Many tasks require students to take control over the spoken and written language they produce, typically by collecting data for writing, negotiating with teachers and peers on how to carry out assignments, and interpreting the meaning of tasks.

Teachers' and students' roles are to a large extent complementary as giving students greater responsibility means teachers can adopt less controlling and more facilitative roles. Teachers' roles can change from one task to another or from one stage of an activity to another, and an ability to be flexible in moving between roles can contribute to the success of a class. Harmer (2001: 57–62) identifies eight major roles that teachers can perform to assist classroom learning: controller, assessor, organizer, prompter, resource, participant, tutor, and observer. Hedge (2000: 28–9) adds a number of interpersonal roles to these pedagogic ones, noting that teachers may be called on to counsel, mediate, and support learners as well as work to create a positive classroom atmosphere. Roles are partly influenced by the task, for example, whether the teacher is providing instruction on a language point, organizing group discussions of a reading, monitoring pair work, or assessing the accuracy of a finished product. Such role variation is essential to facilitate learning and to cater to the different learning style preferences of students.

Reflection 5.4

What do you consider to be the most effective settings for learning to write: individual, group or pairs, in-class, or outside? What roles for teachers and learners do these settings imply? Which roles and settings might be most difficult for new teachers to manage and how could these difficulties be overcome?

Activity, which specifies how the input will actually be used, is the final component of tasks. In writing classes activities can be placed into three main categories according to the type of knowledge or skills they target, dealing with *mechanics, language, and composing*, respectively. The first seeks to develop *graphological skills* and focuses on handwriting, punctuation, and paragraphing skills. *Language scaffolding* tasks provide support

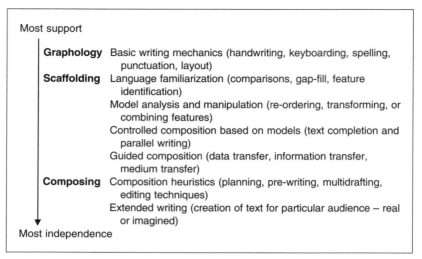

Figure 5.2: Tasks and relative support for writing.

for writing by familiarizing and developing the linguistic and rhetorical skills students need to understand and engage in particular types of writing. *Composing* concerns those activities that develop and practice actual writing skills.

Clearly student proficiencies, learning experiences, and writing needs will determine the kinds of tasks teachers devise and use, but it is important to note that in addition to providing a variety of student learning experiences and skill foci, activities also range along a cline of assistance, provided by either the materials or the teacher, from highly specific and controlled language analysis and practice tasks to free writing from prompts. Later in this chapter I will discuss how tasks can be sequenced to effectively scaffold learning, but the possibility of varying both the support we provide and the skills we target offers a helpful way of selecting different task types. A possible cline of support, together with representative tasks, is shown in Figure 5.2 and discussed more fully in the following sections.

Graphological tasks

Graphological tasks develop the mechanics of writing, and while they typically offer the most support for basic writers, they are also the least provided for in commercial materials. Such tasks address the conventional presentation of written work and deal with handwriting, spelling, and punctuation. In most current methodologies, graphology is practiced in tandem with other writing skills, but this may also be a main focus. Handwriting tasks are

---

Working in groups of two or three, compare the following pairs of sentences, and decide whether (a) or (b) is correct. In some cases both are possible, but with different meanings. What is the difference in meaning in these cases? Then compare your answers with those of other groups.

1. (a) Everest which is the highest mountain in the world was not climbed until 1953.
   (b) Everest, which is the highest mountain in the world, was not climbed until 1953.
2. (a) The river that runs through Paris is called the Seine.
   (b) The river that runs through Paris, is called the Seine.
3. (a) The girls who worked hard were given a bonus.
   (b) The girls, who worked hard, were given a bonus.

Now, working individually, punctuate the following sentences. If there are two possibilities, decide what the different meanings would be. Then compare your answers with those of others.

11. Winston Churchill who was unpopular with many people became Prime Minister.
12. We will have to return the parcel that was delivered today.
13. The Pyrenees which divide Spain from France are often covered with snow.

Source: Coe, Rycroft, and Ernest, 1992: 26–7.

Figure 5.3: A punctuation task.

obviously essential for beginners unfamiliar with roman script, and this skill requires a highly supportive environment which frequently involves learners copying individual letters and then words, moving from left to right across the page. Graphological tasks also address the conventions of capitalization, punctuation, and paragraphing and activities to improve spelling accuracy and keyboarding. Beginners are not alone in experiencing problems with these aspects of writing and many L2 students may benefit from tasks that develop their understanding of punctuation, particularly in the use of semicolons, reported speech marks, paragraph divisions, possessive apostrophes, and commas signaling relative clauses. Figure 5.3 is typical of this type of task.

With writing increasingly being done on computers rather than paper, tasks that support learners in the acquisition of basic word processing can also be vital in improving writing skills. Research suggests that the greatest benefits of using a word processor are not immediately available to students (e.g., Pennington, 1993) and at least one semester may be needed for positive changes in writing behavior (Phinney, 1991). Teachers can provide considerable support in this regard by integrating computer writing tasks into their courses. Techniques such as oral dictation, for example, can help develop keyboarding abilities while also encouraging freewriting as learners do not have time to stop and correct minor punctuation or spelling errors until they have finished (Hyland, 1993). Word processors also lend themselves well to a range of well-established writing activities, the cut and paste facilities, for instance, assisting the development of both composing and computer skills through substitution, reordering, and insertion tasks. (See Chapter 6.)

Reflection 5.5

Graphology tasks often require students to work in isolation from other learners. Is this inevitable because of the skills being developed or can teachers make these tasks more interactive and cooperative? Think of a task that involves learners working together to practice the mechanics of writing.

Language scaffolding

how much? when?

In designing writing tasks, a central question for teachers is the extent to which it is necessary to focus on linguistic form and at what stage in the writing process this focus should occur. I noted in Chapter 1 that language activities are central to structural and genre-oriented writing classes, while process-based instruction typically addresses language issues at the editing stage, responding to student errors rather than predicting areas of need. In both cases, however, language exercises are a staple of ESL writing instruction and most teachers acknowledge that language proficiency can seriously frustrate their L2 students' attempts to create effective texts.

Despite variations in teaching practices, there is a strong case for providing learners with the linguistic and rhetorical resources they need to express themselves at the point they need them: when they are beginning to draft. An inductive, discovery-based approach to writing can work well for high-proficiency students, but risks disadvantaging weaker learners. As the discussion in Chapter 2 suggests, we cannot assume that all L2 writers will possess the necessary cultural understandings of key genres or access to knowledge of the typical patterns and possibilities of variation within the texts they are asked to write (Hyland, 2003). So although postponing explicit language teaching until editing may allow learners to focus on formulating their ideas, it denies them a systematic understanding of the ways language is patterned in particular domains. It treats language instruction as a reactive and extemporized solution to learners' writing difficulties rather than the central resource for constructing meanings. In other words, we need to make plain what is to be learned and assist students toward a conscious understanding of how different texts are codified in terms of their purpose, audience, and message.

"Scaffolding" refers to providing this kind of support for learners as they build their understanding of a text and their linguistic competence to create them. Central to this idea is the view that teachers are in a position to bring learners to the point where they can write a target text without assistance. *goal* This involves providing input and instruction that both support and challenge students, gradually increasing their competence as they move toward independence. By creating learning situations that are cognitively and interactionally demanding for learners, it is possible to push them to higher levels of performance than they could reach by working alone (e.g., Ohta, 2000).

I noted in the previous chapter that learning to write involves acquiring an ability to exercise appropriate linguistic choices, both within and beyond the sentence, and teachers can assist this by providing students with an explicit grammar. As Knapp and Watkins (1994: 8) observe: "Grammar is a name for the resource available to users of a language system for producing texts. A knowledge of grammar by a speaker or a writer shifts language use from the implicit and unconscious to a conscious manipulation of language and choice of appropriate texts." Obviously this means going beyond simply providing learners with heuristics for generating content and drafting, but teachers should guard against the real danger that their language support will just present grammar as an end in itself, rather than as a resource for making meanings. The grammar we teach and the ways that we teach it need to be clearly related to the kinds of writing students are expected to do in their target contexts. Language tasks should have the goal of contributing to the writer's ultimate independent production of a well-written target genre and so should closely relate to that genre.

Reflection 5.6

The explicit teaching of grammar as an element of teaching writing is a controversial issue. What are your own views? When do you think it is appropriate to focus on language and how can this be done most effectively?

Because teachers are concerned with how learners use language, it is often a good idea to begin language scaffolding by working down from the entire text rather than approaching it in a piecemeal fashion from the bottom up. This involves considering how a text is organized at the level of the text in relation to its purpose, audience, and message, then working on how all parts of the text, such as paragraphs and sentences, are structured, organized,

---

Social Purpose

Recounts "tell what happened." The purpose of a factual recount is to document a series of events and evaluate their significance in some way. The purpose of the literary recount is to relate a sequence of events so that it entertains, and this generally includes the writer's expressions of attitude about the events.

Structure

- an orientation providing information about who, where, and when;
- a record of events usually recounted in chronological order;
- personal comments and/or evaluative remarks interspersed throughout the record of events;
- a reorientation, which rounds off the sequence of events.

Grammar

- use of nouns and pronouns to identify people, animals, or things involved;
- use of action verbs to refer to events;
- use of past tense to locate events in relation to the writer's time;
- use of conjunctions and time connectives to sequence the events;
- use of adverbs and adverbial phrases to indicate place and time;
- use of adjectives to describe nouns.

Source: Board of Studies, 1998a: 287.

Figure 5.4: General features of a recount genre.

and coded so as to make the text effective as written communication. An example of how a text might be seen in this way is shown in Figure 5.4, taken from an Australian primary school syllabus. This provides the teacher with a description of the purpose, structure, and main grammar points of a recount text which can be used to select examples and devise tasks to help learners understand the genre and guide them to construct texts of their own. Without this support, weaker students may not have the resources to produce quality pieces of writing.

Language scaffolding tasks

A wide variety of tasks dedicated to improving students' language competencies for writing was discussed in Chapter 4 and categorized into four main groups in Figure 5.2 above (language familiarization, model analysis, controlled composition guided composition). These scaffolding tasks are designed to gradually increase learners' independence and control, moving from basic noticing activities through manipulation of models to tasks that vary the degree of guidance. This section summarizes these approaches and outlines the tasks they suggest.

Language familiarization: Familiarization tasks focus on raising awareness of language forms and patterns without requiring production. They therefore link tasks closely with texts, drawing students' attention to how language is used in relevant contexts and helping them to see that the language they are learning is directly relevant to creating their target genres.

Reflection 5.7

What are the potential advantages and disadvantages of using tasks to raise students' awareness of the features of target genres in the L2 writing class? In what situations are they appropriate? How would you work to maximize the advantages?

Familiarization tasks allow learners to examine aspects of the whole text and then go on to identify and practice selected features of grammar and vocabulary. At the text level it is possible to look at the visual layout of a text, its move structure, its use of headings, or the way it is divided into paragraphs. Students can be asked to compare a formal and a personal letter, for instance, and discuss the ways in which they are similar and different, or they could explore patterns of cohesion by underlining pronouns and linking them back to referents. Familiarization can also involve learners in collecting examples of a feature, perhaps using a concordancer, and seeing how it is used in a particular genre – which tenses are most commonly used, for instance, or what are the preferred ways of addressing readers.

It is important that students are able to study a number of text examples as this can encourage reflection on similarities and differences. They could, for instance, examine the strategies writers use to open or close their texts or the kinds of paragraph development they use, while comparison activities are also helpful in raising awareness of features such as personal pronouns, politeness markers, or hedges to see how removing or adding these features can alter the style, tone, or presentation of the genre. Figure 5.5 shows a task that focuses on the overall effectiveness of a text, encouraging L2 graduate students to evaluate two consecutive drafts of a summary in terms of specific criteria. More often, this kind of consciousness raising is achieved through questions that focus attention on specific features to encourage an understanding of a text's organization or features of its construction. Figure 5.6 is an example task of this kind.

When you write a formal summary of someone else's ideas, you should keep in mind the following guidelines.

1. Always try to use your own words except for technical terms.
2. Include enough support and detail so the presentation is clear.
3. Do not try to paraphrase specialized vocabulary or technical terms.
4. Include nothing more than what is contained in the original.
5. Make sure the summary reads smoothly. Use enough transition devices and supporting detail.

Read these two summaries and answer the questions that follow

(texts omitted)

1. How closely do the two summaries follow the five guidelines?
2. Does the rewrite summary present the main idea of the original text in Task Three? Is there adequate support and explanation?
3. Is the rewrite summary objective?
4. Is it too long or too short?
5. Has the writer used his or her own words?
6. Is there anything missing from the rewrite summary?
7. What changes were made from the draft summary to the rewrite?
8. Which vocabulary items were not paraphrased in the rewrite? Why?

Source: Swales and Feak, 1994: 114–16.

Figure 5.5: Evaluative focus questions on a text.

Analyzing paragraph organization

1. This paragraph describes three different ways of looking at adolescence. Which sentence or sentences discuss: (a) the first way?_____ (b) The second way?_____ (c) The third way?_____

2. Which words signal the transition from
(a) The first to the second way?_____(b) The second to the third way?_____

3. Words like *this*, *that*, and *such* refer back to previous ideas in the paragraph. What previous ideas do the following refer to? (a) In that case . . . (b) This approach . . . (c) Such views . . .

4. You are often taught in writing classes that a well-written paragraph should have a topic sentence that expresses the main idea of the paragraph. Does this paragraph have a topic sentence? If yes, which one? If no, write a suitable one. Compare answers with a partner.

Source: Adapted from Seal, 1997: 51.

Figure 5.6: Focus questions on a reading passage.

Manipulation of models. Models are central to familiarization tasks as they encourage students to reflect on the features of target texts. In the next stage in learners' acquisition of a language competence for writing, models are a source of manipulation activities.

The use of models is controversial. Process-oriented teachers often object to text models on the grounds that they may focus students on the rhetorical form of texts too early and so risk undermining the development of inventing, drafting, and revision processes (Zamel, 1983). Clearly there is a danger of simply concentrating on models as the one-right-way of writing a particular kind of text, and this needs to be countered by ensuring that students are exposed to a range of readings, texts, and activities. There is, however, no reason why an understanding of genre should mean sacrificing content generation and drafting skills; indeed, students need to know what is expected of them to approach the writing task with any hope of success. Good models therefore provide students with a reliable genre schema to prepare them effectively for authentic writing situations.

Reflection 5.8

What is your view of using models in the writing class? Do you believe they restrict inventiveness and creativity by encouraging imitation, or do they help L2 writers understand how rhetorical and grammatical features are used effectively?

Model-based tasks involve students in combining, inserting, reordering, or deleting text segments. Combining tasks, for example, require learners to match the first part of a sentence with an appropriate second part, a cause with an effect, an event with a consequence, and so on. Insertion tasks include cloze activities, where target words or features such as topic sentences have to be inserted into a text, and storyboarding, where students use their knowledge of format and topic to predict all the language needed to recreate a text from a skeleton. Deletion tasks are often designed to encourage succinctness and good style, while reordering tasks require students to (re)construct a cut-up text like a "jigsaw" or to reorder scrambled sentences or other elements into a coherent whole (Figure 5.7). In all cases students use their knowledge of a model to carry out the activity.

Controlled and guided composition. Model texts can also provide the foundation for controlled composition tasks, developing learners'

Rearrange the sentences in the following paragraph so that they follow a logical order.

1. Because of kumara cultivation and the abundance of other food resources available in the North, permanent settlements could be established.
2. In pre-European times Northland was the most densely inhabited part of the country.
3. Some settlements were occupied by several hundred people.
4. The kumara flourished in this climate and became the dominant crop.
5. Clearly the warmer climate in the North made it more attractive to the early Maori.

Source: Rowntree, 1991: 164.

Figure 5.7: A scrambled paragraph exercise.

confidence and fluency by providing a text frame to complete, a parallel text to write, a draft text to edit, or other activities that involve reworking or finishing a model. Example activities include rewriting a text from another viewpoint, writing the middle or end of a story, or writing a shorter version of a text. Figure 5.8 shows how models can be used to create a parallel writing task. The input for the task provides examples of student writing as authentic models of essay introductions, clearly labeling functional stages of the model and giving alternatives. The activity then asks learners to draw on these to draft an introduction of their own.

As students gain familiarity with the genre, they can move away from models and use their increasing knowledge of purpose, structure, and language to create texts in specified contexts and with controlled input. These more guided composition tasks include:

- Information gap, where two students must exchange information to complete a writing task
- Information transfer, where information is translated into text form from a graph, a table, or notes
- Key word writing, where students write from a given set of key words
- Picture writing, where a text is produced from a picture sequence

These kinds of controlled and guided tasks are primarily intended for beginning and intermediate level students and those trying to gain familiarity with a new genre. Here an explicit emphasis on rhetorical structure, context, and the grammatical realization of meanings provides L2 learners with the supportive writing environment that they may need.

The following are examples of effective introductions.

[General statement, engages the reader] [Limited background Information]	Vitamin D is the sunshine vitamin, and Vitamin D is essential for good health. Until the 20th century, however, little was known about this important vitamin, and people who lived in temperate climates tended to suffer every winter from the lack of Vitamin D. Even today, although knowledge about Vitamin D has been available for more than 50 years, many people still suffer from Vitamin D
[Thesis statement of intent]	deficiencies. This essay will describe the chemical makeup of Vitamin D, the group of diseases called "rickets" that afflict people who are deficient in this vitamin, and solutions to avoid such deficiencies.
	Saleh Saeed, United Arab Emirates
[Scene set to interest reader] [Limited background info]	Early in the 1960s, the only way to eat pigeon meat in France was by hunting. Then people began to raise this fowl to sell. At that time the market was full of promise, but today, the market for pigeon in France is still marginal; it has not developed as expected. There is one main
[Thesis statement of intent]	reason for this failure: price. This essay examines the causes that make pigeon meat in France so expensive.
	David Soulard, France
[General, engaging] [Limited background info]	Almost all the small towns in El Salvador are similar in their general appearance. In addition, many of the people who live in these towns have a special lifestyle. In contrast to life in the larger cities, people in small towns share many
[Thesis statement of intent/opinion]	cultural things and experiences. This unusual sharing contributes to a familial relationship among neighbors.
	Rita Saravia, El Salvador
Writing assignment	Draft the introduction for your Explaining essay. Be sure that your introduction: • Interests your audience. • Gives brief but necessary background information about the topic of your essay. • Leads to your thesis statement (of intent and/or opinion) at the end of the introduction.

Source: Reid, 2000: 84–5.

Figure 5.8: A parallel writing task.

Reflection 5.9

Consider how you might set up a guided activity using one of the four approaches listed above. What input would you use, how would you contextualize the task, and what instructions would you give?

Table 5.2: *Pre-writing invention techniques*

Listing	List details for an essay topic (people, place, actions, feelings, objects, etc.)
Freewriting	Rapid "stream of consciousness" writing ignoring grammar, punctuation, spelling
Looping	Expanding a freewriting idea through reflection and further freewriting – limited time
Clustering	Pattern of circled ideas joined by lines showing connections between them (see Figure 1.5)
Cubing	6 way exploration – description, comparison, association, analysis, application, argument
Questioning	Ideas for writing generated by who, what, where, when, how, why questions

Composing tasks

All writers need to develop strategies and skills for writing fluently and independently, regardless of their proficiency in English, and these *skill-using* tasks are often seen as the core of writing instruction. This section looks at the two remaining categories of task listed in Figure 5.2, focusing on those concerned with the development of composing techniques and those that allow learners to use the knowledge they have gained and to practice their writing skills in extended compositions.

Composing heuristics. Fluency in writing is partly the result of having strategies for generating content, drafting, re-writing, editing, and polishing texts, and students need some initial support in developing these skills. In devising tasks of this kind it is important to remember that there is no one composing process. Different kinds of writing require different strategies and learners should be provided with a variety of ways of getting started in their writing and bringing it to fruition. This is perhaps most obvious with pre-writing activities. Unstructured pre-writing tasks are trademarks of process-oriented writing classes, providing learners with ways of stimulating invention through uninhibited, private writing, or the careful accumulation of ideas for writing. Kroll (2002) and Spack (1996: 44–50) suggest a number of ideas for exploring a topic (see Table 5.2).

Many of these techniques are found in process-oriented textbooks as ways of building writing fluency without the compulsion to correctness which can block novice writers. Listing and freewriting may be conducted as short sessions of just a few minutes, then lead into other tasks such as a discussion, a related reading or writing planning, as in Figure 5.9.

Freewriting is one way to start writing.
Freewriting is writing you do for yourself.
Freewriting is writing nonstop, usually for ten to fifteen minutes.
How to freewrite: Start writing on a topic and don't stop until your time is up. Don't worry about grammar, punctuation, or spelling. Don't worry about the order of ideas. If you can't think of a word, leave a blank space.
Choose an experience from your list of early experiences. In the space below and on the next page, freewrite about your experience for fifteen minutes.

Source: Benesch, Rakijas, and Rorschach, 1987: 34–5.

Figure 5.9: Speedwriting activity for pre-writing.

While many learners benefit from tasks that encourage the free release of ideas, it is also true that students have different learning styles and some L2 learners prefer more careful planning before they write. It should also be noted that longer or more complex writing tasks often require more elaborate generation techniques. Clustering, cubing, and questioning facilitate more systematic and heuristic pre-writing practices that help scaffold organized planning. These are more thoughtful tasks which may be conducted by small groups to provide learners with the confidence to both explore topics and begin writing. Figure 5.10 shows how cubing can be used as a basis for writing.

Reflection 5.10
What is the relationship between pre-writing, planning, and writing? Why is this relationship less clear-cut than we might expect? Where do scaffolding tasks and models fit into this relationship?

Pre-writing typically leads learners into constructing an outline for their writing. Outlines vary in detail and formality, but they help learners to set out a structure for their text and to consider the rhetorical patterns they will need to effectively express the ideas they have generated. Many L2 learners find an outline an invaluable piece of scaffolding, helping them to see how ideas become points that are connected in different ways, say via *cause-effect, comparison, problem-solution, hypothetical-real,* and so on, and to construct the linear or hierarchical structure of their texts. Not all learners are able to do this, however, and some, like Maho, a Japanese

Explore a topic through these different viewpoints:
1. Describe or define it. What is it?
2. Compare and contrast it. What is it similar to? What is it different from?
3. Associate it. What does it remind you of? What comes to mind?
4. Analyze it. What parts can it be broken down into? What is their relationship?
5. Apply it. What can you do with it?
6. Argue for and against it. Why are you in favor of it? Why are you against it?

Figure 5.10: Cubing activity for pre-writing.

student, even find it counterproductive: "I know that my writing is quite bad. Even I write in Japanese it still does not make sense sometime. I think because I don't make a plan. Why I t. y to make a plan, my ideas disappear" (Maho, quoted in F. Hyland, 1998: 275). Some students therefore just want to get their words onto paper and leave organizational matters until later, a process referred to as *zero drafting*. Others work better with rough plans that are fluid and open to change as drafting progresses. These allow writers to pull their ideas and data into a tentative structure for development with the freedom to discard, expand, and alter as they progress.

Getting started on a draft can be difficult for students even when they have an outline, and they may need encouragement to get beyond the first words and keep going. Strategies can involve rewriting the first sentence and continuing, or helping students to start later in the text and return to the opening sentence afterward. Tasks should also push students to the end of the first draft, with timed exercises, for example, to encourage them to keep going through a draft and correct errors and fill in difficult spellings or blocked words later. Students can read their drafts to each other to encourage sharing and to listen for problems. Similarly, some of the scaffolding tasks discussed above can be used to practice and develop revising skills. Models can be compared with weak texts to target particular items, and poor or inappropriate texts can provide learners with opportunities to target particular areas: reordering or linking sections together, removing repetitions, combining sentences, or reducing long sentences, changing the formality, rephrasing, correcting spelling or grammar, and so on.

Extended writing. Independent, extended writing is really the goal of the L2 writing class, for while writers do not learn to write *only* by writing, they cannot learn to write without writing. Some advantages of extended writing tasks are shown in Table 5.3. It helps novice L2 writers if they can have class time to conduct at least one complete multiple drafting sequence. This provides supported practice and a chance to draw on their teacher and

Table 5.3: *Advantages of extended writing assignments*

- Provides practice in entire writing process: planning, drafting, formatting, editing, and polishing.
- Encourages students to get started and maintain momentum via deadlines and classroom support.
- Provides opportunities for students to create a textually cohesive, stylistically appropriate, and ideationally coherent piece of discourse for an audience.
- Offers students the chance to develop and express ideas in response to the ideas of others or to a real-world/realistic situation.
- Provides opportunities for students to create a text product on which they can receive feedback.
- Provides learners with the experience of an independent performance in which they combine a knowledge of content, process, language, context, and genre.
- Provides teachers with a means of determining whether students have achieved a required level of competency in the genre.

their peers to develop confidence in planning and polishing a piece of work through several drafts. However, scaffolding and heuristic development consume a considerable amount of time and students typically must do a great deal of writing out of class.

Extended writing assignments are typically based on an input stimulus of some kind and a rubric instructing students about what is required. Teachers need to take care in providing rubrics which are not only clear and unambiguous in specifying what students should do, but which also engage all learners and offer them an opportunity to both display and extend the skills they have learned (see Chapter 8). Such extended writing tasks typically require learners to respond to a reading text or visuals or to collect and synthesize data collected from out-of-class sources such as the library, the internet, and so on.

Extended writing assignments therefore need to be carefully designed to ensure that they both draw on the skills that have been taught and that they contribute to course goals. Reid and Kroll (1995) suggest the following guidelines for the preparation of effective writing assignments:

- The context should be clearly stated so that students understand the purpose of the assignment.
- The content should be accessible to students, feasible given their knowledge and abilities, and allow for multiple approaches.
- The language used should be unambiguous and comprehensible.
- The task should be sufficiently focused to allow for completion in the given time and length.
- The task should draw on and extend students' knowledge of the genre and the topic.

- The task should require a specific and relevant genre and indicate a specific audience.
- There should be clear evaluation criteria so that students know how their work will be assessed.

Reflection 5.11

Consider these rubrics for extended writing tasks. What are their strengths and weaknesses? How might you improve them using the guidelines above?

give model, context / ex. titles

1. Choose a well-known legend or fairy tale and rewrite it. You can:
   - Imagine a different or unexpected ending;
   - Write it from the point of view of another character (e.g., a minor one);
   - Give the tale another context or background (making it a "Fable for our Time," as Thurber did);
   - Use the new story to make a point, political or social, etc.

   (Grellet, 1996: 58)

2. Culture shock happens when a person has to operate within a new set of cultural rules and values. Write a text, for American travellers to your country, alerting them to the existence of "culture shock," and giving them some advice on how to cope with it. Before you begin planning your essay, discuss the following texts with two or three other students (texts omitted).

   (Hamp-Lyons and Heasely, 1987: 122)

As noted above, not all extended writing is done in the same way and students may also have their own preferences for writing. But while multidrafting tasks should not be prescribed as a rigid sequence of invariant steps, many teachers find it useful to plan for a series of drafts, each of which focuses on a separate aspect of writing, such as revising for rhetorical organization, for grammar and vocabulary, for content and voice, and for audience. Not all assignments or students require a separate draft for each feature, however, and targeting different elements in different assignments is a good way of varying the writing experience for learners. Nor do students need to be thrown entirely back on their own resources when composing. Teacher or peer feedback on intermediate drafts (see Chapter 7) can encourage students to expand or compress parts of their text, to reorganize it, or to develop ideas in different ways.

An important element of drafting and editing is considering one's audience, the ability to see the text through another's eyes, and therefore

A	B	C	D
What do I know about the topic?	What does my reader already know about it?	What does my reader not know?	What is my reader's attitude likely to be?
Customer bought some biscuits. There was something hard in one of them.	Customer bought some biscuits. There was something hard in one of them.	What the company will do about it, e.g., apologize, refund the price.	Customer is probably very annoyed. She will expect compensation.

Source: White and Arndt, 1991: 32.

Figure 5.11: An audience awareness heuristic.

anticipate where the message might be unclear. Novice writers often find it difficult to anticipate their readers' comprehension needs and cannot flesh out a mental image of their readers in the same way as experienced readers (Flower and Hayes, 1980). Peer review may assist learners here, but they may also need practice to shift their attention from their topic and language to consider readers as real people. Elbow (1998) encourages teachers to design assignments that provide "intended" readers other than the teacher in order to "adjust the transaction" between themselves and the reader, while Schriver (1992) recommends asking writers to predict readers' problems with a text and then provide them with detailed reader responses gathered from think aloud protocols.

One major source of potential miscommunication is misjudging the knowledge and attitudes that writer and readers share. White and Arndt (1991) suggest a simple checklist to sensitize students to the importance of attending to shared knowledge with an example response to a letter of complaint (Figure 5.11). Most centrally, however, students need a clear context for writing. Professional and academic environments typically oblige writers to present arguments or information to known audiences, and Johns (1997) suggests that students can be asked to research the interests and expectations of such readers. Assigning tasks that involve interviewing clients, colleagues, content subject teachers, experts, and so on, can improve students' writing through a better understanding of the interaction between their purposes, the interests and values of real audiences, and the genres that are appropriate for specific contexts.

Another technique that has been widely used to encourage students to think of their reader and to write freely is that of dialogue journals (Peyton and Staton, 1993). Originally developed for children and adult literacy learners, teachers in L2 classrooms have found journal writing a fruitful means of building confidence, fluency, and audience awareness among writers, particularly in early stages of writing proficiency. While journals can form the basis of an entire course and represent an alternative way of conceptualizing writing curricula (e.g., Vanett and Jurich, 1990), they more usually form a small part of the daily activity of the class, allowing students the opportunity to select and discuss topics they care about rather than ones assigned to them.

This approach has been found to enhance communication in L2 classes by providing students with the motivation to write and to express themselves clearly through private interaction with the teacher. This can improve students' writing abilities, their competence to handle rhetorical and grammatical forms, and their capacity to reflect on writing. Clearly, dialogue journals can do little to familiarize learners with particular academic or professional genres, but they represent an interesting and effective way of encouraging writing and providing a context for exploration, meaning, and the exchange of ideas.

Reflection 5.12

One consideration when setting extended writing tasks is whether to offer students a choice of topics. A single prompt has the advantage of providing practice with a focused theme and with a restricted set of rhetorical and grammatical patterns, while a choice may encourage a more motivated response. What is your view on this? In what circumstances may one work better than the other?

Sequencing writing tasks: the teaching-writing cycle

An important issue for teachers is how to organize their syllabus to form a coherent progression of tasks. There is no single "right way" to sequence learning tasks, however, and several possibilities are suggested in the literature. Nunan (1989), for instance, proposes that activities can be graded according to the cognitive and performance demands they make upon the learner, moving from comprehension-based activities through controlled production to tasks that require engagement in communicative interaction. In the L2 writing class this psycholinguistic processing approach is similar to the task-structure cline shown in Figure 5.2, which presents categories of writing activities as simultaneously utilizing and extending the skills learned at the previous stage. For Breen (2001), tasks are about meanings rather than the accumulation of forms, so sequencing is determined by the logic of chaining tasks to solve a series of problems. Other commentators have sought to integrate pedagogic tasks with more "unfocused" communicative tasks, so Ellis (1987), for instance, suggests two parallel strands where a progression of real-world activities enables students to use the forms they have acquired in an accompanying strand of graded language tasks.

Reflection 5.13

Are the proposals for sequencing tasks sketched in the previous paragraph relevant to L2 writing classes? Which approach seems most effective to you? Why? Are there any other principles teachers should consider when sequencing writing activities?

An alternative approach to sequencing tasks, influential in genre pedagogy, draws on Vygotsky's (1978) views of collaborative learning and Bruner's (1986) ideas of scaffolding. This approach, as noted in Chapter 1, is often represented in the form of a cycle of teaching and learning designed to make clear to students what is to be learned and assessed and to build their confidence and abilities to write effectively (Rothery, 1986). The main idea underlying this approach is that novice L2 writers are likely to require greater support during the early stages of working with an unfamiliar genre and less later. Learners move toward their potential performance through appropriate input and interaction with a teacher, who contributes what the students are initially unable to do alone, scaffolding their progress by providing information, appropriate language, and opportunities for guided practice. As they gain control of the new genre, this support is gradually removed and more responsibility shifted to the learners. This cycle therefore suggests how teachers of writing can sequence tasks to achieve particular purposes at different stages of learning. As each stage is associated with different activities, the cycle offers an explicit model of how teachers can move through successive phases of classroom tasks and interaction to develop writing abilities. Feez (1998) represents these phases diagrammatically (Figure 5.12).

It is possible to enter the cycle at any point, and instruction can therefore be modified to suit the needs of individual learners, skipping stages if they do not need them or returning to stages for review. In most cases, however, especially when a genre is being introduced for the first time, teachers and students work through them all. As we can see, a whole section is devoted to building students' understanding of the context in which the target text is

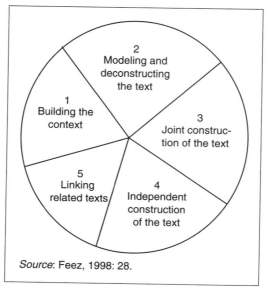

Source: Feez, 1998: 28.

Figure 5.12: Stages of the teaching-learning cycle.

used. This can be a crucial step for learners in foreign language learning or new migrant contexts who may have little idea of the cultural and situational aspects of the genre. Here teachers establish the purpose of the text, the roles and relationships of those who use it, and generally build an understanding of the social activity in which it is used. In learning to write a job application, for example, students might read newspaper advertisements, research company publicity documents, visit prospective employers, build up vocabulary lists, and study how relationships between prospective employers and job-seekers are structured.

During the modeling and deconstruction stage, the teacher's role is again strongly directive as he or she presents examples, identifies the stages of the text, and introduces activities to practice salient language features. Learners' attention is drawn to the structure and language of the genre through the different stages of language scaffolding tasks, moving from consciousness-raising through model manipulation and controlled composition exercises. Here, then, tasks assist students to learn the grammar they need in the context of relevant and purposeful teacher-directed activities. In the joint negotiation stage the teacher begins to relinquish responsibility to the students as they gain control of the genre and confidence in writing. Students' growing understanding allows them to create a target text in collaboration with the teacher and their peers. They are guided through all steps of the planning and drafting process, developing a text together through composition heuristic tasks and teacher questions which shape the text (e.g., Where did we go first? What did we see? Where did we go next? Then what happened?).

During the independent construction stage, the scaffolding is removed to allow students to create texts by themselves. Students individually construct the genre, basing their drafts on notes and summaries they have made in researching a topic, working through several drafts consulting the teacher and peers only as needed, and evaluating their progress in terms of the characteristics of the texts they have studied. The teacher no longer directly intervenes in learning but withdraws to a more encouraging and monitoring role, advising, assisting, and providing feedback on drafts. Achievement assessment can be conducted at this stage of the cycle or following it. At the end of the stage links are made to other contexts, either to compare the use of the genre in other situations – sales letters in different companies for instance, or other genres in the same situation – such as orders, customer complaints, and so on. Tasks here can draw on the same familiarization activities used at the beginning of the cycle.

Reflection 5.14

Consider the strengths and weaknesses of the teaching-learning cycle as a way of sequencing tasks to scaffold L2 writing. In what ways might the use of the cycle depend on the specific teaching context? Is this an approach you would feel comfortable using in your teaching? Why or why not?

The model offers both teachers and learners clear pathways in learning to write. It gives students clear goals and a sense of how language, context, content, genre, and process are connected and relate to their work in the writing class. For teachers it provides a principled way of planning writing activities and sequencing tasks without restricting them to one particular teaching method or set of tasks. Each stage of the cycle allows students to focus on different aspects of writing and makes it possible for teachers to interact with students in different ways and use different types of writing tasks. Table 5.4 summarizes these points.

Summary and conclusion

Tasks form the heart of writing teaching. Not only are they a fundamental planning tool for teachers uniting syllabus goals, materials, and

Table 5.4: *Tasks and teacher roles in the teaching-learning cycle*

Stage	Purpose	Teacher role	Sample tasks
Contextualizing	Assist students to understand purpose, audience, and context	Initiator/ guide Resource	Reading, site visit, research, library study, questioning, jigsaw reading, brainstorming, vocabulary building, role-play
Modeling	Investigate prototypical patterns and language of genre examples	Instructor/guide Controller	Familiarization, model manipulation, controlled and guided composition tasks
Negotiating	Teacher and students jointly create examples of the text	Prompter Resource	Composition heuristics, guided composition work on individual text stages
Constructing	Students create texts independently. Performance used for assessment	Observer Responder Assessor	Extended writing, planning, drafting, conferencing, editing, peer review, polishing
Connecting	Students relate work to other texts in similar contexts	Observer Guide	Journal reflections, project work

methodology, they are the ways that students come to understand and develop the abilities to write effectively. This chapter has explored tasks from a practical perspective to help teachers select, design, and plan their use. The key points can be summarized as follows:

- Tasks differ in the extent to which they focus on language, content, context, rhetorical structure, and writing processes; in the cognitive and performance demands they make on learners; in the support they offer writers; and in the emphasis they give to real-world or pedagogic goals.
- Teachers can provide task variety by manipulating the main task components: input, goals, settings, roles, and activities.
- Tasks can be grouped according to whether their main focus is graphology, language scaffolding, or composing, although teachers should ensure that all activities contribute to students' current and target needs.
- Tasks which scaffold L2 novice writers' gradual control of the grammatical and rhetorical features of target texts, can be crucial to their ability to reach potential levels of writing performance.

- The development of writing skills is greatly facilitated by the analysis and manipulation of authenic text models and the use of composing heuristics.
- The teaching-writing cycle, which is based on the idea of different interactional stages in learning, offers a principled way of selecting and sequencing writing tasks.

Discussion questions and activities

1 Select one task-type from Figure 5.1 and develop materials in order to present the task to a particular group of students. Contextualize the activity by noting who the students are, their proficiency and target goals, and identify the language focus and content of the materials. Write a clear rubric instructing the learners how to use the materials and complete the task.

2 Choose a text you think might be suitable for a group of learners you are familiar with and analyze it to identify its main moves or stages or three salient language features. Now develop language scaffolding tasks that focus attention on these features drawing on the different task types suggested in this chapter. Finally, plan a lesson that uses these tasks.

3 Identify the cognitive and pedagogical benefits of employing a variety of task types to teach L2 writing. What are the advantages for students of different inputs, goals, roles, settings, and activities?

4 What are the main pros and cons of using models in the writing class? Set out your own views on the issue, giving reasons for your position and addressing opposing arguments.

5 Select a writing task from a textbook. What are its five task components and what are the main pedagogic functions it seeks to develop? Could the task be improved to address additional functions, provide more interest, or give greater support to learners? Modify the task and show which components have been changed.

6 Look at the writing prompts below which have been taken from writing textbooks. What pedagogic goals and student roles does each imply and for what population of writers would each be appropriate? Select two and evaluate their potential effectiveness by considering the extent to which they develop control of content, system, context, process, and genre; their possible relevance as real-world rehearsal; and the specification of an audience, a purpose, and a context. What other criteria might you apply to evaluate them?

   a. Imagine a friend of yours has either just entered college or is about to enter college. What advice would you give your friend to help him or her cope with the stress of college?

b. Discuss the dangers of smoking and the benefits of exercise.

c. Describe an effective foreign language teacher by explaining what he or she does or doesn't do.

d. Buy a postcard of the city or town in which you live. Think of a friend overseas who would like to hear from you. Write the postcard and *send it*!

e. Read the newspaper articles given and choose one that interests you. Write a letter to the editor of the class magazine or the editor of the newspaper expressing your opinion on the subject. (In your opening sentence, refer to the letter you are responding to.)

f. You share a small two-bedroom apartment with one other person. You receive a notice saying your rent will increase by $20 per week. You feel the rent increase is unfair for the following reasons:

- The apartment is in great need of repair.
- The last rent increase was three months ago.
- You are a very good tenant.
- The increase will mean you have to get a third tenant, and it is a very small apartment.

You write to the agent or a residents' help organization.

7 Rewrite two of the above prompts so that they meet the criteria of effectiveness you used in question 6. Justify your changes.

8 Select a genre that you consider suitable for a particular target group of learners and write a rubric for an extended writing task to practice that genre. Be sure to specify an audience, a context, a topic, and any other information you consider necessary.

6 *New technologies in writing instruction*

Aims: This chapter explores the place of the computer in L2 writing instruction and provides a critical overview of its main uses, implications, and practical applications for writing teachers.

Technology has had a massive impact in L2 classrooms over the last decade or so and writing instruction now makes considerable use of computer technologies. Some teachers have welcomed these developments enthusiastically, seeing the integration of new technology-based pedagogies as a means of enlivening instruction, improving students' writing skills, and facilitating collaboration and interaction both within and beyond the classroom. Others have been more cautious, regarding this expansion as another manifestation of the escalating corporatization of education or as a threat to the essentially human interactions on which teaching is based. It is true that many of the early claims and fervor for the medium now seem rather naïve, but while unbounded optimism has been tempered by increasing experience of the medium, the pressure on teachers to take up technology is becoming increasingly difficult to resist. It is important, therefore, that we have a critical appreciation of what computers offer.

This chapter considers the ways that computers are currently used in L2 writing instruction and explores some of the research on their effects. In particular it will examine the following areas:

- The use of word processors in L2 writing instruction
- Online writing
- Internet resources for writing teachers
- Computer Assisted Language Learning materials
- Corpora and concordancing in writing teaching

Orientation

In what ways do computers influence the ways we write? How do you think computers might be used to effectively assist the teaching and learning of L2 writing?

Computers, writing, and language learning

In a world increasingly dominated by electronic Information and Communication Technologies (ICT), it is unsurprising that writing teachers are often faced with demands to integrate these technologies into their classes. It is also the case that new technologies have had a major impact on writing. They have had a fundamental influence on the ways we write, the genres we create, the forms our finished products take, and the ways we engage with readers. Most significantly, new technologies:

- Influence drafting, editing, proofreading, formatting, and publication processes
- Facilitate the combination of written texts with visual and audio media
- Encourage nonlinear writing and reading processes
- Alter the relationships between writers and readers
- Blur traditional oral and written channel distinctions (e.g., email, ICQ)
- Facilitate entry to new online discourse communities
- Increase the marginalization of writers and texts isolated from new writing technologies

These developments are very uneven in their effects and are confined mainly to the developed world. They have been sufficiently important, however, for many observers to talk of a "new literacy" (e.g., Snyder, 1998; Tyner, 1998), and teachers need to come to grips with what this means for them professionally. One important point is that writing, in the sense of making language visible, always involves the application of technology of some kind, whether quill, pencil, typewriter, or printing press, and each innovation involves new skills applied in new ways (Lankshear and Snyder, 2000). Writing is, therefore, not fixed but constantly evolving and each new mode of communicative practice requires different skills and understandings. A word processor, for example, offers the writer different opportunities and challenges than writing with pen and paper, and composing an email requires different skills to writing a letter. These effects are still not completely understood.

In addition to the implications they have for *what we teach*, new technologies also have influenced the *ways we teach*, providing alternative approaches to traditional materials and methodologies. Word processors, for instance, provide composing environments which facilitate writing by making drafting, revising, and editing much easier and quicker. This obviously offers opportunities for learners to engage with the creative process of construction and for teachers to help make their writing processes more transparent and effective (e.g., Pennington, 1993).

Similarly, the enormous possibilities for remote communications which technology has opened up enable teachers to link students to a far greater range of information, advice, and people than was ever possible before. The Internet now makes it feasible for learners to collect and publish texts online and to extend their communicative experiences beyond the classroom (e.g., Dudeny, 2000), while classroom networks increase interaction between students for brainstorming and peer feedback more locally (e.g., Knobel et al., 1998). Some key teaching possibilities in these areas are the ability of students to utilize online information as resources for writing (Taylor and Ward, 1998), to post their writing on the Internet for peer feedback, to communicate electronically with "keypals" or via chat sites, to draw on corpus or research data, or to participate in online writing workshops.

It is important to recognize, however, that computers are no more likely to bring about learning improvements by themselves than other teaching tools such as blackboards, overhead projectors, or video players. Technology is not a method but a resource which can support a variety of approaches (Warschauer, 2002). Like all tools and methodologies, it is the ways they are used that can change student writing behaviors. Nor do our uses of technologies simply reflect changes in technology. As I noted in Chapter 1, methods and approaches always reflect beliefs about teaching and learning which are influenced by current broad perspectives of language teaching.

Warschauer and Kern (2000) have recently argued that the use of computers in language teaching reflects a move from structural through cognitive to sociocognitive orientations to teaching. The earliest CALL (Computer Assisted Language Learning) programs were consistent with a structuralist model which emphasized grammar and vocabulary drill and practice activities with the computer acting as a tutor. In line with cognitivist conceptions of learning, the second generation of CALL shifted agency to learners by requiring them to use computers to solve problems and navigate through simulated environments. Current uses reflect sociocognitive approaches, shifting "the dynamic from learners' interaction *with* computers to interaction with other humans *via* the computer" (ibid., 11). Warshauer and Kern observe that these shifts in perspectives and methods have paralleled developments in technology from the mainframe, to the personal, to the networked computer.

This characterization of the ways that theory and technology interact in language teaching reflects definite trends in computer-mediated learning toward the view that learning depends on exposure to authentic language and using language for communication. But despite this, computers are still being used in a variety of different ways in L2 writing classes: as instructors, as communication tools, and as informants about language. The following sections explore these different uses in more detail.

Reflection 6.1

Based on your own experience and the brief overview given above, what do you think might be the main advantages and drawbacks of computers in the L2 writing class? Which of the uses mentioned above would you feel most comfortable in using with a writing class and why?

Word processing and writing teaching

Perhaps the most immediately obvious feature of computer-based writing is the way that electronic text facilitates composing, dramatically changing our writing habits and laying bare the processes that we use to create texts. Commonplace word processing features allow us to cut and paste, delete and copy, check spelling and grammar, import images, change formatting, and print to publishable quality, all of which mean that our texts are now generally longer, prettier, and more heavily revised. The ability of these programs to create and manipulate text easily was immediately taken up by writing teachers so that word processing is the most widely accepted and researched use of computers in education today. The impact of word processing on writing has been so great, in fact, that other uses of computers in L2 writing instruction are sometimes neglected entirely (e.g., Ferris and Hedgecock, 1998).

Features of word processors

The interest in the word processor stems from the fact that it is an environment which encourages users to experiment with different means of expression and organization. Liberated from linear constraints, writers can play around with the text until they are satisfied with the result, and this

Table 6.1: *Potential pros and cons of word processor writing*

Advantages	Disadvantages
Greater motivation – more writing time	Increased focus on surface features
More revisions	Increased anxiety
Greater development of content	Local revisions rather than global
Improvements in quality	Premature completion of work
Removal of handwriting barriers	Decreased writer collaboration
Awareness of writing as a process	Increased plagiarism and cheating
Greater fluency and accuracy	Quantity at the expense of quality
Longer compositions	Preoccupation with physical appearance
Increased experimentation with language	Isolation of student writers

flexibility initially suggested that this might encourage students to write more, and with more care, than with traditional methods. Unfortunately, this optimism was quickly dispelled as improvements in student writing turned out to be slow and limited. Research has produced mixed results. Some studies have confirmed that the medium improved students' attitudes to writing and led to increased revisions and improved products (e.g., Snyder, 1993). Others have discovered little difference between hand-writers and computer-writers, or even that the medium inhibits writers and restricts their composing and revising (e.g., Gerrard, 1989). Table 6.1 summarizes some of the major findings of L2 word processed writing (Hawisher and Selfe, 1989; Pennington, 1996; Pennington and Brock, 1989).

These inconsistent findings on the role and impact of word processors are influenced by both variations in participants and contexts, but it is doubtful whether such studies can ever tell us much of interest. While word processors may make writing easier, they are only machines and no inherent advantages can be directly attributed to them. As I noted above, writing cannot be developed by new tools but only by proper instruction, and this involves providing learners with appropriate tasks and support. In fact, arguments about the effectiveness of word processors in improving writing have become largely irrelevant as writing is now increasingly produced on computers by necessity, particularly in business and university settings. As with most arguments about technology, the important issue is not whether we should use it, but rather how it can best be used.

Reflection 6.2
What changes do you think word processing has made to the ways you write? How might you use your understanding of writing with a word processor to develop students' writing with computers?

Word processors in the writing class

Computers do not replace teachers. As with conventional composing, students need help to improve their writing. Instruction should therefore both support student writing and be related to their goals, with teaching oriented to the following general principles (Hyland, 1993):

1. A training in keyboard skills and word processing software
2. The provision of explicit instruction in computer composition
3. The integration of computer writing activities into the writing course
4. The provision of opportunities for collaboration and peer support

Obviously students can only write freely on computers if they feel comfortable with the software, can exploit its potential, and are not deterred by typing. A central aspect of writing effectively on computers therefore involves learning basic computer literacy and understanding what the software can offer, but writing teachers do not generally devote much time to these skills. Although L2 students now tend to be "computer savvy" and familiar enough with word processors to be free of any anxiety in using them, even the most experienced users often fail to take advantage of many of their capabilities for revision and editing (Susser, 1998). Successful adaptation to the word processor is more likely if composition classes incorporate a familiarization course in keyboarding and basic skills. The most useful of these direct students' attention away from a fixation on local editing, such as cursor moves and block text moves, delete and restore text, scrolling and split screen functions, which encourage more global editing. Help in using the thesaurus, and spelling and grammar checkers is also essential to avoid an overreliance on these very fallible features and their ad hoc, de-contextualized advice.

Reflection 6.3

What are the potential dangers of L2 writers developing an over-reliance on thesaurus, spelling and grammar checking tools? Can you think of any tasks that might help students recognize these dangers and use these features cautiously?

In addition, to write on word processors, students must be provided with ways to generate, revise, and organize material on them. Word processors facilitate rapid, nonlinear drafting by removing the apprehension created by the need to produce clear, accurate prose at the first attempt, but students tend to get bogged down in detailed tinkering. Techniques such as oral dictation,

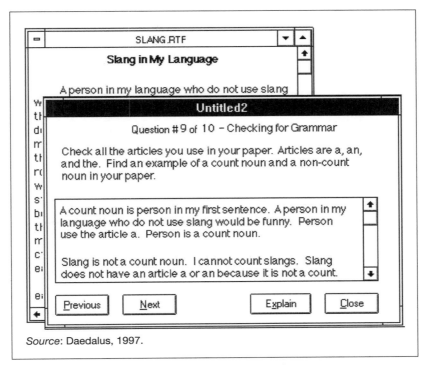

Figure 6.1: The revision heuristic program Respond.

brainstorming, and focused freewriting, which force learners to type quickly, can help them get ideas out and build the confidence to put errors right later. Editing can be assisted by the fact that word processors facilitate the jumbling and rearrangement of texts, so that the kinds of transformation, substitution, insertion, reordering, and text completion tasks discussed in Chapter 5 are easily converted to the computer (Hyland, 1990).

Teachers can also use revision heuristics, an example of which is provided by the *Respond* module of the *Daedalus Integrated Writing Suite* (Daedalus, 1997). This steers students through an evaluative process using a series of teacher modifiable prompts as they revise their drafts. As shown in Figure 6.1, the questions appear in the upper half of a window and students respond in the lower half while consulting their texts in another window. Switching back and forth between windows, students can work independently through the prompts and refer to the original text to make comments.

The third pillar of support involves effectively integrating word processing with other activities and within the writing course itself. Word processors are valuable teaching tools, but if writing classes only involve writing and writing only occurs in the computer lab, then lack of variety is likely to stultify learning. Intelligent scheduling of computer use is essential to provide adequate access to computers for students, both within and out-side class time, while ensuring that computers do not come to dominate activities. Research suggests that computer sessions tend to be more pro-ductive when conducted as writing workshops, allowing students to receive individual attention from a roving teacher and plenty of time to focus on their writing (e.g., Bernhardt et al., 1989). Dividing class sessions between classrooms and regular use of the computer lab enables in-class instruction and discussions to take place as pre-writing and post-writing work, while providing frequent and productive opportunities for writing in a structured and supportive context.

Reflection 6.4

What are some of the potential advantages in holding a writing class exclusively in a computer lab using word processors? What are the advantages of using a mixture of both a lab and regular classroom?

Finally, students often prefer to work on their texts alone when using word processors and teachers may need to encourage cooperation through joint assignments, collaborative writing tasks, and opportunities for peer feedback. While writing involves individual effort, there are clear benefits to students sharing both their texts and experiences with others as they grow as writers, and word processors can facilitate this. The computer screen, for example, is a more public space than a page of paper, providing access to a text by a small group working together. Collaboration is also fostered by the ease and speed of distributing electronic files and hard copies of texts for comments and reworking. Most word processors allow revisions by multiple authors to be tracked in different colors. Microsoft Word, for instance, displays the name and comment of each reviewer in a separate window when the cursor is moved to the text. Collaboration is most fully achieved, however, only with computers through online writing.

Online writing

Word processors are important writing and teaching instruments but they do not fully exploit available technologies for writing and communication. This is partly because word processors are, in a sense, only transitional tools which prepare texts that will eventually be translated back into ink on paper, whereas much written communication is now entirely electronic, employing hypertext environments with their own conventions and genres. Second, and more importantly for writing teachers, word processors fail to make use of the advantages of connectivity that technology now offers. A powerful extension of the computer's role in writing instruction is achieved through networked computers. This comprises:

- *Synchronous writing*, where students communicate in real time via discussion software on Local Area Networks or Internet chat sites with all participants at their computers at the same time.
- *Asynchronous writing*, where students communicate in a delayed way, such as via email.

Reflection 6.5

To what different kinds of writing and communication tasks might these two forms of interaction best be suited? Are students more likely to prefer one type over the other? Why?

Synchronous writing environments

Teachers sometimes observe that when using word processors students tend to work in relative isolation with minimal interaction with other students. Absorbed by the machine and concentrating on the development of their own texts, they rarely discuss their unfolding prose or exchange ideas to gain a deeper understanding of texts, audiences, and their fellow students. Linking computers together attempts to build on the advantages of individual machines through learner collaboration. This reflects both educational theory (Vygotsky, 1962) and research (e.g., Gere, 1987) which suggest that learning is improved through collaboration. Students appear to value peer support while actually composing, rather than simply receiving comments on written products (F. Hyland, 2000), and this also seems to benefit the revision practices of reviewers themselves by helping them to gain an increased awareness of their own writing processes (Stoddard and MacArthur, 1993).

Reflection 6.6

How might networked synchronous interaction improve students' writing? What kinds of activities, discussion tasks, and topics might make best use of this approach?

LAN conferencing software

A *Local Area Network* (LAN) is a number of computers linked through a server for the purpose of sharing information. It offers real-time conferencing between students or between students and teacher in a "virtual environment" which encourages greater peer involvement and interaction than in non-networked contexts. Networks are used in writing classes to provide for synchronous writing discussions, online teacher feedback, and peer conferencing on texts. These communication contexts require specialized writing software such as *CommonSpace*, *InterChange* (Daedalus, 1997) or *ytalk*, which allow students to simultaneously co-construct a discourse.

Such programs typically display two windows. The bottom portion is the student's writing space where he or she can compose a contribution before clicking the "send" button to post it to the network. The top window is a shared read-only space where posted messages appear sequentially in a continuous flow preceded by the poster's log-in name. While they cannot alter anything in the conference window, students can usually paste text from it into their own window which allows them to respond easily to a specific part of a message. In some programs, a third window allows smaller groups to break off and hold discussions separately from the main conference, a useful facility for peer review sessions. Figure 6.2 shows an L2 chat session on *Bridge*, a chat program run by Washington State University.

LANs have been slow to attract research interest, although many teachers claim that they increase both the quantity of student writing and the amount of student interaction. Clearly networks potentially have advantages for teaching writing that go well beyond those of word processing (Swaffer et al., 1998). The fact that students have relative autonomy and are interacting for a genuine purpose encourages writing. However, if discussions get lively, then messages fly past at a rapid rate and weaker students are forced to catch up, making the sequence of contributions difficult to follow (e.g., Braine and Yorozu, 1998). Table 6.2 summarizes the pros and cons of LANs.

Electronic conferencing is probably most effective when used as a sustained learning activity with clear goals and teacher support. The following comments by teachers on their experiences of using LAN conferencing software in writing classes, taken from discussions on the online bulletin boards *Neteach-L* and *Teach*, suggest some of the problems and possibilities:

> I find conferencing on computers fast-paced and conversational. It takes a little time to get used to, and I've generally had a few lurkers early in the semester. I've also had a class or two that could not stay on task at all and moved into somewhat juvenile flaming. Students learn quickly that the teacher cannot control the conversation – which can be great in some circumstances.

Generally, I've used Interchange as a substitute for face-to-face class discussion, on the premise that students writing their comments are students learning the reality of audience and gaining practice in expressing their opinions through text. I am not too directive and the free-wheeling conversations have functioned well as heuristic and planning sessions, moving from a discussion of an assigned reading into trying out some of their ideas for essays.

In my session tonight I asked the students to reflect on the essay they just completed (three drafts). I asked them what they thought of the writing task, what was difficult, what was easy, what do they think they did well and not so well, what they would do if they had more time to work on the essay. We did this for about 45 minutes. Most responses were on task. A traditional discussion on those questions would not have lasted as long, nor elicited comments from as many students.

I use CMC for focused discussion; I remind students that they are working in a writing medium and encourage a degree of formality. After the conference I sort the transcripts by student, and show each of them how much work they've done toward an essay. In this way their transcripts can function as drafts, because I've fed them questions to answer in Interchange in a sequence that produces essays.

Internet conferencing resources

An obvious problem with specialist software is that access is restricted to sites with the program installed, and this can make it difficult to find a lab for

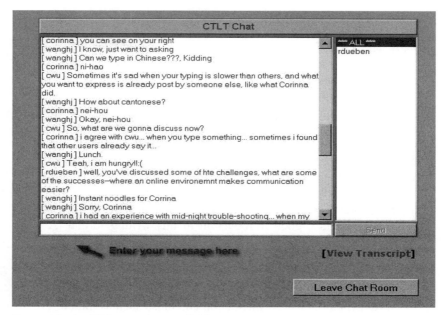

Figure 6.2: An L2 interaction on *Bridge*.

Table 6.2: *Potential advantages and disadvantages of networked writing instruction*

Potential advantages	Potential disadvantages
• Allows all users equal rights and opportunities • Encourages weaker and shy students to participate • Decentralizes teacher role • Facilitates more student talk • Encourages interaction and sense of audience • Minimizes social cues such as color, age, gender, and accent and so encourages participation • Teachers can discreetly moderate small-group work • Provides conference printouts for students to develop ideas or consider feedback later • Hard copy of transcripts gives teachers a record of individual participation	• Unclear whether it improves writing quality • Rapid addition of messages means flow is disjointed and incoherent to learners • Weaker students unable to keep up with fast scrolling messages • Relinquishing of teacher authority may lead to reduction in constructive discussion • Lack of physical co-presence among students may mitigate against careful feedback • Feedback is not sustained or developed, 1 or 2 lines only • Technophobic students may fail to participate • Requires access to labs with network software and so restricts out-of-class work.

classes and for students to work outside of the classroom. A solution to this is to go online and communicate through a chat site, a MOO (Multi-user, Object Oriented text-based virtual reality site), or a group site. These do not usually have the features of specialized writing software, but they are free, open up the possibility of long-distance exchanges, and facilitate writing for unknown audiences.

Perhaps the most widely used synchronous chat resource is ICQ (ICQ.com), an onomatopoetic acronym for *I Seek You*. This is a free program that allows conferencing at any time with groups of two or more participants. Users can initiate chats, page other registered users, be notified when other users are online, and save their interactions. Figure 6.3 shows an example from an L2 ICQ session.

A MOO is different in that users navigate around and interact with other online participants in a virtual space. Lingua MOO at http://lingua. utdallas.edu/ offers a good introduction to this writing format. A good teaching MOO environment is *Tapped In* (http://www.tappedin.org). This is a virtual building where teachers can have free offices and conduct classes there with their students with transcripts of interactions emailed to the teacher after logging out (see Figure 6.4). Some group chat sites provide for synchronous text interaction and those such as Yahoo! groups

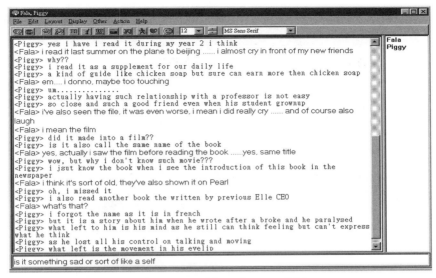

Figure 6.3: Synchronous chat among L2 students on ICQ.

(http://groups.yahoo.com) provide good environments for classwork as they allow teachers to place controls on who can join the group and who can post messages, although transcripts of discussions cannot be kept.

Like any other teaching approach, Computer Mediated Communication needs careful thought before being implemented. While this can be a motivating environment for writing, relinquishing control to learners can result in short, undeveloped contributions and may degenerate into off-task personal exchanges. In fact, the absence of co-presence can weaken interaction norms and result in aggressive or antisocial "flaming." More importantly, there is, as yet, no conclusive evidence that networked communication actually leads to an improvement in written products. Although it is great for collaborative writing and exchanging ideas on writing projects, teachers are still experimenting with ways of making the best use of this tool for writing instruction.

Reflection 6.7

How would you use synchronous communication as a tool for writing teaching? How would you ensure that discussions were focused and how would you facilitate interaction? Would you monitor interaction and what would be the best way to do this? What kind of writing assignments would you set?

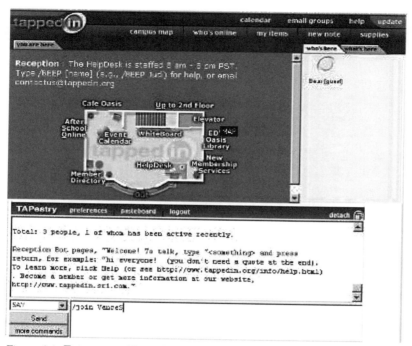

Figure 6.4: Entrance to Tapped In.

Asynchronous writing environments

Asynchronous, or time-delayed, communication using networked computers includes email, news groups, and conferencing software. Its main advantage for L2 writing teachers is that the nonsynchronicity of the communication means that a text can be composed and edited prior to transmission
at a more leisurely pace, rather than being co-constructed by participants.
This tends to mean more reflective and considered responses with greater
participation from less proficient students. Topics change less rapidly and
contributions do not rush past in an incoherent sequence so that responses
are typically more thoughtful, more carefully edited, and more closely reflect
conventions of written communication.

Email is likely to be familiar to many students as text files that can be
read, saved, edited, and forwarded to other users. It is a useful tool for writing instruction as it allows teachers to set up both classroom interaction
and long-distance exchanges, encouraging students to focus on fluency and
meaning while writing for a real audience and purpose. Within a single class,

most information gap tasks can be accomplished by email, encouraging written accuracy and clarity of expression. In addition, the fact that writers can respond to parts of an email, delete unnecessary parts, and then send it on to another student allows question-answer sessions or serial stories to be developed. A slightly more ambitious use is to establish discussion groups, putting all group members into a collective "alias" so that students can send an email message to their classmates simultaneously, discussing ideas, exchanging vocabulary lists, passing on useful Websites, and so on.

The creation of such online learning communities can also encourage collaboration and a sense of what it means to write for an unknown audience beyond the classroom. Email is an effective medium for intercultural exchanges and collaborative writing projects between students in different countries, perhaps even assisting L2 learners corresponding with native speakers to notice and incorporate L1 discourse patterns into their writing (Davis and Thiede, 2000). As a result, a growing number of teachers now use email for class projects with great success. A list of sources for arranging *keypals* is given in Appendix 6.1, and ideas for using email in L2 writing classes can be found in Warschauer (1995).

Reflection 6.8

How might keypals be used as a resource in the writing class? What kinds of assignments would be appropriate and what would be interesting cross-cultural topics for keypal exchanges?

Another form of asynchronous communication used by L2 writing teachers is discussion lists (or mailing lists). Each list has its own purpose and scope and serves to connect people with similar interests. Subscribers send questions, opinions, announcements, responses, and other information of interest to members via email to the list and these are distributed to all other members. Lists can be an excellent way of communicating with fellow teachers to exchange information, get advice, or keep up to date with conferences or new ideas. Most lists have archives organized by themes (or threads) which allow subscribers to refer to previous topics of interest. There are also student lists where learners can communicate with others with the same interests, do their own cross-cultural studies, conduct research projects, and so on. Again, some sources are given in Appendix 6.1, while a good introduction for teachers is Kenji Kitao (www.ling.lancs.ac.uk/staff/visitors/kenji/kitao).

Internet resources for writing

The Internet is a massive online database that gives users access to several hundred million multimedia documents, an overwhelming abundance which may make it seem like we are quenching our thirst for information by drinking from a firehose. This vast source of information has also changed many aspects of writing teaching. Not only does the Internet facilitate the modes of computer-mediated communication discussed in the last section, it also enables both teachers and learners to easily find and read online texts which provide (a) data for projects; (b) information, tasks, and materials for classes; (c) authentic language for analysis; and (d) a place for students to publish their work.

The Internet as a source of content

Perhaps the Internet's most widely used role is as a research source, providing students with data that they can use in writing assignments. Its vast stock of statistics and information provide a rich source of data on the environment, economics, literature, politics, current affairs, entertainment, pop culture, and so on which can be used in essays or writing projects. In addition to independent cyber searches, teachers can set guided information-gap tasks which require learners to treasure hunt for specific information. Thus, students can surf the Web or trawl specific Websites to collect information, about celebrities, travel destinations, and so on to complete a worksheet. Books by Windeatt, Hardisty, and Eastment (2000) and Dudeney (2000) provide a number of ideas for these kinds of Internet tasks. Figure 6.5, for instance, encourages students to analyze the content and style of different online newspapers.

Teachers need to be aware, however, that this immense retrieval potential of computers also offers opportunities for writers to construct texts from other texts without acknowledgment and even the chance to simply download complete essay-length responses to familiar assignment topics. Sites such as *Evil house of cheat* (www.cheathouse.com), *12,000 term papers* (www.12000papers.com), and *cheater.com* all distribute plagiarized papers. The battle has been engaged on the other side by sites such as *plagiarism.org* and *turnitin.com* which offer "document source analyses" of submitted papers, comparing them against millions of texts on the net and documenting similarities.

	Electronic newspaper 1	*Electronic newspaper 2*
Are the headlines the same?		
Are there any photos to accompany the article? Are they the same?		
Are the captions to the photos different?		
Are the stories the same length?		
Is the beginning of the story the same in each newspaper?		
Is the conclusion the same?		
Does one story have more direct speech than the other?		
Are the same facts reported in both articles?		
Do the articles emphasize different aspects of the story?		
Is one article more "personal" than the other? Is one more "factual"?		
Is one article easier to understand than the other? Is the language easier?		
Source: Windeatt, Hardisty, and Eastment, 2000: 1.7.		

Figure 6.5: Web-task writing awareness worksheet.

Reflection 6.9

What Websites are you familiar with which might serve as useful resources for a writing class? What genres or writing tasks could they assist students to complete?

The Internet as a source of language data

An alternative way of exploiting this wealth of textual material is to collect and analyze the patterns of language it contains, drawing on journalistic, business, scientific, or academic texts as language corpora which can provide insights into written genres. There are excellent reasons for studying real data, and online editions of newspapers, magazines, and academic papers make it fairly easy to collect large amounts of specific and relevant machine-readable English language texts, although copyright laws may complicate their long-term storage. A database of authentic writing of this kind can help us to understand features of written language and make these salient to our students. With the help of concordancing software (discussed below) it can also give the computer an informant role, allowing learners to see the ways in which language is typically used in their target genres.

The Internet as a source of language learning materials

In addition to the resources it contains for researching content and compiling corpora, the Internet is also a rich source of language learning materials and advice on writing. There are now hundreds of sites with quizzes, puzzles, grammar activities, and writing tips for L2 students. These sites generally offer an attractive interface and varied tasks and options for learning and interacting, although their use of multimedia is generally poor and many sites tend toward repetitive and mechanical exercises.

Among the most useful Websites for L2 writing teachers are the On-Line Writing Labs (OWLs) hosted by many university language centers or rhetoric departments. These sites often focus on academic writing, but typically have links to other sites. In addition to online information and tasks, OWLs may allow teachers to register and download handouts and tutor manuals. Some of the best of these sites are given in Appendix 6.1, and a list of over 200 U.S. writing centers can be found at the National Writing Centres Association (http://departments.colgate.edu/diw/NWCAOWLS.html). As with all sources of materials, however, teachers need to be sure of its accuracy and that they agree with its approach before recommending it to students. Figure 6.6 shows a screenshot from the Purdue University OWL, providing information on writing a research report.

The Internet as a publishing outlet

Finally, the Internet provides an alternative outlet for students to publish their work. This gives them the satisfaction and pride of displaying their writing for a potentially enormous audience and encourages greater care in presenting their texts. Student magazines such as *Write Now!* are possible outlets for student writing, or Web-savvy teachers can set up class Web pages or encourage students to create their own sites to post their work. There are now numerous Websites that provide advice and examples to help new users create Websites, and several Internet Service Providers (ISPs – the

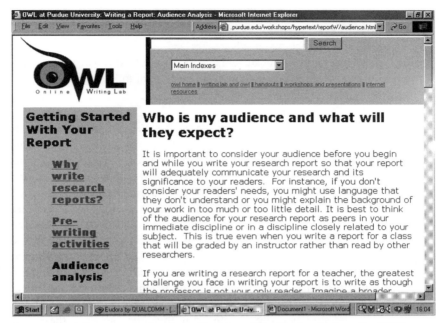

Figure 6.6: Advice on academic writing from The Purdue University OWL.

companies that provide Internet connections) offer free space to host these (see Appendix 6.1).

It is now almost as easy to create a Web page as to word process a document. While specialist Web editors such as *FrontPage* and *Dreamweaver* may have more features than most teachers want to handle, the editors supplied with Web browsers, such as *Netscape Composer*, allow writers to create Web pages quite simply and most word processors enable documents to be saved in Web-readable HTML format. It should be noted, however, that students and teachers need a reason to create a site, as the style and content of the pages and the material that is posted will depend on this. If the page is going to be displayed for a restricted audience on a local area network, it is likely to be different than if work will be posted for anyone to see. Another consideration is whether only final copies of work will be published or also in-progress drafts for peer or teacher comment, providing online response forms for classmates or keypals to comment on the work (e.g., Kahtani, 1999). A further important point is that of copyright; although most teachers have assumed they can simply post their students' work on their Websites, it is perhaps more ethical, and legally more sensible, to get written permission from students first.

Reflection 6.10

What are likely to be the major advantages and difficulties in setting up and using a Website to publish your students' work? How could you overcome these problems and how would you seek to make best use of the resource?

An important consideration of writing on the Web is that the Internet is not simply a distribution channel for students' work, but a medium in its own right. Its power lies in the fact that it frees writers from the constraints of the page, allowing them to author documents that are layered, linked, and nonlinear. This kind of fully electronic, fluid, interactive writing is called hypertext. This is the glue that holds the Internet together, where writers are able to provide active connections to different parts of the current text and beyond it to digitized graphics, video, sounds, animation, and other texts. This provides readers with different pathways through the text according to their own interests and decisions. Hypertext capabilities therefore require a pedagogical response and draw the writing teacher into new, and as yet unexplored, realms of discourse which many of us may prefer to avoid. For teachers and students with an interest in this area, however, these new literacy skills present fascinating and challenging opportunities for writing teachers.

CALL resources for writing

In addition to CMC (Computer Mediated Communication) there are numerous CALL (Computer Assisted Language Learning) programs which support L2 writing instruction. Again, these vary enormously in their appearance, their effectiveness, and the teaching philosophies that underlie them, and care needs to be taken when selecting resources for learners.

Two decades after the first simple gap-fill and matching programs, CALL is still largely distinguished more by its potential than its performance, with multimedia gee-whiz failing to disguise serious pedagogical weaknesses in much software. Obviously some exciting and useful materials have emerged, but good, intelligent software has not been widely available. Most of the big commercial software houses and publishing companies have been reluctant to invest in the field and professional programmers usually have little knowledge of the principles of language learning. On the other hand, few teachers have the necessary time or programming skills to produce sophisticated courseware based on a sound understanding of language acquisition

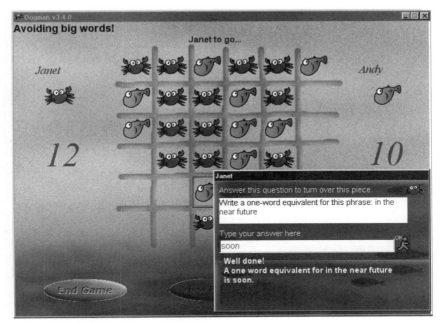

Figure 6.7: A Mindgame activity encouraging awareness of succinct expressions.

and learner psychology. Consequently, there has been a wide gap between much CALL software and current communicative teaching methods.

Programs that exclusively address writing are relatively rare as software developers have tended to focus on what computer programs do best: relieving teachers of grammar and vocabulary drill and practice tasks. These can take many imaginative forms, such as *Mindgame*[1] (Figure 6.7) which requires players to answer a language question each time they capture a piece from their opponent, with questions frequently repeated for reinforcement. Such programs offer interesting variations on scaffolding tasks. Although they need to be carefully integrated to ensure their relevance to particular genres and purposes, these tasks frequently offer more entertaining ways of building language competence than those found in textbooks. They also allow students to learn and practice at their own pace and receive instant feedback on their understanding of words or grammar rules.

Writing programs themselves tend to be very procedural, guiding student users through exercises to help them identify the features they need to create

---

[1] I am grateful to Andrew Stokes and Clarity Language Consultants of Hong Kong for permission to reproduce the screenshots in this section.

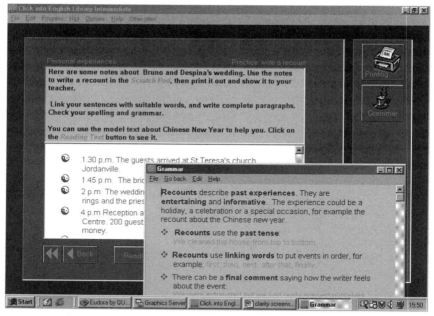

Figure 6.8: Constructing a recount essay from notes and grammar help in *Click into English*.

particular kinds of texts. A good example is *Click into English* developed for the Australian Adult Migrant Education Service (Figure 6.8).

This program is unusual in that it follows a genre approach, with a series of instructional sequences built around model texts from different genres. Each sequence highlights structural, stylistic, or grammatical features of the genre and leads the learner through a series of screens with different practice and self-test multiple choice, gap-fill, and drag and drop activities. The program is self-paced and interactive, allowing students to recall the text at any time, get instant feedback on their answers, consult pop-up screens for genre information and usage advice, and access a dictionary through hyperlinks in the text itself. Like many programs, *Click into English* provides an environment for students to work either alone or with teacher support. Most software, however, is best used when students work collaboratively to maximize human interaction and when the software is integrated into a coherent writing program employing writing assignments and noncomputer activities.

A specialized writing program is *Report Writer*, designed to help more advanced students with the organization, style, and grammar of special-ized professional genres. There are different versions of the program for

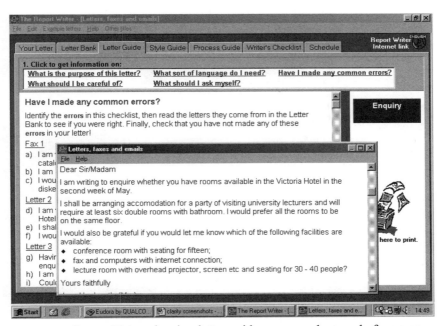

Figure 6.9: Report Writer showing letter guide screen and example for an enquiry letter.

technical or business reports and for letters, faxes, and emails. In this program students are led through each step as they write a particular type of report or letter, following online prompts supported by pop-up advice on the purpose of each stage and explanatory notes on key language, style, and content. Students also have access to a resource bank of models which they can paste into their own report. The technical report program, for instance, begins with typical forms of report titles with definitions of key words such as *describe, analyze*, and *investigate*, together with an explanation of the purpose of each kind of title and authentic examples. After completing their own title, the student then proceeds to acknowledgments, abstract, introduction, and so on, through the structure of a report. Figure 6.9 shows a language guide screen for an inquiry letter with a pop-up example.

An advantage of this software is that teachers can add their own sample texts and advice on style and grammar to the database through a procedure known as *teacher authoring*. Authoring is a dimension of many CALL programs allowing teachers to customize off-the-peg software to the needs of their own learners without the use of specialized programming skills. Teachers can add new texts and exercises for the particular proficiency

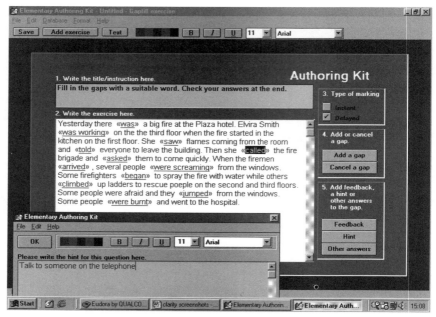

Figure 6.10: Authoring an on-screen gap fill exercise with hints for *Tense Buster*.

levels and target needs of their students. This might involve adding content from a local newspaper story or class project, highlighting features of a specific professional or academic genre, or providing back-up material for a course textbook. Some programs have multimedia capabilities enabling teachers to add sound, video, and pictures to their texts in addition to creating gap-fill, multiple choice, matching, proofreading, and drag and drop exercises. Figure 6.10 shows an authoring screen from the program *Tense Buster*.

CALL programs offer students a very different learning experience than either computer-mediated communication or the Internet. Language learning and writing software represent motivating, multimedia environments for studying finite language areas at the student's pace and with control over the directions they take, the material they focus on, and the time they devote to it. In essence, however, these are tutors in another guise, digital textbooks with many of the same advantages and disadvantages. Also like traditional paper materials, their effectiveness in writing classes ultimately depends on the teacher's ability to use them in ways that respond to students' proficiencies, interests, and target needs.

Reflection 6.11
Which of the CALL programs discussed above do you think offer most to the teacher of L2 writing? How might you effectively integrate your choice of program into a writing course for L2 students?

Corpora and concordancing

The use of language corpora and concordancing offers one of the most exciting applications of new technologies to the writing class, providing teachers with evidence of language use not available from other sources and moving away from preprogrammed CALL to redefine the computer as a tool. Electronic corpora are becoming increasingly important in second language writing instruction as teaching becomes less a practice of imparting knowledge and more one of providing opportunities for learning. Essentially a corpus is a collection of computer-readable texts, sometimes comprising many millions of words, considered more or less representative of a particular domain of language use. Concordancing software[2] is used to search a corpus for a particular word or phrase and display the results as a KWIC (Key Word in Context), a list of unconnected lines of texts with the item studied at the center of each line surrounded by the immediate words in that sentence. Figure 6.11 shows the results of an "approximate pattern match" of *benefit* using *WordPilot 2000*.[3]

Concordancing software is used to reveal particular language features of a corpus and determine the relative importance of recurring patterns. The principle is that if a particular pattern is found to occur frequently across a range of texts from the same genre, then it can reasonably be assumed that it will occur frequently in future texts, allowing us to treat it as a significant feature of that genre. Thus, regularity provides a basis for predictability and helps us to understand how particular genres are typically written. Lines in a KWIC display can be sorted in different ways to show the most frequent collocates, or words which typically occur in its environment. So to identify the adjectives that most frequently modify a target noun, it is helpful to sort on the word left of the keyword, while the collocates of a specific adverb would require a right-sort. *Wordpilot* then gives a summary of these words (Figure 6.12).

---

[2] The two leading commercial concordancers for learners are *WordPilot 2000* (www.compulang.com) and *MonoConc* (www.athel.com).

[3] I am grateful to John Milton for permission to reproduce screenshots of his program *WordPilot 2000*.

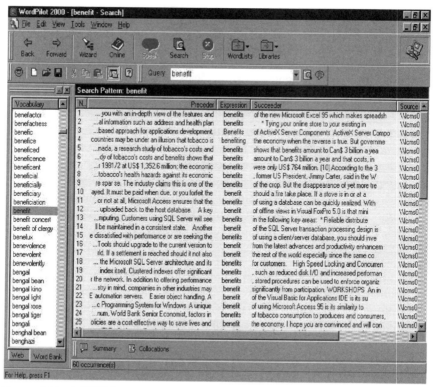

Figure 6.11: A KWIC concordance of forms of 'benefit' in *WordPilot*.

Collocations therefore allow frequently occurring patterns to be seen and show how words typically behave in particular genres (e.g., Partington, 1998; Wichmann et al., 1997). For instance, teachers (or their students) might use a concordance to answer the following questions:

- What adjectives are most often used to describe places in recount genres?
- What tense is most commonly used in the methods section of physics lab reports?
- What preposition most commonly follows *grateful* in inquiry letters?
- In what context is *besides* used to add information and where is it used to emphasize information?
- What contexts determine whether *quite* is used to strengthen or weaken a statement?
- What is the most common salutation/closure in a business letter?
- How do *since* and *for* differ?

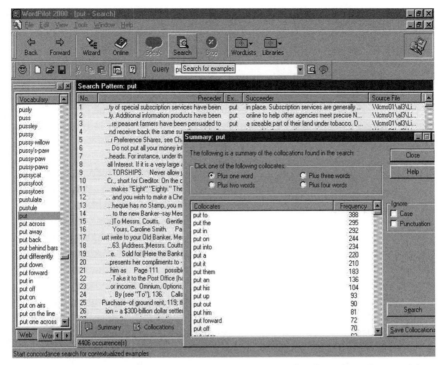

Figure 6.12: A KWIC concordance and a summary of collocations for 'put' in *WordPilot 2000*.

Reflection 6.12

How might a concordance be useful to you as a writing teacher? What kinds of corpora would be most useful to your students and how would you use them as part of a writing course?

Tribble and Jones (1997) discuss activities for using language corpora in L2 classes, but essentially corpora have been used in two ways in the classroom. In the first, the teacher examines a corpus and writes materials based on the results. For instance, we can consult a corpus to determine the most common words or patterns to teach when introducing a target genre and, drawing on the examples we find there, illustrate authentic uses of those forms in worksheets and exercises. The second, and perhaps more interesting approach, is to teach students how to use a concordancer to study corpora themselves. This raises students' awareness of conventional patterns in writing and encourages a more inductive understanding of the texts they need to write. Wu (1992: 32) summarizes the advantages of this method: "Only when words are in their habitual environments, presented in their most frequent forms and their relational patterns and structures, can they be learnt effectively, interpreted properly and used appropriately." This kind of direct learner access suggests two further lines of approach (Aston, 1997). Corpora can be treated as *research tools* to be systematically investigated as a means of gaining greater awareness of language use, or as *reference tools* to be consulted for examples when problems arise while writing.

Even though some students may be stimulated by the research approach to corpora, there is a danger that others will be bored by an overexposure to concordance lines. Research approaches presuppose considerable motivation and a curiosity about language that is often lacking, and teachers have generally confined student searches to key features through tasks which guide them to what is typical in target genres. Such concordance activities can both suggest the appropriacy of using one word rather than another in specific circumstances and indicate the rarity of true synonymy among semantically related items. For many learners, however, language only becomes important when they need it to communicate, and here concordancers are more usefully employed as reference tools.

Novice writers are often faced with the problem of a relatively limited lexicon and set of formulaic expressions when composing, and this is not greatly improved by a discovery approach to lexical acquisition. As a result, "learning is more effective when students have direct access to information and timely advice on its use" (Milton, 1997: 239). By linking concordancers to word processing software, writers are able to call up a concordance for a word by double clicking that word while they are typing. This gives them information about the frequency and contexts of the expressions they need when they need it. Thus, if a writer is unsure whether to use *possible for* or *possible that* in a given context, retrieving concordance lines should provide sufficient examples to make the choice clear. Information searches can be extended into the Internet to provide instant access to online English and multilingual dictionaries, writing tutorials, and additional corpora. Figure 6.13 shows definitions from an online dictionary called up from within a word processor by *WordPilot*.

Finally, concordancers also offer teachers interesting possibilities for innovative uses of feedback. If students submit their writing electronically, then teachers can hyperlink errors in an essay directly to a concordance file where students can examine the contexts and collocations of the words they have misused. This kind of reflective, active response to a teacher's feedback can contribute a great deal to a student's writing development.

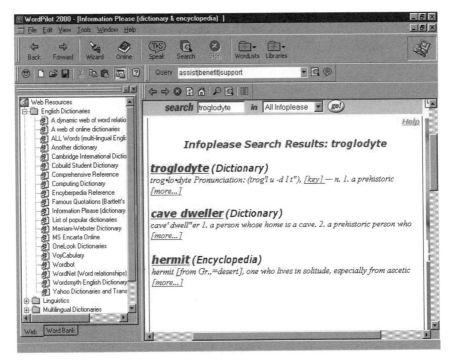

Figure 6.13: Online dictionary information in *WordPilot*.

These kinds of immediate online assistance can be extremely useful for raising students' awareness of genre-specific conventions, developing independent learning skills, and improving writing products, but this is perhaps an approach to be used cautiously. No method can be effective if participants are uncomfortable with it, and concordancing challenges common perceptions about how writing should be taught. It is useful, however, for writing teachers to be aware of this approach and able to employ it. Shifting the pedagogic role of computers from communication channel or virtual instructor to that of *informant* presents considerable opportunities as well as challenges and it would be foolish to ignore what corpora can tell us and our students about texts.

Reflection 6.13

Which of the three ways of using corpora discussed above appeals to you most? What do you see as the potential advantages of using corpora in the writing class? Can you envisage any problems?

Summary and conclusion

Although writing teachers may be hesitant to make use of computers in their classrooms, this chapter has sought to show that we should not be immune to the possibilities technology offers. In many circumstances, computer-based instruction presents stimulating alternatives to traditional paper materials and tasks, and much commercial software, Internet sites, and chat facilities are easy to learn, straightforward to use, and technically robust. However, teachers should consider carefully why they want to use computers, how students might benefit from them, and how best to integrate them into a coherent writing course. The main points of this chapter are listed below.

- Evidence suggests that the use of computers provides a stimulating learning and communication environment and can improve L2 students' motivation, attitudes, and confidence about writing.
- Computer-mediated communication and instruction has implications both for the kinds of writing that students do and the ways that teachers teach, suggesting alternative or parallel materials and methodologies to those used in traditional writing classrooms.
- Computers do not represent a method but can be used to support a variety of methods.
- Computers offer a range of different opportunities for writing instruction including word processing, synchronous and asynchronous computer-mediated communication, Internet writing and resources, CALL programs and concordancing.
- Like any other learning activity, the use of computers in a writing course is only effective when they are integrated into a sustained, coherent program that offers learners some control over their learning and guidance from teachers.
- The choice of programs, sites, and tasks should be carefully based on students' target needs and current abilities as well as the teacher's views of learning.
- Computers do not replace teachers but crucially depend on them, both so that technology is used effectively in the time available and so that students receive adequate support.

Discussion questions and activities

1 A word processor enables the rearrangement of a text by removing words, inserting superfluous words, and by mixing up words, sentences, or paragraphs. How might this feature be useful in teaching word processing and computer composing skills?

2 What are the main differences between synchronous and asynchronous channels of communication in terms of the types of writing and activities they allow? Devise two activities for each channel, setting out clear goals for the tasks and describing what the students are expected to do before, during, and after that activity.

3 One difference between online and traditional classes is that students are only present when they are participating, when they are actually writing, and so a major challenge for teachers using Computer-Mediated Communication is how to encourage their students to contribute to discussions and form an online community. What kinds of topics, activities, assessments, and principles of engagement might best foster such a community among students you are familiar with?

4 What makes a good language learning program? How important is the use of multimedia or the way it provides feedback? Devise a set of criteria for evaluating the value of an ELT Website or CALL software for a particular group of learners. You may want to draw on the lists of criteria discussed in Chapter 4, but in addition to pedagogic criteria, you will probably want to include features that relate to technical design, multimedia features, and ease of use.

5 Visit the ESL Websites listed in Appendix 6.1 or follow the links you find there to others. Evaluate six sites using the criteria you devised in the previous task and select the best two. What features of these sites are most useful and how would you incorporate them into a writing class for a particular group of students? Write a lesson plan to do this.

6 One advantage of the Internet over individual CALL programs is that students do not need to learn how to use a large number of programs. However, the Internet does require a set of specialized competencies which students may have to learn. What competencies would you require of your writing students? Add another five items to this checklist and be prepared to justify your choices.
a. Use a search engine to locate a list of sites.
b. Start a browser and type in a URL.
c. Copy and paste text or graphic from a Web page into a word processor.
d. Bookmark and organize Web pages.

7 Look back to the tasks discussed in Chapter 5. Which of these could be adapted for use on the computer? Select three tasks and rewrite them as computer activities, either for word processing, local networked communication, synchronous or asynchronous C-M-C, or CALL. Write lesson plans to show how you would incorporate these tasks into a lesson.

8 Design a writing project that requires a particular group of students to contact students in another country via email or the Internet. How would you present the project to students? How would you make contact with students from the other school? What kinds of tasks would you set for the project? Describe how you would integrate the project into a writing syllabus and how it might influence the assignments you give.

9 It was noted that one danger of the Internet was the great temptation it offers students to cut and paste portions of articles that they find into their own essays or to download ready-made essays. Teachers obviously need to spend some time with students discussing acceptable practices when using Web-based material, but what steps could you take to practically prevent this? Suggest some assignments that might prevent electronic copying.

10 Explore one of these computer resources as a participant, then write up your experience and reflections on how you would use it to improve your teaching. You can either set up your own Website, join a synchronous chat program or discussion list, or correspond with a keypal.

Appendix 6.1: Some useful Websites for writing teachers

Web Search Engines

Search Engine	Colossus (directory of search engines)
	http://www.searchenginecolossus.com/
Altavista	http://www.altavista.digital.com/
AskJeeves	http://www.askjeeves.com
	(allows users to make full sentence queries)
Google	http://www.google.com
Hotbot	http://www.hotbot.com/
Infoseek	http://www.infoseek.com/
Lycos	http://www.lycos.com/
WebCrawler	http://www.webcrawler.com/

Free space for student Web pages

http://www.geocities.com
http://www.tripod.com
http://www.angelfire.com

Free email: Free Web-based email for student exchanges

http://www.mail.yahoo.com
http://www.hotmail.com
http://www.newtaddress.com

Synchronous writing sites

ICQ	http://www.icq.com/download/ New users information at
	http://www.mirabilis.com/ icqtour/

mIRC	http://www.mirc.co.uk/get.html
Dave's Internet Café Discussion Centre	http://www.eslcafe.com/discussion/dv/
The Speakeasy Studio and Café	http://morrison.wsu.edu/studio/About.asp
Remarq Discussion Site	http://www.remarq.com/home.asp
ESL and Language Teachers' Chatboard	http://www.teachers.net/mentors/esl_language
CRIBE (Chat Room In Broken English)	http://www.cup.com/bm7/cribe.htm

Keypal lists
1. *Sites where students can find keypals*

Dave's E-Mail for ESL Students	http://www.pacificnet.net/~sperling/student.html
ePals Classroom exchange (Over 850,000 users in 90 countries)	http://www.epals.com/
The E-Mail Key Pal Connection	http://www.comenius.com/keypal/index.html
Keypals Club	http://www.mightymedia.com/keypals/
The Meeting Place	http://www.encomix.es/~its/newdoor.htm
Keypals	http://www.reedbooks.com.au/heinemann/global/ global1.html

2. *Sites for teachers to arrange keypal exchanges*

Dave's ESL E-mail for Teachers	http://www.pacificnet.net/~sperling/guestbook.html
E-mail Pen-Pals for Students	http://math.unr.edu/linguistics/teslpnpl.html
Intercultural E-mail Classroom	http://www.stolaf.edu/network/iecc
International E-mail Project	http://www.enst.fr/~benenson/lgv/
Key Pals	http://www2.waikato.ac.nz/education/WeNET/key/khome.html
Keypals Club	http://www.mightymedia.com/keypals/
Keypals International	http://www.collegebound.com/keypals
International EFL/ESL discussion lists	http://www.latrobe.edu.au/www/education/sl/sl.html

Discussion lists
1. For teachers

Linguist List Information:	http://www.baal.org.uk/baalf.htm
Writing discussion group:	http://kalama.doe.Hawaii.edu/hern95/pt035/writing/wholalist.html
TESL-L (TESL list)	List: listserv@cunyum.cuny.edu
	Mail: eslcc@cunyum.bitnet
Linguist	Listserv@tamvm1.tamu.edu
NETEACH-L (net ESL teaching)	listserv@raven.cc.ukans.edu

2. For students

LaTrobe University	announce-sl@latrobe.edu.au
Tile.Net (info on lists)	http://tile.net/
Liszt directory (info)	http://www.liszt.com/
Inter-Links (info)	http://alabanza.com/kabacoff/Inter-Links/listserv.html

ESL Teaching and learning sites

Dave's Internet Café	http://www.eslcafe.com
Its-online	http:its-online.com
Virtual Language Centre	http://vlc.polyu.edu.hk/
EF Englishtown	http://www.englishtown.com/
HKUST Language Centre	http://lc.ust.hk/
Writing Machine	http://ec.hku.hk/writingmachine/

Online Writing Labs

National Writing Centres Association:	http://departments.colgate.edu/diw/NWCAOWLS.html.
Purdue OWL	http://owl.english.purdue.edu/
The Online Writery (Missouri)	http://web.missouri.edu/%7Ewritery/
The Writing Machine (HKU)	http://ec.hku.hk/writingmachine/
HK PolyU Writing Centre	http://elc.polyu.edu.hk/CILL/writing.htm
Garbl's Active Writing Links	http://members.home.net/garbl/writing/action.htm
Bemidji State Writing Center	http://cal.Bemidji.msus.edu/WRC/WRChome.html
Colorado State Writing Center	http://www.colostate.edu/Depts/English/wcenter/ecenter.com
Michigan State Writing Center	http://pilot.msu.edu/user/writing/

Style guides and information on writing

APA Style resources	http://www.psychwww.com/resource/apacrib.htm
Columbus guide to citation style	http://www.columbia.edu/cu/cup/cgos/idx_basic.html
Resources for writers	http://webster.commnet.edu/writing/writing.htm
Writing resources	http://www.indiana.edu/~wts/wts/resources.html
Way to Write	http://www.ucalgary.ca/UofC/eduweb/writing/
Steps in the Writing Process	http://karn.ohiolink.edu/~sg-ysu/process.html
Research & Writing Step by Step	http://www.ipl.org/teen/aplus/stepfirst.htm
Tools for Your Writing	http://www.usc.edu/dept/LAS/writing/tools/process.html
Research Paper Writing	http://www.researchpaper.com/
How to write an essay	http://www2.actden.com/writ_den/tips/essay/index.htm
Online Technical Writing	http://www.io.com/~hcexres/tcm1603/acchtml/acctoc.html
PIZZAZ (Creative writing)	http://darkwing.uoregon.edu/~leslieob/pizzaz.html

7 Responding to student writing

Aims: This chapter examines central features of teacher oral and written feedback and peer response to student writing, exploring the potential effectiveness of different methods and the main issues for teachers.

Providing feedback is often seen as one of the ESL writing teacher's most important tasks, offering the kind of individualized attention that is otherwise rarely possible under normal classroom conditions. Writers typically intend their texts to be read, and in the classroom feedback from readers provides opportunities for them to see how others respond to their work and to learn from these responses. This kind of formative feedback aims at encouraging the development of students' writing and is regarded as critical in improving and consolidating learning. Vygotsky (1978), for example, discusses a stage in cognitive growth he calls "the zone of proximal development" where skills are extended through the guidance and response of expert others. Feedback therefore emphasizes a process of writing and rewriting where the text is not seen as self-contained but points forward to other texts the student will write. It helps the writer work out the text's potential and to comprehend the writing context, providing a sense of audience and an understanding of the expectations of the communities they are writing for.

why feedback

The nature of this response can vary widely and feedback practices differ according to the teachers' preferences as well as the kind of writing task they have set and the effect they wish to create. But while a response to written work is probably essential for the development of writing skills, there is less certainty about who should give this response, the form it should take, and whether it should focus more on ideas or forms. This chapter explores the practical issues of responding to student texts, addressing:

- Teacher written feedback
- Teacher-student conferencing
- Peer feedback

Orientation
What kinds of factors are likely to influence the type of feedback you give? What do you need to know – about language, writing, or the writer – to give your students usable and effective feedback?

Teacher written feedback

Despite increasing emphasis on the importance of oral response and the use of peers as sources of feedback, teacher written response continues to play a central role in most L2 writing classes. Many teachers do not feel that they have done justice to students' efforts until they have written substantial comments on their papers, justifying the grade they have given and providing a reader reaction. Similarly, many students see their teacher's feedback as crucial to their improvement as writers.

A great deal of research, however, has questioned the effectiveness of teacher feedback as a way of improving students' writing. Research on first language writing suggests that much written feedback is of poor quality and frequently misunderstood by students, being too vague and inconsistent (e.g., Sommers, 1982), and often "authoritarian," "formalist," and "insensitive" (Connors and Lunsford, 1993). Comments tend to be directed to form rather than content and responses can appropriate, or take over, student texts by being too directive (Sommers, 1982). Zamel (1985: 86) suggests a similar picture in ESL contexts:

ESL writing teachers misread student texts, are inconsistent in their reactions, make arbitrary corrections, write contradictory comments, provide vague prescriptions, impose abstract rules and standards, respond to texts as fixed and final products, and rarely make content-specific comments or offer specific strategies for revising the texts. . . . The teachers overwhelmingly view themselves as language teachers rather than writing teachers.

Reflection 7.1
Look at this comment from Knoblauch and Brannon (1981:165) which summarizes their survey of the L1 research on teacher feedback:

Commenting on student essays might just be an exercise in futility. Either students do not read the comments or they read them and do not attempt to implement suggestions and correct errors.

Do you agree that this is also true of ESL contexts? What could you do as a teacher to make your written feedback effective in improving students' writing?

Despite these negative findings, feedback on early drafts of a paper does seem to lead to improvements in subsequent drafts (e.g., Knoblauch and Brannon, 1981) and this also appears to be true in L2 writing (F. Hyland, 1998). The following sections highlight key aspects of the research relevant for teacher feedback.

Student preferences and uses of feedback

Clearly teachers need to consider what students want from feedback and what they attend to in their revisions. Research suggests that teacher written feedback is highly valued by second language writers (F. Hyland, 1998) and that many learners particularly favor feedback on their grammar (Leki, 1990). Error-free work is often a major concern for L2 writers, possibly because of prior learning experiences and the fact that many will go on to be evaluated in academic and workplace settings where accuracy may be essential. In contexts where they are asked to write multiple drafts, however, students claim to prefer comments on ideas and organization in earlier drafts and on grammar in later drafts, perhaps influenced by process-oriented feedback practices. Both proficiency and academic level can muddy these waters, however, as students may come to see the writing instructor's expertise as increasingly restricted to grammar correction as they progress through university (Radecki and Swales, 1988).

The effect of written feedback on student revisions in subsequent drafts has not been extensively studied, although it seems that students try to use most of the usable feedback they are given (F. Hyland, 1998). Students' claims that they value feedback are largely supported through their actions in response to it and, equally importantly, most feedback-linked revisions seem to result in text improvements (Ferris, 1997). In Hyland's study students either followed a comment closely in their revision (usually a grammar correction), used the feedback as an initial stimulus which triggered a number of revisions (such as a comment on tone or style), or avoided the issues raised by the feedback by deleting the problematic text. While these changes largely improved the text, Hyland found that students often revised their texts with no real understanding as to why it was necessary and that in many cases deletions were not rephrased, so that the original idea was lost rather than amplified. In other words, although revisions may make an improvement to the current text, it is possible that they are contributing little to students' future writing development.

It is also important to note that what individual students want from feedback – and the use they make of it – varies considerably. Some students want praise, others see it as condescending; some want a response to their ideas, others demand to have all their errors marked; some use teacher commentary effectively, others ignore it altogether. It can be difficult for teachers to cater to all these different perceptions and expectations, but a full dialogue with individual students is often beneficial. This can take the form of a "revise and resubmit letter" (Ferris, 1997) in which students detail the changes they have made in the subsequent draft, journal reflections on the feedback they have received, or a precourse questionnaire in which students set out the areas on which they want feedback to focus.

Reflection 7.2

What factors might influence individual students' preferences and use of feedback? How could you discover your students' past experiences and expectations concerning feedback? How could you encourage them to try new responses to feedback and abandon ones that have not been effective?

Forms of teacher written feedback

A variety of techniques have been proposed to provide teacher feedback to students, the most common being commentary, cover sheets, minimal marking, taped comments, and electronic feedback.

Commentary. Probably the most common type of teacher written feedback consists of handwritten commentary on the student paper itself. This kind of feedback is best seen as responding to students' work rather than evaluating what they have done, stating how the text appears to us as readers, how successful we think it has been, and how it could be improved. If time allows, responses may take the form of both marginal and end comments. A comprehensive end note allows more space and opportunities for the teacher to summarize and prioritize key points and to make general observations on the paper. Comments in the essay margins, on the other hand, are both immediate and proximate, appearing at the exact point in the text where the

Symbol	Meaning	Symbol	Meaning
S	Incorrect spelling	λ	Something has been left out
W	Wrong word order	[ ]	Something is not necessary
T	Wrong tense	*PM*	Meaning is not clear
C	Concord (subject and verb do not agree)	*NA* *P*	The usage is not appropriate Punctuation is wrong
Wf	Wrong form		
S/f	Singular or plural form wrong		

Figure 7.1: Correction codes.

issue occurs. This not only ensures relevance and creates a strong sense that the reader is responding to the text "on the fly," but is also more effective than an end comment in making sure that the student understands precisely what is referred to.

Rubrics. A variation on commentary, and often accompanying it on final drafts, is the use of cover sheets which set out the criteria that have been used to assess the assignment and how the student has performed in relation to these criteria. Different rubrics can be used for different genres and, while they restrict the range of issues that can be addressed, they are useful in making grading decisions explicit and showing what the teacher values in a particular piece of writing. An example of a rubric for an expository essay in a university writing class is shown in Appendix 7.1.

Minimal marking. This refers to a type of in-text, form-based feedback. It follows research which suggests that indicating the location and perhaps type of error, rather than direct correction, is more effective in stimulating a student response (e.g., Bates et al., 1993; Ferris, 1997) and also perhaps in developing self-editing strategies. One way of accomplishing this is to use a set of simple "correction codes" such as that suggested by Byrne (1988) and reproduced in Figure 7.1. This technique makes correction neater and less threatening than masses of red ink and helps students to find and identify their mistakes. A disadvantage, however, is that it is not always possible to unambiguously categorize a problem, particularly when it extends beyond a sentence boundary. Extending the code merely makes the procedure un-wieldy and confusing, so some teachers adopt a more minimalist approach by broadening the categories to focus on a limited number of general areas (Hyland, 1990).

In the example below, codes identify three such areas: surface form (GR), expression (E), and logical development (L).

> GR The mining industry are able to bring two things to the country. First a
> E large amount of revenue to the country and also jeopardy to the natural
> environment. BCL and other mines all over the world are a good
> L example of this. Therefore we must only have local companies to
> mine.

A true minimal marking method, however, makes a virtue of providing even less information to students as nothing is underlined and no symbols are used. Surface errors are indicated only by a cross in the margin alongside the lines in which they occur, encouraging students to identify the problems and correct them before returning the paper. While various rhetorical and communicative aspects remain outside its reach, the simplicity of the approach allows more time for making more substantive comments and generates peer discussion as students collaborate in correction:

> XX *We apologise for the inconveniency. It was all because certain*
> X *reasons that things turned out that way. We did sent a*
> X *driver to the airport but it broke on the way. Secondly about the hotel. The group had to take another. We booked the cheapest and a reasonably good one. Going to the Hilton was*
> X *impossible because bookings are made one month early.*

Taped commentary. An alternative to marginal comments is recording remarks on a tape recorder and writing a number on the student paper to indicate what the comment refers to (Hyland, 1990). This not only saves time and adds novelty, it provides listening practice for learners and assists those with an auditory learning style preference. It also shows the writer how someone responds to their writing as it develops, where ideas get across, where confusion arises, where logic or structure breaks down. This example gives some idea of how this works:

> *Student paper*
> 6. *Although its construction and building materials have been constantly changing, with the influence of the western technology, the basic engineering application is still the foundation of its operating principle.*

> *Teacher commentary*
> Are you clear about what you're trying to say at six? It's a good general rule to keep your language simple and your sentences short so that your message

gets across. Try reading this sentence again after checking the grammar and removing the commas. The last two lines are not clear and you need to rewrite them as a separate sentence.

Electronic feedback. Finally, as discussed in Chapter 6, computers have opened up new opportunities for responding to writing. Teachers can provide comments on electronic submissions by email or by using the comment function, which allows feedback to be displayed in a separate window while reading a word processed text. Feedback on errors can also be linked to online explanations of grammar or to concordance lines from authentic texts to show students examples of features they may have problems using correctly. These new channels of written feedback offer teachers greater flexibility in their responding practices, but ultimately convenience is likely to be the deciding factor in which are used.

Reflection 7.3
What do you see as the main advantages and disadvantages of each of these approaches? Are there any you would not use to give feedback to students? Why?

Types of teacher feedback

Both the communicative approach to language teaching and the process approach to writing emphasize the need for language production uninhibited by language correction, but since errors of grammar are an obvious problem for L2 writers it is not surprising that teachers may feel the need to respond to form. Cumming (1985), for example, found that teachers try to make "comprehensible order" of their students' scripts by focusing on surface features, and Zamel (1985) argues that teachers respond as language teachers rather than writing teachers. The effectiveness of such correction, however, has been questioned, and in a much quoted review of the research, Truscott (1996) concluded that error correction is ineffective in improving student writing. As a result, teachers are often encouraged to focus on global issues of meaning and organization and on the process of writing.

While Truscott's assertion may be correct as far as it goes, it is also true that writing teachers have not been well served by the literature he summarizes. Much of this research reflects experimental or analytical research techniques that ignore classroom realities and the preferences of students.

Written feedback is more than marks on a page, yet research procedures often remove it from the real classrooms and teacher-student relationships within which it occurs. Master (1995), for instance, found that corrective grammar feedback was valued by students and effective when combined with classroom discussions. Moreover, while marking mechanical errors can be frustrating, the view that there is no direct connection between correction and learning is greatly overstated. Fathman and Whalley (1990) discovered that texts improved most when students received feedback on *both* content and form, while Ferris (1997) found that teachers' attention to form led to a reduction in errors in later assignments, particularly when it contained comments rather than corrections.

It is also the experience of many teachers that students vary greatly in their response to grammar feedback and in their ability to benefit from learning how to construct and edit their prose. ESL students themselves, particularly those from cultures where teachers are highly directive, generally welcome and expect teachers to notice and comment on their errors and may feel resentful if their teachers do not provide this. It should also be borne in mind that teachers respond to *students* in their comments as much as texts, considering students' backgrounds, needs, and preferences as well as the relationship they have with them and the ongoing dialogue between them (F. Hyland, 1998; 2001).

A further important consideration is audience. Students may be learning to write for a particular discourse community for whom accuracy can well be important, such as in business or academic environments. Numerous studies of university subject teachers, for instance, suggests that there is little tolerance of typical ESL errors and that linguistic errors tend to interfere with subject teachers' comprehension and influence their overall grading of papers (e.g., Janopoulos, 1992). While we might also seek to encourage these readers to modify their demands, we cannot ignore the immediate needs of our students to both produce texts that are regarded as competent and successful by their intended audiences and to become self-sufficient in constructing acceptably accurate prose.

Admonishments to teachers to avoid attention to form and focus on meaning therefore seem misplaced, the result of a view of writing which sees ideas and language as distinct. Although teachers should not be excessively focused on eradicating errors, they should also be careful to avoid emphasizing ideas to the neglect of form. Teachers may feel that they can only help learners to engage in the writing process by responding to their ideas, but, in fact, the separation of form and content is largely an artificial one, of dubious theoretical value and impossible to maintain in practice. As I have noted in earlier chapters, we only successfully articulate our meanings *through* the selection of appropriate forms. Language is a *resource* for making meanings, not something we turn to when we have worked out what we are going to say, and the two cannot be realistically separated when responding to writing.

Reflection 7.4
How important do you think linguistic form is in writing? What strategies do you think might be effective in developing ESL students' abilities to notice and correct the accuracy of their writing?

Responding to errors

Teacher written feedback should respond to all aspects of student texts: structure, organization, style, content, and presentation, but it is not necessary to cover every aspect on every draft at every stage of the teaching-writing cycle. In a personal experience essay, such as a response to a reading for instance, it is important to help students generate, focus, and organize their ideas by providing feedback that addresses the development and clear expression of content material. Attention to sentence-level errors generally can be delayed to a later draft as major parts of the paper may be changed or revised. But teachers cannot ignore cases where students have confused text stages, used an inappropriate text structure, or made tense and vocabulary choices that grossly interfere with the successful expression of their ideas. The key to effective written feedback is to reinforce the patterns which were taught when modeling the genre so that it becomes part of the process of learning to write a genre rather than an extemporized response to error.

As discussed in Chapter 5, the teaching-writing cycle offers an explicit model of how teachers can move through successive phases of classroom activities to develop writing abilities, with each stage associated with different purposes. Feedback on appropriate language and organizational features of the genre is likely to be most effective during the joint construction stage after students have received considerable input on the structure and language of the target genre and before scaffolding is removed to allow students to create their own texts independently. Feedback can then build on what is currently salient to students because attention is given primarily to the features that have just been taught. This approach allows indirect techniques such as minimal marking, which are more successful in encouraging a response and in developing longer term editing and proofreading skills.

It makes sense for teachers to address text features associated with the genre in question and that have been the subject of earlier scaffolding activities, yet some errors seem to be blind spots for particular students and persist in their work. It is obviously counterproductive to attend to all errors and teachers need to prioritize problems for feedback and review. Numerous factors can influence the errors students make and, once again, teachers will need to consider individual differences and students' particular preferences for feedback. Ferris (2002) offers a practical resource on this topic for teachers, but more generally in deciding which errors to target in feedback, the following criteria are useful:

- Genre-specific errors – those particular to the current target text-type.
- Stigmatizing errors – those that most disturb the particular target community of readers.
- Comprehensibility errors – those that most interfere with the clarity of the writing.
- Frequent errors – those consistently made by the individual student across his or her writing.
- Student-identified errors – those the student would like the teacher to focus on.

Reflection 7.5

Which of these types of error should receive most urgent attention? Which are likely to be the easiest and most difficult to address through teacher-written feedback?

Writing feedback: purposes and forms

This discussion has suggested that teachers do not simply respond to grammar or content, but have a number of different purposes in mind. Reid (1993: 205), for example, distinguishes responses that are descriptive (the main idea in this essay is X), personal (the part I like best was Y), and evaluative (comments that justify a judgment). Ferris et al. (1997), on the other hand, identified eight broad functions of response in over 1,500 teacher comments, ranging from "Asking for unknown information" ("what is your focus here?") to "Giving information on ideas" ("This is a bit off track"). Different stages of writing are also characterized by different purposes. Teachers can only judge and evaluate a finished product and hope the writer will improve in the next assignment, for instance, while the goal of feedback on a text in progress is to respond and influence the writing. Bates et al. (1993) suggest the following ways to achieve these purposes:

- Write personalized comments – maintaining a dialogue between reader and writer
- Provide guidance where necessary – avoiding advice that is too directive or prescriptive
- Make text-specific comments – relating comments to the text rather than general rules
- Balance positive and negative comments – avoiding discouraging students with criticism

In practice, it may be quite difficult, and unhelpful, to follow specific rules too strictly as different assignments and different students require different types of responses. The most flexible approach may be for teachers to select from the overarching functions of *praise, criticism*, and *suggestions* in their comments (Hyland and Hyland, 2001). Some teachers believe that providing too much praise, especially at early stages of the writing cycle, can make students complacent and discourage revision. Praise, however, is widely used to encourage students, particularly in responding to ideas in a text, but is often reserved for final drafts where it can act to reward students for their efforts:

You have dealt with this topic well. There is a good flow of ideas and a very clear plan.

An excellent essay, the ideas are clear and easy to follow and there are few vocabulary problems.

An interesting and comprehensive essay. Well-organized and well-written.

There is no doubt that positive remarks can be motivating and that many L2 learners attach considerable importance to them (all quotes from Hyland, 1998; Hyland and Hyland, 2001):

If teacher give me positive comments it means I succeed. (Japanese student)

I always look for what she says is good in the essay first, this gives me the support. Then I can look at the corrections I must do. (Spanish student)

However, while students appreciate and remember positive comments, they also expect to receive constructive criticism (e.g., Connors and Lunsford,

1993). Nor do all students welcome empty praise, regarding it as insincere, looking instead for comments they can act on:

Sometimes maybe the teacher doesn't mean it, but they just try to encourage you. [...] Because there is always "but" after the positive. Sometimes the teacher just tries to find something good in my essay and then may be that strength is not the main point. (Chinese student)

Reflection 7.6

What are your own feelings about the value of praise? Is it best reserved for final drafts only? Can it be used for margin comments as well as end comments? Should it be used for all aspects of texts or only ideas? At what location, stage, and focus is praise likely to be most effective in improving writing?

Teachers therefore need to use positive comments with care, but a lack of positive comments can affect both students' attitudes to writing and their reception of feedback.

I am very interested in teacher's comments every time. I like to read it and when I read it and if it says "it's good but your problem is grammatical problem," then I will turn back to see how many mistakes I have. But if the comment is very bad and maybe not good enough, maybe I'll stop for a while and keep it and take it out and look at again later. (Thai student)

... If feedback is not so good, I mean that teacher criticize many mistake I have, then I feel – "Oh I don't like writing." (Taiwanese student)

Because of this, some teachers seek to stress the most important or most generalizable problems in their feedback in order not to overwhelm the students by criticizing all their problems. This experienced teacher described why she is reluctant to be directly critical (F. Hyland, unpublished Ph.D. thesis):

I had a Korean student who was kind of a fossilisation problem I guess. And her writing was just full of errors and like you didn't even have paragraphs and it was very short. On the very first test I think I made some criticisms ... and she wrote in her journal that she found this very devastating and "please try and encourage me" and so after that I modified my feedback to try and be more positive. I mean I had been positive but I felt it was my duty to point out that there were major problems here. I mean it's hard sometimes to get a balance between being a realist and being positive. But once she told me that, I made a conscious effort.

Reflection 7.7

How do you think a teacher might achieve this balance between being realistic in pointing out errors and problems to learners and being encouraging?

Suggestion and criticism can be seen as opposite ends of a continuum ranging from a focus on what is done poorly to measures for its improvement, so while criticism is negative comment on a text, suggestions contain a retrievable plan of action for improvement, a do-able revision of some kind. Thus, in (i) the teacher provides a fairly clear suggestion for revision, while in (ii) she has chosen to express her comment more forcefully as a criticism:

> (i) *Try to express your ideas as simply as possible and give extra information.*
>
> (ii) *There is no statement of intention in the essay – what is the purpose of your essay and how are you going to deal with it? You are not giving me any direction.*

It is important to note here that it may be difficult for students to extract the implications of a criticism as it contains no explicit advice on what they should do to rectify the problem. If students fail to understand what is being said, they may simply ignore it or delete the passage from their revised draft. To guard against this, teachers can pair a criticism with a suggestion:

This conclusion is all a bit vague. I think it would be better to clearly state your conclusions with the brief reasons for them.

This is a very sudden start. You need a more general statement to introduce the topic.

Suggestions can focus on a student's text and propose revisions to it, or can refer to general principles which extend to future writing behavior:

Maho, as I said on your first draft, a lot of this essay is about your learning history and therefore not directly relevant to the topic. At least you haven't shown how it is relevant. At university you must answer the question you choose and keep on the topic.

Interesting content, but difficult to understand. I think you need to ask for help from flatmates, classmates, friends, to read your writing and see if they can understand it.

Although this moves away from strictly text-specific issues, summary comments of this kind help communicate concepts and principles that students can make use of in subsequent assignments.

Reflection 7.8

Do you think that either praise or criticism can be an effective choice in encouraging revision and proofreading strategies? How can criticism be made constructive in facilitating student revisions?

Interpersonal aspects of written feedback: mitigation strategies

The form that feedback takes also shows that teachers consider the potential interpersonal impact of positive and negative feedback. While it is an important pedagogic resource, teacher feedback also involves delicate social interactions that can affect the relationship between a teacher and student and influence instruction itself. ESL writers are often insecure about their writing and can be heartened by positive comments or devastated by criticism. Because of this, teachers often soften the force of their comments using the various mitigation strategies shown in Figure 7.2 (Hyland and Hyland, 2001).

The use of such mitigation strategies can also help moderate the teacher's dominant role and tone down what might be seen as overdirective interventions in students' writing. Many teachers are anxious about the issue of *appropriation* and concerned about how students might respond to comments that are too directive and prescriptive. Knoblauch and Brannon (1984: 118) have argued that writing can be "stolen" from a writer by the teacher's comments and that if students follow directive feedback too closely they may develop neither their cognitive skills nor their writing abilities, but merely rewrite texts to reflect their teachers' concerns. In ESL writing classrooms, however, nondirective approaches may not only violate the cultural expectations of students from backgrounds where explicit advice and correction is expected, but fail to give L2 students the direct and concrete help they need (Reid, 1994), leaving them ill-prepared for the demands of their target contexts (Johns, 1997). Once again, it can be seen that feedback does not occur in a vacuum and teachers always need to respond to their particular contexts.

However, despite these laudable interpersonal and pedagogic reasons for mitigating feedback, indirect comments have the very real potential to cloud issues and create confusion. Mitigation allows teachers to minimize the risk of demotivating students or of taking over their texts, but it is possible to forget that students are reading feedback in a foreign language and that

---

Paired comments Combining criticism with either praise or a suggestion

> *Vocabulary is good but grammar is not accurate and often makes your ideas difficult to understand.*

> *Good movement from general to specific, but you need to make a clearer promise to the reader.*

Hedged comments Modal verbs, imprecise quantifiers, usuality devices

> *Some of the material seemed a little long-winded and I wonder if it could have been compressed a little.*

> *There is possibly too much information here.*

Personal attribution teacher responds as ordinary reader rather than as expert

> *I'm sorry, but when reading this essay I couldn't see any evidence of this really. Perhaps you should have given me your outline to look at with the essay.*

> *I find it hard to know what the main point of each paragraph is.*

Interrogative form express element of doubt or uncertainty in the comment

> *The first two paragraphs - do they need joining?*

> *Did you check your spelling carefully? Why not make a spelling checklist of words you often get wrong and use this before handing in your final?*

Figure 7.2: Mitigation strategies in end comments.

being indirect may actually result in significant misunderstandings (Hyland and Hyland, 2001). Students are often confused by indirectness and so either ignore the comment or make unnecessary revisions, while more serious cases can lead to frustration and hostility toward the teacher which might prevent effective learning.

Reflection 7.9

How can teachers ensure that their comments are clear and effective while simultaneously softening the potentially damaging impact of criticism and avoiding the dangers of appropriation?

In sum, written feedback from teachers can play a significant role in improving L2 students' writing, but this role is complex and requires careful reflection to be used effectively.

Teacher-student conferencing

Teachers can also give feedback on student writing through face-to-face conferencing. Conferencing has important advantages as it can supplement the limitations of one-way written feedback with opportunities for "the teacher and the student to negotiate the meaning of a text through dialogue" (McCarthey, 1992: 1). The interactive nature of the conference gives teachers a chance to respond to the diverse cultural, educational, and writing needs of their students, clarifying meaning and resolving ambiguities, while saving them the time spent in detailed marking of papers. For students, writing conferences not only assist learners with auditory learning styles, but give them a clearer idea of their strengths and weaknesses, develop their autonomy skills, allow them to raise questions on their written feedback, and help them construct a revision plan (F. Hyland, 2000; Riley, 1997).

Advantages and disadvantages of conferences

Both teachers and students tend to be positive about the opportunities for detailed discussion that conferences offer, and research suggests that students typically receive more focused and usable comments than through written feedback (Zamel, 1985). Conferences vary considerably in the extent to which they improve student writing, and the literature stresses the need for careful planning. The most successful conferences are those in which students are active participants, asking questions, clarifying meaning, and discussing their papers rather than passively accepting advice. Where they are successful, however, oral conferences can not only lead to revisions in subsequent drafts but have more lasting effects on improving writing in later assignments (e.g., Patthey-Chavez and Ferris, 1997).

Some researchers have expressed reservations about oral conferences, however. While learners have the opportunity to get individual attention and fully discuss their writing face-to-face with their teacher, second language students are not always in a good position to make the most of this. Conferences differ considerably from the typical classroom situation, and some students may lack the experience, interactive abilities, or aural comprehension skills to benefit. Some learners have cultural inhibitions about engaging informally with authority figures, let alone questioning them (Goldstein and

Conrad, 1990), and this can result in students passively incorporating the teacher's suggestions into their work without thought, leading to the kind of "appropriation" of student texts discussed earlier. The disadvantages for teachers are that conferences consume considerable amounts of time and require good interaction skills.

A further important issue is the potential mismatch of participant expectations, as these diary extracts by teachers reflecting on their student counseling sessions indicate:

Felt on my guard, felt as if I might be being taken advantage of as Linda hadn't done what she said she would. Felt she wanted to present me with different pieces of work to check and suggest ways to correct, but she wasn't prepared to work systematically on developing changes to the work I had already assessed. I couldn't see how she was developing her skills or meeting her goals.

She is a dependent student and expects me to practise English discussion with her. (Pemberton, Toogood, Ho, and Lam, 1999: 6)

These notes show that while students may be getting valuable experience communicating in English, their purposes in the conferencing sessions may be only marginally related to those of the teacher. Instead of using the opportunity to develop their writing skills and genre awareness, the first student is hoping for proofreading and the second for conversation practice. The fact that the teachers and students are working at cross-purposes is likely to undermine the effectiveness of the conference.

The use of conferences is intuitively attractive and supported by the experiences of numerous teachers, although the empirical research is rather limited. However, like any kind of teaching, conferences have the potential for both success and failure and as a result require careful planning and preparation.

Reflection 7.10

What do you see as the major advantages and disadvantages of teacher-student conferences? How might you overcome the potential problems created by mismatched expectations outlined above?

Forms of conferences

All conferences involve students talking about their writing with their teacher, but they can take a variety of forms. Typically they are conducted as one-to-one activities between a teacher and a student outside the classroom. In cases where time is a serious constraint, however, or where students are likely to find such intimate discussions intimidating or unrewarding, then conferences are run as small groups, adding the support and advantages of peer feedback to the interaction. Conferences can also be brief consultations on topics, sources, or outlines, explorations of strategies for writing or future conferences, or reviews of already completed writing, but more usually they focus on a paper in progress, examining the current draft and ways of improving it.

Some teachers organize their classes as writing workshops where the students work on their writing and consult their teachers or classmates when necessary. Conferences are a regular feature of such environments as teachers encourage students to come up and discuss matters as they need to while the remainder of the class is engaged in group work or individual writing at their desks or on computers. Such ad hoc conferencing allows the teacher to quickly read and comment on a short piece of writing the student has just completed, such as a thesis statement or conclusion, or to quickly go through the teacher's written comments when handing back a draft.

Other teachers prefer to set aside regular times and see each student for fifteen minutes every month during their office hours to discuss progress. For some the conference is an optional extra which students can take advantage of or not as they choose, while for others it is a compulsory aspect of their teaching. These decisions will be partly influenced by teacher and student preferences, and it is a good idea to ask students in their feedback preference questionnaires at the beginning of the course whether they would like to participate in conferences. Equally, however, decisions about frequency, timing, and duration of meetings will also be influenced by issues such as scheduling and the availability of rooms. In crowded timetables or where teachers are working part-time, for instance, scheduling conferences outside class time may be difficult.

Conferences can also vary in their purpose and focus. It may be that the student has initiated the meeting to get advice on a particular problem or to obtain clarification from the teacher on a written feedback point. It may be an additional once-only conference called by the teacher to discuss a particular aspect of the student's draft or to underline a specific point covered in class. Alternatively, the session may be part of a regular program of feedback with no clear agenda but to read and discuss an ongoing assignment. Whatever the format, however, the conference should always offer the student something to address in his or her writing, a doable course of action for improvement.

Table 7.1: *Teacher-student conference planning decisions*

- Whether to hold conferences in class or outside class hours
- Whether to work one-to-one or in small groups
- How frequently to hold conferences
- How much time to allocate to each student
- Which topics to cover
- Whether to ask students to prepare for the conference
- How to manage the conference
- How to follow it up

Planning for conferences

Clearly, conferences need to be prepared. In addition to basic logistical is-sues such as finding time and rooms, planning involves the decisions set out in Table 7.1. It is also the teacher's responsibility to ensure that students are well-prepared to get the most from the conference. Most generally this means making sure that the purpose of the activity is understood by brief-ing learners about the role of one-to-one feedback in the first class of the course. This can help overcome any divergent expectations that teachers and students may have about how the sessions will operate and the desired outcome of the activity. For many L2 students it might also be necessary to provide some training, via both explicit instruction and role play, in the basic interaction patterns required to make the sessions work, such as requesting and giving information, seeking clarification, and so on.

Reflection 7.11
While teachers may plan carefully for conferences, students vary considerably in how they interact in these settings and there is no guarantee that they will participate actively. What kind of preparation can a teacher do to help encourage such participation?

More specifically, many teachers also take steps to ensure that students take an active role in the conference by asking them to prepare for sessions in advance. This can mean students reading through and annotating their drafts by putting a number in the margin at points where they need advice and writing out the corresponding question or comment on a separate sheet.

Initial Conference (about a topic)
1. Topic for my essay . . . .
2. Intended purpose of my essay . . . .
3. Intended audience for my essay . . . .
4. Pre-writing about my topic . . . .

Essay Draft Conference
Statements 1–3 above plus
1. In group work my peers asked the following question about my topic . . . .
2. In group work my peers made the following suggestions . . . .
3. The problem(s) I'm having with this draft are . . . .

Revision Planning Conference
1. I thought the best part of my essay was . . . .
2. I thought the weakest part of my essay was . . . .
3. According to the teacher's comments, the strengths and problems in the draft are:

Strengths	Problems
(a)	(a) . . . .
(b)	(b) . . . .
(c)	(c) . . . .

4. Based on the feedback, here is my plan for revising the essay (list specific steps you intend to take and specific paragraphs you intend to revise):
(a) . . . .
(b) . . . .
(c) . . . .
Three questions I want to ask you (the instructor) are:
(a) . . . .
(b) . . . .
(c) . . . .

Source: Reid: 1993: 222–3.

Figure 7.3: Sample worksheets for conference planning at different stages.

More simply, students might just underline what they want feedback on or circle possible errors to discuss. In these ways students are able to develop their self-evaluation skills while shy or less proficient learners can ensure they have some control over the interaction with the teacher. Alternatively, some teachers give students planning worksheets before the conference which address the goals of the session and require learners to think about the meeting and to reflect on their writing. Reid (1993) provides several examples of these (see Figure 7.3). In addition to providing students with worksheets and encouraging them to plan for the session, teachers can also prepare for a conference themselves by making notes of points to discuss on a draft or listing features of the student's writing that need attention.

Conducting conferences

In the conference itself teachers need to ensure that the discussion both involves the learner and addresses salient issues effectively. Research cautions against being overly directive as there is a danger that the teacher's authority will be played out in "find and fix" correction routines, and Newkirk (1995) argues that the conversational and evaluative responsibility should be given to the student. This means teachers have to adjust to the student's individual discourse style and act to support writing rather than edit it. Questions about the work and encouragement to participate are perhaps more effective here than instructions, although teachers should be alert for misunderstandings that can result from indirectness.

Participation implies collaboration and involves creating a relaxed and supportive atmosphere. The tone should be positive to allow the student to talk about the issues that concern him or her and opportunities to think about text improvements. Students should be encouraged to initiate issues rather than just respond to the teacher's comments and to close the sessions with an explicit plan for action. White and Arndt (1991: 132) suggest the following procedures for conducting a conference:

1. Help the student to relax. Make the situation nonthreatening by finding something to praise.
2. Interact with the student. Establish a collaborative relationship.
3. Engage the student in the analysis process. Give every opportunity for the student to do the talking and make the revision decisions.
4. Attend to global problems before working on sentence and word level problems.
5. Respond to the writing as work in progress or under construction.
6. Ask the student to sum up the changes they need to make for revision.
7. End the session with praise and encouragement.

Finally, as with other kinds of feedback, students need to be accountable for following up the discussion with a task to show that the feedback has been taken seriously. This need not involve incorporating every suggestion into a revised draft but can simply be a journal entry or brief letter summarizing what was discussed, how the feedback was used, or what the student found useful. This can help focus the student, encourage reflection, and ensure that the teacher's feedback is considered carefully.

Reflection 7.12

When do you think oral feedback may be more effective than written feedback? How would you employ the two forms to best advantage in a writing course?

Peer feedback

The idea of students receiving feedback on their writing from their peers developed from L1 process classes and has become an important alternative to teacher-based forms of response in ESL contexts. Peer response is said to provide a means of both improving writers' drafts and developing readers' understandings of good writing, but teachers have generally been more positive than students, who tend to prefer teacher feedback, and its benefits have been hard to confirm empirically in L2 situations.

Pros and cons of peer review

The theoretical advantages of peer response are based largely on the fact that writing and learning are social processes. Collaborative peer review helps learners engage in a community of equals who respond to each others' work and together create an authentic social context for interaction and learning (e.g., Mittan, 1989). Practically, students are able to participate actively in learning while getting responses from real, perhaps multiple, readers in a nonthreatening situation (Medonca and Johnson, 1994). Moreover, students not only benefit from seeing how readers understand their ideas and what they need to improve, but also gain the skills necessary to critically analyze and revise their own writing (Leki, 1990; Zhang, 1995).

On the negative side, the fact that learners are rhetorically inexperienced means that they may focus heavily on sentence level problems rather than ideas and organization. Moreover, peers are not trained teachers and their comments may be vague and unhelpful, or even overly critical and sarcastic (Leki, 1990). There is also some concern that students from collectivist cultures may be more concerned about the need to emphasize a positive group climate than critically appraise peers' writing, making feedback less beneficial (Carson and Nelson, 1996). This is clear in the disappointment expressed by one of F. Hyland's (2000: 41) respondents:

Just now I asked Chan for some comments for my presentation. Well, he said "oh it's all right." Nothing important, nothing useful. Maybe he didn't like to comment.

Table 7.4: *Potential pros and cons of peer feedback*

Advantages	Disadvantages
Active learner participation	Tendency to focus on surface forms
Authentic communicative context	Potential for overly critical comments
Nonjudgmental environment	Cultural reluctance to criticize and judge
Alternative and authentic audience	Students unconvinced of comments'
Writers gain understanding of	value
reader needs	Weakness of reader's knowledge
Reduced apprehension about	Students may not use feedback in
writing	revisions
Development of critical reading	Students may prefer teacher feedback
skills	
Reduces teacher's workload	

Especially for Chinese, for Chinese people you know, they seldom comment on some other people's work. . . . I think it is not good. I want to know more about how I done.

Research on the effectiveness of peer response in ESL contexts has found that writers do make some use of peers' comments in their revisions, although L2 proficiency, prior experience, and group dynamics are likely to influence the extent of this (e.g., Mendonca and Johnson, 1994). Active collaboration and an openness to suggestions are important factors in adopting comments for revision but, like L2 students' revision practices from any source of feedback, most revisions tend to be surface changes (Connor and Asenavage, 1994). In discussions, students vary in their ability to maintain a task focus. Most talk is reported to be about peers' drafts (Villamil and de Guerrero, 1996), but authoritative reviewers, operating in an evaluative and prescriptive mode, may tend to dominate the interactions (Lockhart and Ng, 1995). Students themselves are rather ambivalent about the quality of their peers' suggestions and many both mistrust them and fear ridicule due to their poor proficiency, generally preferring feedback from teachers (Zhang, 1995). These perceptions and findings are summarized in Table 7.4.

Reflection 7.13
What are your own views of peer feedback? What circumstances do you think are required to make it work successfully? Would you use it in an ESL writing class? Why? / Why not?

Forms of peer response

Peer response can take a number of different forms and occur at various stages in the writing process. Most typically it consists of assigning students to groups of two, three, or four who exchange completed first drafts and give comments on each others' work before they revise them. This normally occurs during class time and can take up to an hour to complete, especially if readers are asked to produce written comments and writers are required to provide written responses to these. Some peer sessions involve the free exchange of reactions to a piece of work, but L2 learners typically work with a set of peer review guidelines to help them focus on particular aspects of the writing and the conventions of the genre.

Peer review need not be confined to first drafts. Students can collaborate in pre-writing tasks to generate ideas for an assignment before any draft-ing is done, commenting on each other's brainstorms and outlines to raise awareness of the rhetorical issues involved and to develop writing strate-gies (Flower, 1994). The goal here is to encourage negotiation of rhetorical planning by involving a reader, drawing on Vygotskian ideas of activity in the "zone of proximal development" and the intersubjective construction of goals. Alternatively, peers can contribute to later stages of the teaching-writing cycle. As they develop their knowledge of relevant features of con-text, system, content, and genre, learners are better able to intervene with helpful advice. In early drafts they may comment on the clarity and rele-vance of the ideas and their coherence for readers or the appropriateness of contextual factors such as the role the writer is adopting or the relationship being established with the reader through the choice of particular features. At later stages they might address elements of grammar and expression and how the text is structured rhetorically to effectively present the writer's message.

In many peer group sessions students give their paper to another student for comment, although some teachers prefer writers to bring copies for each member of the group to read so that they get a range of responses. Other variations include conducting discussions of a student's paper online as a synchronous chat exercise or asynchronously through email. In some cases students read their own papers aloud while others listen, or a member of the group reads another student's paper aloud. However, while reading aloud can provide additional oral-aural practice with considerable motivation to attend and comprehend, many ESL writers are uncomfortable with this public presentation of their work and others may lack the speaking-listening skills to benefit from it. Respondents can provide comments orally after the reading, or they can give written comments to the student privately.

Reflection 7.14

Which type of peer feedback do you think is likely to be most effective? Think about it in the context of a writing class you are familiar with or with students you are likely to teach. Do you think the same type would be effective for all stages of writing and all kinds of written genres?

It should also be noted that not all peer response occurs in classrooms. Many students report independently seeking help from classmates, friends, or family who are either native English speakers or at higher levels of proficiency than themselves. More importantly, such informants are typically of equal status and in a relationship with them that is socially close and relaxed, so that constructive criticism can be freely given and correction can be supplemented by detailed discussion. This journal extract from a mature Taiwanese student illustrates the value of such feedback.

I got the long essay yesterday. There were some mistakes and some sentences were not clear. I didn't ask my husband to revise the first draft, so there were lots of grammar mistakes. When I finish an essay, I usually give it to my husband. My husband corrects my mistakes and points out which sentence is not clear. I think it is good for me to learn how to write a correct essay. Sometimes I have good ideas, but I cannot explain very well in English. My husband can give me advices to improve my writing. I always discuss some sentences with my husband and he teaches me grammar. In this way, I think I can improve my English ability. I like this kind of feedback. I can have more ideas about my essay during the discussion. (F. Hyland, 2001)

Reflection 7.15

Not all teachers are comfortable with the kind of informal peer feedback discussed by Hyland that occurs outside of their control. In fact, the journal entry above was actually written by the student in response to her teacher's disapproval of this assistance. Do you think it is more important for the teacher to control feedback in order to get an idea of their students' abilities and improvements or to encourage this kind of autonomy and out-of-class feedback?

Integrating peer review into a writing course

Peer review sessions are generally more effective as an integral part of a course rather than isolated occurrences. By informing learners from the

---

What Is Peer Editing?

Peer editing means responding with appreciation and positive criticism to your classmates' writing. It is an important part of this course because it can:
- Help you become more aware of your reader when writing and revising
- Help you become more sensitive to problems in your writing and more confident in correcting them

Rules for Peer responding:
- Be respectful of your classmate's work
- Be conscientious – read carefully and think about what the writer is trying to say
- Be tidy and legible in your comments
- Be encouraging and make suggestions
- Be specific with comments

Remember: You do not need to be an expert at grammar. Your best help is as a reader and that you know when you have been interested, entertained, persuaded, or confused

---

Figure 7.4: A peer review introduction sheet.

outset that peer response will be required and utilizing it frequently and consistently, teachers can emphasize its importance to students, ensure that it is taken seriously, and reduce anxieties that individuals may have about sharing their writing. Sufficient time should be built into the course to allow for both written response and oral discussion of the reviews and a clear structure for grouping students adopted. Some teachers allow students to self-select their groups and this seems a good practice until a better idea of their writing abilities is gained. Later, pairs can be based on their ability to offer mutual assistance, with one participant of slightly higher proficiency than the other.

To effectively integrate peer response into a writing course, the purpose of the activity needs to be clearly stated and rules for responding suggested. Students need to feel comfortable about sharing their work and collaborating, and time should be taken to ensure they see the activity as nonjudgmental and as a means of learning to consider readers' needs in expressing their purposes. An introductory information sheet can be a useful way of outlining such advantages and purposes (Figure 7.4).

Reflection 7.16

Are these general rules for peer response adequate and comprehensive? What would you add to them? How would you ensure that they were observed?

Another way of integrating peer response tasks into a course is for teachers to collect and read all feedback, perhaps responding to it with a brief comment or even assigning a grade on its quality and substance. Writers themselves can be asked to write a brief reaction to the comments they have received, including whether, and how, they have incorporated them into their subsequent draft. Developing peer response skills takes time, however, and students cannot be expected to assume full responsibility for feedback immediately or to overcome their doubts about the quality of their peers' comments. Most importantly, integrating peer response into a writing course involves patience and a supportive environment in which students can take increasing responsibility for their interactions and feedback.

Peer response training

Because L2 students generally lack the language competence of native speakers who can often react intuitively to their classmates' papers, peer response practices are most effective if they are modeled, taught, and controlled. Berg (1999), for instance, found that peer response training led to significantly more meaning changes and higher marks on L2 writers' second drafts regardless of proficiency levels, and the peer response literature strongly advocates teacher input prior to the first feedback session (e.g., Carson and Nelson, 1996; Leki, 1990; Lockhart and Ng, 1995). While appropriate schemata for responding partly comes from students' understanding of appropriate genre, system, and context which they develop in the early stages of a writing cycle, they also need strategies for reading and responding: knowing what to look for and how to comment on it.

Training in peer response practices can begin by students working on their own papers with a reflective note to the teacher explaining what he or she was trying to do in a paper, what worked, what didn't, what was learned, and so on (Reid, 1993: 210). Alternatively, students can be given a short list of attributes to look for in their papers. This may involve checking for a particular rhetorical feature that was the subject of a scaffolding task from the modeling stage, such as topic sentences, transition paragraphs, problem-solution patterns. If the list is submitted with the draft, then the student begins to learn to take responsibility for carefully reading his or her paper. Asking students to write down their reflections can increase their understandings of the genre and the writing process, focusing their attention on texts, encouraging revision, and providing them with ways of proofreading and editing texts.

Building on this self-awareness training, students can watch videos of peer discussions taken in other classes (Carson and Nelson, 1996), or examine transcripts of peer review sessions (Lockhart and Ng, 1995). In addition, explicit instruction can be given in the "language of response" and expressions students would find useful to compliment, suggest, and mitigate criticism. Most importantly, students need experience in exploring "safe" essays written by students from other classes, either in groups or as a whole class, following a list of questions that elicit a general response and some suggestions. This training in response strategies can follow general directives on how to approach the task (a) or address specific issues in the papers (b):

(a) What to look for when reading your partner's draft:
 • Clarity – Are you given all the information you need in a clear order?
 • Interest – Does the paper interest you?
 • Effectiveness – Does the paper make an impact on you?
 • Accuracy – Are there any errors of spelling, grammar, definitions?
(b) Try to answer these questions as you read:
 • What is the main idea that the writer is trying to express in this paper?
 • Are there any parts that do not relate to the main idea?
 • Which part of the paper do you like the best?
 • Find two or three places where you would like more explanations, examples, or details.
 • Did you lose the flow of writing at any point or find places where the writer jumped suddenly to another idea?
 • Did the beginning capture your attention and make you want to read on? Why or why not? (Raimes, 1992: 64)

Another approach is to give students a number of core response principles which they can build on through the course with increasing detail on what they like and dislike and greater explanation on how their suggestions will improve the text. Mittan (1989) suggests the following principles:

• Offer a positive response and encouragement to the writer.
• Identify the purpose and main points of the text.
• Direct questions to the writer.
• Offer suggestions.

It is worth noting that students often unconsciously follow the feedback patterns of their teachers (Connor and Asenavage, 1994), adopting the response forms they are exposed to: prioritizing form or function, questioning or informing, providing rules or making suggestions. Recognizing that they implicitly model response patterns should encourage teachers to offer clear, positive, and focused feedback.

Reflection 7.17

Do you think these forms of training are likely to overcome the reservations some students have about the quality of feedback they get from their peers? How would you address the reluctance of students from some cultures to engage in collaborative activities of this kind?

Peer response sheets

Response sheets help structure peer review activities by providing guidance on what participants should look for as they read. Again, these can be more or less specific, but the objective is to build students' responding skills and to focus their attention on relevant issues. However, while students should have precise instructions and clear directions concerning the tasks they are expected to complete, some teachers believe that if such sheets are too directive, students' behavior will simply mirror their own priorities, effectively resulting in an indirect form of "appropriation." However, many L2 learners need a focus for their interaction, particularly in the early stages of peer feedback activities, although these constraints can be gradually relaxed and the students given greater autonomy as their confidence and metacognitive awareness of writing increases.

Response sheets can therefore provide a valuable form of indirect instruction about good writing practices and genre formats. They can be written by students but are more commonly provided by teachers, often with space for writers to specify particular areas they would like the reader to comment on. The format of response sheets can vary greatly and the precise focus will depend on the proficiency of the students, their experience of peer reviewing, the stage in the writing process, and perhaps the particular features that the teacher wishes to stress. Appendix 7.2 shows an example response sheet for a first draft of a research essay and Figure 7.5 illustrates a more interactive response sheet for an argument paper.

Peer Response Sheet: Argument

Author's Name . . . .   Title of Draft . . . .
Write three questions you would like your responder to answer.

1

2

3

Responder's Name . . . .
Read the questions above. Listen to the author read his/her draft aloud. Read the paper again if you want to. Then write a response for the author.

Author's Reflection

Read the response you have received carefully. Reflect on it and write what you have learned and what you intend to do next below.

Figure 7.5: Peer response sheet for an argument essay.

Mittan (1989: 216–17) suggests the following principles for designing a peer response sheet:

1. Begin with clear instructions as to the purpose, audience, and procedure for completing the form, for example:

   Your purpose in answering these questions is to give an honest and helpful response to your partner's draft and to suggest ways to make his/her writing better. Before beginning, be sure to read the writing carefully, then respond to each of the following questions. Be as specific as possible; refer directly to your partner's paper by paragraph number.

2. Limit the sheet to one page. The amount of white space will help determine the length of response.
3. Use questions that follow this format:
   - Give encouragement. *What do you like most in this writing?*
   - Identify the purpose or main idea. *In your own words state what you think the focus is.*
   - Questions and suggestions. *Which part needs to be developed? How could the writer help you understand this idea better?*
4. Vary the question types. These can include open-ended types, reformulation of ideas, selecting the most appropriate response from several choices, a letter to the writer.

In sum, there are good reasons to believe that peer feedback can be effective in improving second language writing, although it is uncertain which are the most effective forms, how frequently it should be used, how much training and guidance should be provided, and how best to group

Table 7.7: *Principles of effective peer response*

1. Make peer response an integral part of the course.
2. Model the process.
3. Build peer response skills progressively throughout the term.
4. Structure the peer response task.
5. Vary peer response activities.
6. Hold students accountable for giving feedback and
   for considering the feedback they receive.
7. Consider individual student needs.
8. Consider logistical issues, including
   - the size and composition of groups
   - the mechanics of exchanging papers

Source: Ferris and Hedgcock, 1998: 178.

students and encourage participation. Ferris and Hedgcock (1998) offer general guidelines, given in Table 7.7.

Summary and conclusion

Feedback is central to learning to write in a second language. Not only can it provide writers with a sense of audience and sensitize them to the needs of readers, but it offers an additional layer of scaffolding to extend writing skills, promote accuracy and clear ideas, and develop an understanding of written genres. The three kinds of feedback discussed in this chapter each have their advantages and possible drawbacks, and teachers might use them in tandem to offer students the best of all worlds. The key points of the chapter are:

- Teachers should ask students for their feedback preferences at the beginning of the course and address these in their responses.
- The response practices the teacher intends to use in the course should be explained at the outset. This should include the focus of the feedback that will be given on particular drafts, any codes that will be used, whether written, oral, or peer forms will be employed, and so on.
- Expectations concerning student responses to feedback need to be clearly explained at the beginning so that students understand what is required from them in terms of followup to feedback.
- Teachers should provide both margin and end comments in their written feedback if time allows and, remembering that students may find comments vague and difficult to act on, seek a balance of praise and doable suggestions for revision.

- Criticism should be mitigated as far as possible while bearing in mind the potential of indirectness for misunderstanding.
- Both teachers and students need to prepare carefully to make the most of face-to-face conferences.
- Peer response can be helpful in providing learners with an alternative audience and a different source of commentary, but students may need to be trained to respond effectively in these contexts.
- Students should be encouraged to reflect on the feedback they receive from any source by keeping journals or writing summaries in which they respond to the comments.

Discussion questions and activities

1 Research suggests that teacher written feedback might be more effective if it targeted areas of most concern to students. Devise a pre-course self-report form that would help you gather information on individual preferences for feedback.

2 What is the difference between intervention and appropriation? Write an essay that sets out the arguments concerning possible conflicts between the needs of L2 students for advice and the reluctance of teachers to be too directive. Consider whether this is a "real issue" or not and explain your own point of view. How can teachers give effective feedback without taking over the learner's text?

3 Tribble (1996: 119) argues that there are four basic roles available to teachers as readers:
   - *Audience*: Responding like any reader to the ideas or perceptions the student has tried to convey in the text.
   - *Assistant*: working with learners to improve the text and make it as effective as possible in relation to its purpose by helping with language, genre, and content.
   - *Evaluator*: commenting on the learner's overall performance and strengths and weaknesses – usually at the final draft stage.
   - *Examiner*: providing an objective assessment of the student's writing abilities based on explicit criteria. A more "summative" feedback.

   What do you think are the main advantages and disadvantages of each of these roles? Can teachers adopt each of them at different times, or are they mutually exclusive? At what stage of the writing process might each role be employed to provide the most effective feedback?

4 Look at the example of a cover sheet for an expository essay assignment in Appendix 7.1. Are these the criteria you would use to provide feedback

on this kind of assignment? What aspects do you think are neglected or emphasized? Design a rubric for a narrative and a research essay assignment and justify your choice of criteria.

5 Consider the peer feedback sheet for a research essay in Appendix 7.2. Note that this is designed for a first draft. Design a peer response sheet for a second (intermediate) draft for this genre. What are the main differences between the two and what principles underlie these differences?

6 If possible, collect some student scripts that either you or another teacher has marked. Analyze the end-comments and determine if they constitute Praise, Suggestion, or Criticism. What functions predominate? How are the comments expressed and how are they mitigated? Do you think the comments would be clear to the intended students?

7 If possible, arrange a series of three or four one-to-one conference sessions with a second language student to discuss a paper he or she is working on. Make a plan for each session in advance and give clear feedback on the drafts, requiring the student to make and carry out a revision plan. Keep a journal of what happened at the meetings and your reflections on them. At the end of the series, consider the extent to which the drafts and the student's understanding improved as a result of your input and what you would do differently another time.

Appendix 7.1: A rubric for the first draft of a university expository essay assignment

Name . . . .   Title . . . .   Group . . . .

Content	Excellent	VG	Good	S	Weak	Unacceptable
• The piece is engaging and alive						
• It contains valuable information and insights						
• Writer shows good understanding of topic						
• Details are clear and helpful						
• Voice of narrator is honest and convincing						

Reader Awareness
- The piece has clear organization
- Writer relates topic to reader's knowledge
- Effective lead, engaging the reader
- Satisfying ending
- Clear transitions and signposts

Style
- Language is clear and precise
- Sentences are varied and effective
- Unnecessary words are eliminated
- Style is consistent and appropriate

Mechanics
- Grammar
- Spelling
- Punctuation
- Proofreading

Process
- Presentation (double-spacing, legibility)
- Effective revision
- Peer response and self-evaluation
- Paper is on time

Your Strengths: **Possible Improvements**:   **Grade**:

Source: Holst, 1993: 48.

Appendix 7.2: A peer response sheet

Assignment: Write a 6–8 paragraph essay in which you defend or explain your own view in relation to a topic you have researched, either in this or another course you are taking. Your aim is to write an informed, clear essay for an educated but uninformed audience. You should refer to, and acknowledge, at least three different sources, one of which can be the source you used for the summary assignment.

Research Essay: First Peer Response

Writer ....   Title ....

Reader ....

Read your partner's essay and respond to the following questions.

A full sentence answer is only required for the thesis/focusing statement.

1. What is the topic of the paper?
2. What is the focus/thesis statement? If the writer has not written a full sentence, suggest one.
3. Why is the topic important? What background information has the writer provided?
4. Number the paragraphs and name the topic of each paragraph. Are the topics clear?
5. What evidence has the writer provided to support his or her position?

Can you suggest any more points that he/she could use?

6. Has the writer used sources? Are there enough sources to support the evidence?
7. What are the main conclusions? Do you think these follow from the evidence?
8. Can you think of one aspect that would improve the essay?

8 *Assessing student writing*

Aims: This chapter examines the roles and processes of assessment in the L2 writing class. Different purposes and methods of writing assessments are discussed and types of scoring examined.

Teachers often regard assessment as an unwelcome task with the potential to undermine the relationship they have created with their students and the confidence students have gained in their writing. But evaluating student performance is a crucial aspect of teaching, a formative process closely linked to the planning, design, and teaching strategies examined in earlier chapters and to the issues of teacher response discussed in Chapter 7. Assessment is not simply a matter of setting exams and giving grades. Scores and evaluative feedback contribute enormously to the learning of individual students and to the development of an effective and responsive writing course. As a result, an understanding of assessment procedures is necessary to ensure that teaching is having the desired impact and that students are being judged fairly. Without the information gained from assessments, it would be difficult to identify the gap between students' current and target performances and to help them progress.

Needs analysis, course design, materials selection and evaluation are not separate, linearly related activities but represent phases that overlap and influence each other. Assessment thus provides data that can be used to measure student progress, identify problems, suggest instructional solutions, and evaluate course effectiveness. This chapter explores the main practical issues that teachers face when making decisions about evaluating written work, particularly:

- Purposes of assessment
- Validity and reliability issues
- Designing assessment tasks
- Approaches to scoring

- Reducing student anxiety
- Portfolio assessments

Orientation

In what ways can teachers collect information about a student's writing performance? How can this information be analyzed and used to make decisions about course design and the tasks and materials to be used?

Purposes of assessment

Assessment refers to the variety of ways used to collect information on a learner's language ability or achievement. It is therefore an umbrella term which includes such diverse practices as once-only class tests, short essays, long project reports, writing portfolios, or large-scale standardized examinations.

Although this chapter focuses on classroom assessments, it is worth briefly mentioning the TOEFL (Test of English as a Foreign Language) and IELTS (International English Language Testing System) exams because of their prominence in the assessment of English writing. TOEFL is a standardized test of proficiency administered in over 180 countries and widely used for admission to U.S. universities. It tests listening, reading, and structure using a multiple choice format and includes a thirty-minute written paper (Test of Written English) that requires candidates to write a single short essay. Scripts are scored by two independent markers on a five-point scale. IELTS is administered to about one million candidates annually for immigration and professional purposes and university admissions. All candidates take the same listening and speaking modules and opt for either "general training" or "academic" reading and writing sections. The writing modules comprise two essays (150 words and 250 words) in a sixty-minute period. The exam seeks to provide a profile of a candidate's English language proficiency and each skill is reported on a nine-point band scale. More details of the test formats, sample questions, test venues, and preparation materials are available from the exam Websites (www.ielts.org; www.toefl.org).

In the classroom, any assessment can be either *formative* – designed to identify a learner's strengths and weaknesses to effect remedial action, or *summative* – concerned with "summing up" how much a student has learned at the end of a course. So while the results of the former feed back into instruction, the latter provide information on either individual accomplishment or program outcomes. There are five main reasons for evaluating learners:

1. *Placement*: To provide information that will help allocate students to appropriate classes. Efficiency in administering and marking is generally given high priority as mistakes can usually be rectified later. These tests may also serve a diagnostic function.

2. *Diagnostic*: To identify students' writing strengths and weaknesses. Typically used as part of a needs assessment, this kind of test can also identify areas where remedial action is needed as a course progresses, helping teachers plan and adjust the course and inform learners of their progress.

3. *Achievement*: To enable learners to demonstrate the writing progress they have made in their course. These assessments are based on a clear indication of what has been taught, testing the genres that have been the focus of the course. The results should reflect progress rather than failure and are often used to make decisions for course improvements.

4. *Performance*: To give information about students' ability to perform particular writing tasks, usually associated with known academic or workplace requirements. These use "real-life" performance as a measure and typically seek to replicate nontest contexts. The extent to which these tests can approximate real-world settings depends on how far target performance can be clearly specified.

5. *Proficiency*: To assess a student's general level of competence, usually to provide certification for employment, university study, and so on. Unlike achievement tests, these are not based on a particular writing course, nor are they like performance tests in measuring specific writing skills. Instead, they seek to give an overall picture of ability. Often standardized for global use (e.g., TOEFL or IELTS).

While these broad categories represent the main reasons for carrying out assessment, teachers also use assessments to motivate their learners to work harder or to feel positive about their achievements, to provide practice for national or international exams, to gather information about what to teach next, and to evaluate the success of their methods, tasks, or materials. Writing assessment thus has clear pedagogic goals as it can directly influence teaching and promote learner progress, while informing teachers of their own effectiveness and the impact of their courses. This effect is sometimes called *washback*: "the effect a test has on the teaching environment which has preceded it" (Hamp-Lyons, 1991: 337).

Reflection 8.1

Which of these purposes is most likely to be of interest to writing teachers and contribute most to washback? How might the purpose of a writing assessment influence its design and format?

Validity and reliability issues

The qualities that most affect the value of an assessment measure are validity and reliability, that is, a test should do what it is intended to do and it should do it consistently.

Reliability

A writing assessment task is considered *reliable* if it measures consistently, both in terms of the same student on different occasions and the same task across different raters. It therefore involves minimizing variations in scores caused by factors unrelated to the test.

Many factors can influence a writer's performance. These include the conditions under which tests are taken, the instructions given to students, the genre, the time of day, and so on. Writing is a complex activity in which the writer draws on a range of knowledge and skills and this complexity makes it unlikely that the same individual will perform equally well on different occasions and tasks. So while differences in the same person's scores might reveal particular strengths and weaknesses, there is a need to restrict statements about a student's writing abilities to what has actually been assessed. Hughes (1989) argues that *reliability of performance* can be achieved through taking a sufficient number of samples, restricting the candidate's choice of topics and genres, giving clear task directions, and ensuring students are familiar with the assessment format.

The second component of reliability concerns the consistency with which student writing is rated, and this is potentially problematic as writing assessments involve subjective judgments. This typically boils down to two main issues:

- All assessors should agree on the rating of the same learner performance.
- Each assessor should assess the same performance in the same way on different occasions.

Teachers are often the only evaluators of their students' writing and so they want to feel confident that they are responding consistently across student scripts and that other teachers would evaluate the work in a similar way. Unfortunately, however, raters may be influenced as much by their own cultural contexts and experiences as by variations in writing quality. Even where texts are double marked, research has found that raters can differ in what they look for in writing and the standards they apply to the same text. Novice raters, for instance, tend to focus far more on grammatical accuracy and local errors which tend to be highly visible (see Weigle, 2002: 70–72).

Reflection 8.2

What factors might affect inter-rater reliability (different raters reading the same script) and intra-rater reliability (the same rater reading different scripts) in marking an L2 writing assignment? Consider the factors that could cause variation between several teachers marking the same assignment (e.g., experience, language theory, personal preferences). What might cause you to mark the same assignment differently? How could you minimize this variation to ensure reliability?

One response to the problems of reliability has been to make scoring "rater-proof" by using indirect assessments which seek to minimize variation in test results through the use of objective formats such as multiple choice questions or close tests. These indirect measures are supposed to demonstrate the test taker's knowledge of writing subskills such as grammar and sentence construction which are assumed to constitute components of writing abilities. They are very efficient forms of assessment and have been widely used in large-scale standardized examinations such as the "Structure and Written Expression" section of the TOEFL. But while some researchers claim that indirect assessments are reliable measures of writing skill (DeMauro, 1992), they are largely concerned with accuracy rather than communication, and classroom assessments are now almost always based on a student-generated text. A comparison of direct and indirect measures is given in Table 8.1.

Reflection 8.3

In what circumstances do you think indirect measures could be usefully used to assess writing?

Table 8.1: *Features of direct and indirect assessment*

Indirect assessment	Direct assessment
Claimed objective measurement	Based on production of written texts
High statistical reliability	High validity
Allows standardization	Reflects real-life communicative demands
Inferential judgment of ability	Ability judged directly
Easy to administer	Integrates all elements of writing
Easy to mark	Requires rater training

While indirect writing assessments have been a major response to improving reliability, absolute reliability is no longer a major goal. Test designers are generally satisfied with an agreement between two raters of 75 percent or more and, with appropriate rater training, sufficient reliability can be achieved using direct methods. It is widely agreed, moreover, that direct measures are actually no less "objective" than indirect ones for the reason that test design itself is not an exact science.

Validity

The quality that most affects the value of a writing assessment is *validity*. Although dependent on reliability, validity is crucial to fair and meaningful writing assessment. It means that:

- An assessment task must assess what it claims to assess.
- An assessment task must assess what has been taught.

Thus, it is not valid to give a writing test that does not require students to write, asks students to write in a genre they have not studied, allows insufficient time to plan or develop a topic, or requires specialist knowledge they do not have.

Establishing validity is one of the basic concerns of all language testing. Evidence for validity can be either *internal*, concerned with the prompts and the responses they elicit, or *external*, relating to what is actually being tested and the criteria for judging performance (Davies et al., 1999). A number of different types of validity have been identified, each of which provides a slightly different viewpoint on gathering and interpreting data. The most important are shown in Table 8.2.

Face validity means that assessments seem credible in that both teachers and students believe the task measures what it claims to measure. This means that an assessment should be based on an actual writing sample and be relevant to students' out-of-class writing needs. *Content validity* also addresses authenticity, but it draws on evidence of the topics that writers are

Table 8.2: *Main types of validity*

Face validity	The extent to which a test seems valid by test takers or untrained observers
Content validity	Whether the test adequately represents the content of the target area
Criterion validity	How far the test results match those from other tests or writing tasks
Construct validity	The extent to which an assessment measures particular writing abilities
Consequential validity	The effects of test scores on test takers and on subsequent teaching

required to discuss in target domains, usually through a thorough needs analysis. Both Face and Content validities can contribute to the test takers' motivation, but they can be challenging for the writing teacher especially in ESP contexts where the learner may have greater expertise and familiarity with the assessed genre. *Criterion-related validity* refers to how well assessment results compare with those from other measures such as a public exam. If the two measures rank candidates in the same way, then the task is seen as having criterion validity. This is usually only practicable in large-scale tests, but it encourages teachers to reflect on how far scores relate to students' results in other courses or exams.

Construct validity concerns the qualities that the task measures, how far it actually represents writing abilities. This is a key feature of assessment and means understanding exactly what ability the task is attempting to measure and the domain of writing that the task is seeking to capture. In L2 writing classes, teachers are concerned with measuring abstract constructs such as "writing ability" or "progress" and this is done indirectly by examining the control students display over aspects of writing. Assessment tasks must therefore produce writing that taps these abstract concepts, being based on a close analysis of target texts to effectively elicit the appropriate rhetorical, cognitive, and linguistic processes required to write in a particular domain. So a task designed to assess abilities in writing an argumentative essay, for instance, should encourage writers to present and support a proposition, explore points of view and weigh evidence, address an audience appropriately, and draw on relevant topic material.

Construct validity forms the heart of current integrated conceptions of validity (Messick, 1989; 1996) which emphasize that tasks should measure both the conceptual and linguistic content that interests us, while guaranteeing that they are both useful and clear to those who make use of them. This means that results are not only reported efficiently, but with less likelihood of misinterpretation and misapplication of the results to the disadvantage of the test takers.

This last point is of great importance to writing teachers who, after working hard to help their students write effectively and with enjoyment, are frequently frustrated when administrators insist on using indirect testing methods or apply the results for purposes they were not designed to handle. TOEFL tests, for instance, are widely used for placement or practice purposes, while at one university in Hong Kong the IELTS written module has recently been used both to measure undergraduates' language progress and to judge the effectiveness of the center that had been teaching them. More generally, Messick's integrated validity also encompasses the notion of *consequential validity*, which refers to the potential consequences of the use of test scores and the impact of a test on educational and social systems. This not only includes issues of bias and fairness, but also the expectation that the assessment should do no harm to instruction or learning when studying or teaching to a test.

Reflection 8.4
To what extent do you think writing teachers are likely to have control over these different aspects of validity?

While often seen as impenetrably complex, issues of reliability and validity are important to the ways assessment tasks are designed and scored and have important consequences for students. Because assessments influence what is taught, how learners are evaluated, and judgments of course effectiveness, teachers need a basic understanding of these principles to ensure that the assessment process is fair, useful, and appropriate. To summarize the points in this section, the most effective assessments will:

- Require multiple writing samples of topics and genres from the course (*performance reliability*).
- Have mechanisms for clear and consistent marking across texts and raters (*scoring reliability*).
- Provide opportunities for writing which are as much like the real ability required as possible by reflecting the authenticity of target contexts (*face and content validities*).
- Produce results that broadly match students' performances in other tests (*criterion validity*).
- Only assess skills that are part of the focus ability/skill (*construct validity*).

- Ensure that results are used ethically in the treatment of students/teachers (*consequential validity*).

Reflection 8.5

How can you ensure that a writing task has face validity? To what extent are the following assignments likely to be seen as having face validity by (a) final-year EFL secondary students, (b) first-year science undergraduates, and (c) newly arrived adult migrants? Consider the reasons for your responses.

1. Write a 500-word essay on automobile safety. a c – no
2. Develop the following sentence into a five-paragraph essay: "It seemed like any other morning when my mom woke me up with a cup of tea a few weeks ago." c – no
3. Complete the gaps in this letter requesting a bank overdraft.
4. You are going to write a letter to a local newspaper to support a project that helps old people in your area and have collected the following points. Decide which points are important enough to be included, organize them, and write the letter. a, c – yes
5. Write an article for an airline magazine on a subject you know well such as skateboarding, choral singing, playing a musical instrument, a sport, etc. a – yes
6. Choose an abstract word or a significant term or concept from your subject area and write an extended definition of it aimed at an adult, nonspecialist audience. b, c – yes
7. Find a job vacancy advertised in a newspaper that you are qualified to apply for. Prepare a CV and a letter of application setting out why you are a suitable candidate for the post. (b – maybe) c – ok

---

Designing assessment tasks

So far this chapter has stressed the need to be clear about the purposes of evaluation and to give consideration to reliability and validity in creating fair and meaningful tasks. In the classroom this means providing students with opportunities to show what they have learned and ensuring that their writing is scored appropriately. I will discuss the first of these in this section and the second in the next section.

In practical terms, designing writing assessment tasks involves four basic elements. Although it may be difficult to separate these in practice, considering them as distinct ensures each is given due attention:

- **Rubric**: instructions for carrying out the writing task.
- **Prompt**: the stimulus the student must respond to.
- **Expected response**: what the teacher intends students to do with the task.
- **Post-task evaluation**: assessing the effectiveness of the assessment task.

The rubric

This refers to features "that specify how test takers are expected to proceed in taking the test" (Bachman, 1990), but more generally concerns information about how any assignment should be done. Douglas (2000: 50) suggests that the rubric may include:

- The specification of the objective: describing what the task or each part of the task will assess – for example, "This is a test of your ability to write a coherent and grammatically correct paragraph."
- The procedures for responding – for example, "Answer all the questions in complete sentences," "Complete the table using information from the graph," "Assignments should be eight double-spaced pages."
- The task format including the number and relative importance of the subtasks and distinctions between them – for example, "The questions relate to the case study materials provided," "The writing task is based on your understanding of the reading text and so you should attempt section one first."
- The time allotted or the deadline for submission – for example, "You will have 90 minutes to complete the test," "The assignment should be handed in to your class teacher in week 10 of the course."
- The evaluation criteria: the relative weighting given to each part of the task and information on how it is to be marked (often provided in course materials, although can be included in the rubric) – for example, "Part one carries 60% of the marks," "You will get extra marks for using original examples."

In real-world writing contexts this information is typically implicit, known to the writer as a result of cultural or situational knowledge, but in assessment contexts it needs to be made explicit. Clearly, the level of detail that is provided to the students, both before the assessment in a hand-out, practice activities, or course manual, and in the rubric itself, may have a considerable influence on the writer's performance in the task. Rubrics should therefore be as clear and as comprehensive as possible.

Reflection 8.6

Identify the rubric information from these writing assessment tasks and decide which categories they include. Do you think the information is adequate? Do you think it is excessive? What might be added to help students complete the task without overwhelming them with details?

1. Read the two texts below and write your response in the space provided. You have thirty minutes.
2. *Time*: two hours plus fifteen minutes reading time.
   Instructions: Spend the first fifteen minutes reading the text. Do not begin writing until you are told to do so. Write your answers in the book provided. Answer all the questions in all the sections.
   Information: There are thirty marks for each section. You cannot use dictionaries. You are reminded of the need for good English and will be assessed on the relevance and clarity of your work
3. You have been asked to compile a guide to Hong Kong snakes. Using the information in the table and the illustrations on page 2, classify them into groups and describe their variations. You should write about one side and you have forty minutes to complete the task.
4. From a newspaper or Website, select an advertised post that interests you and write a formal application for it. Prepare and attach a curriculum vitae (CV) or resume in support of your application. Make sure you highlight your strengths and that the information you provide is clear and relevant. The letter carries 60 percent and the CV 40 percent of the marks. Submit your work to your tutor by April 1.

The prompt

In addition to procedural information, writers also need material that will stimulate a written response and this is the function of the *prompt*. Kroll and Reid (1994: 233) suggest there are three main formats:

1. *A base prompt* – states the entire task in direct and simple terms:
   • Do you favor or oppose capital punishment? Why?
   • Discuss the view that women make better managers than men.
2. *A framed prompt* – presents a situation as a frame for the interpretation of a task
   • Many businesses now prevent their employees and customers from smoking in or near their shops or offices and some governments

have banned smoking in all public places – including shopping malls, cinemas, restaurants, and even parks and streets. This is a good idea but removes some freedom from the individual. Do you agree with the policy or disagree? Give reasons for your answer.
- You are an official for the Ministry of Education. You have been asked to write an article for a student magazine in support of the view that university students should be required to pay for the full cost of their education through their own resources or government loans. You expect your audience to disagree with you, so present the argument as a problem that your position will solve.

3. *A text-based prompt* – presents a text to which the student responds or uses in his or her writing
- The advertisement below describes a new product designed to improve our daily lives. Imagine you are a journalist for a local newspaper and write a short report to evaluate the potential advantages and disadvantages of the appliance.
- You are a supervisor of a team of engineers responsible for on-call emergency repairs at a large hospital. Using the technicians' notes, telephone records, job entry sheets, and other data provided, write a one-page incident report for July 13.

As can be seen from the last example, these categories can overlap, with prompts providing both the frame for the task and the texts to be used.

Reflection 8.7
Consider what advantages and disadvantages the three kinds of prompts might have for students.

Prompts can contain both contextual and input data. *Contextual material* is information that is necessary for the writer to engage in the task, "establishing the setting, participants, purpose, and other features of the situation" (Douglas, 2000: 55). These are aspects of the target context (rather than the testing context as in the rubric) which are included to ensure that student writers select the appropriate genre and readership. If the task is designed to elicit a particular genre, or the writer is expected to assume a particular voice, pursue a specific purpose, or address a definite audience, then the prompt is where this is made clear. Like the ideas in the rubric, these contextual aspects ought to be within the writer's experience and relate to what has been taught in the preceding course. They should also be stated precisely, but as briefly as clarity allows.

The *input data*, on the other hand, "consists of visual and/or aural material to be processed during a communicative task" (Douglas, 2000: 57). Students need to be able to activate a relevant schema to address the prompt and so the content and ideas should be accessible to all students equally. This can be a tricky requirement in a timed writing situation as some topics may be more familiar to some learners than others, disadvantaging those with less knowledge of the area who may take longer to get going. It is important to note that L2 learners are unlikely to share a common cultural frame of reference with those constructing the assessment prompt and may therefore be unfamiliar with many issues which might seem commonplace (see Chapter 2). For those who have lived in an ESL context only a short time, questions about current affairs, politics, television, popular culture, and so on may be inaccessible. Teachers can guard against this by offering a choice of equivalent topics in the same genre, although students do not always make the best choices, or by providing appropriate supporting reading texts or other input data.

Reflection 8.8

Look again at the example prompts above and identify the contextual and input features of each.

The expected response

By providing rich input data and clear prompts, teachers seek to elicit a certain response, generating discussion of a topic using appropriate language and generic structures. It is always possible, however, that writers will respond in ways that were not anticipated, misreading the rubric, misunderstanding the prompt, or falling victim to an unseen ambiguity in the task. One of the most common flaws in prompts is that they are too broadly focused, encouraging students to write with no clear direction or rhetorical structure (Reid and Kroll, 1995). In particular, students may be mislead by vague instructions, a directionless topic, or the fact that the task cannot be completed in the time allotted. Alternatively, they may not be able to see what the teacher wants, perhaps the genre or audience is unclear or the instructions concerning length or submission date have not been specified.

It is important that teachers are clear in their own minds about what they want from the assessment task. This is not only because the requirements will then be more clearly communicated to students, but also so that teachers have explicit criteria against which they can judge task performance. An important influence here is the scope of the input, or how much material students need to process before they write. There is a trend in writing assessment toward richer, more contextualized assessment tasks and longer responses. While this may limit the possibilities for misunderstanding, such a broadening of scope also presents opportunities for writers to interpret tasks more flexibly and to produce work that the teacher did not expect.

Reflection 8.9

Look at the following ESL writing tasks and, based on the points raised in this section, identify their strengths and weaknesses. Where possible, rewrite them to maximize students' understanding of the task and their ability to address them effectively.

1. Global warming. Discuss. *[handwritten: too vague – no instructions or expected response; no contextual material; evaluation]*

2. Choose one of the essays from your coursebook and analyze the argument it presents. Your paper should be no more than one page and include all relevant information. *[handwritten: =? evaluation criteria]*

3. You are a member of a tramping party which gets lost in the bush and has to spend a night in the open while waiting to be rescued. You decide to tell each other stories of dangerous situations you have escaped from in the past as a way of passing the time. Write a story that will entertain and encourage your audience. The paper is due on April 4. *[handwritten: Objective? how grade this?]*

4. Read the three short texts which present the research on the relationship between violence on TV and aggression in children. What is the evidence for a cause and effect relationship and what can be done about this? Discuss this in terms of the debate about censorship and freedom of expression. *[handwritten: make clear; lots of input data]*

Post-assessment evaluation of the task

It is worth stressing once again that the rubric, prompt, and input material are crucial to successful writing assessment tasks and need to be as rich and engaging as possible to allow writers to display their strengths. Careful task preparation is essential and this does not end with administering the task and grading papers. Reid and Kroll (1995: 35) identify ways of evaluating the effectiveness of a writing task and suggest a number of questions that teachers can ask of the task and students' responses to it. Good tasks are likely to produce positive responses to the following questions:

- Did the prompt discriminate well among the student group?
- Were the products easy to read and evaluate?
- Were students able to write to their potential?

They also suggest questions to identify problems with writing tasks:

- Context: Is the task relevant to the course and students?
             Is it reasonable given their current needs and abilities?
- Content: Does it address a relevant, authentic audience and purpose?
             Is it accessible to all student writers, culturally or otherwise?
- Genre   Does the task provide clear specification of the required genre
             and suggest the appropriate tone and audience relationships?
- Activity   Is the task sufficiently well defined to be accomplished given
             the parameters?
             Does it allow students to demonstrate their skills and
             knowledge?
- Language   Is the rubric comprehensible, brief, and unambiguous?
             Is the prompt easy to interpret, avoiding cultural bias, obscure
             specialized knowledge, abstract knowledge, etc.?
- Responses Do these avoid simplicity, glibness, emotionality, and show
             differences?
             Do the responses produce what you want to assess?

Approaches to scoring

In addition to designing and administering assessment tasks, teachers must also score the writing students produce in response to them. Traditionally a student's writing performance was judged in comparison with the performance of others, but this *norm-referenced* method has largely given way to *criterion-referenced* practices where the quality of each essay is judged in its own right against some external criteria, such as coherence, grammatical accuracy, contextual appropriacy, and so on. Criterion referenced procedures take a variety of forms and fall into three main categories: holistic, analytic, and trait-based. The first offers a general impression of a piece of writing; the second is based on separate scales of overall writing features; and the third judges performance traits relative to a particular task (Weigle, 2002:108–39).

Table 8.3: *Advantages and disadvantages of holistic scoring*

Advantages	Disadvantages
Global impression not a single ability	Provides no diagnostic information
Emphasis on achievement not deficiencies	Difficult to interpret composite score
	Smooths out different abilities in subskills
Weight can be assigned to certain criteria	Raters may overlook subskills
Encourages rater discussion and agreement	Penalizes attempts to use challenging forms
	Longer essays may get higher scores
	One score reduces reliability
	May confuse writing ability with language proficiency

Holistic scoring

An holistic scale is based on a single, integrated score of writing behavior. This method aims to rate a writer's overall proficiency through an individual impression of the quality of a writing sample. This global approach to the text reflects the idea that writing is a single entity which is best captured by a single scale that integrates the inherent qualities of the writing. The approach contrasts with the error-hunting of earlier assessment methods and instead emphasizes what the writer can do well rather than dwelling on his or her deficiencies (White, 1994). Despite its relative ease of use, however, reducing writing to a single score means that teachers cannot gain diagnostic information which they can feedback into their teaching. Moreover, because the approach requires a response to the text as a whole, readers must be carefully trained to respond in the same way to the same features. Table 8.3 (from Cohen, 1994: 317) summarizes the pros and cons of this method.

Studies suggest that reliability improves when two or more trained readers score each paper, but without guidance raters have trouble agreeing on the relative quality of essays and on the specific features of good writing. Novice teachers develop the confidence and skill to score consistently with experience, but this process also requires reflection and joint consideration of sample papers with other teachers to reach agreement on clear and specific criteria.

Scoring guides, called "rubrics," are used to aid raters by providing bands of descriptions corresponding to particular proficiency or rhetorical criteria. Some rubrics have nine- or ten-step scales, but it is unlikely that raters can reliably distinguish more than about nine bands and most holistic rubrics have between four to six bands. Rubrics are designed to suit different contexts and seek to reflect the goals of the course and what its teachers

Grade	Characteristics
A	The main idea is stated clearly and the essay is well organized and coherent. Excellent choice of vocabulary and very few grammatical errors. Good spelling and punctuation.
B	The main idea is fairly clear and the essay is moderately well organized and relatively coherent. The vocabulary is good and only minor grammar errors. A few spelling and punctuation errors.
C	The main idea is indicated but not clearly. The essay is not very well organized and is somewhat lacking in coherence. Vocabulary is average. There are some major and minor grammatical errors together with a number of spelling and punctuation mistakes.
D	The main idea is hard to identify or unrelated to the development. The essay is poorly organized and relatively incoherent. The use of vocabulary is weak and grammatical errors appear frequently. There are also frequent spelling and punctuation errors.
E	The main idea is missing and the essay is poorly organized and generally incoherent. The use of vocabulary is very weak and grammatical errors appear very frequently. There are many spelling and punctuation errors.

Figure 8.1: A rubric for holistic scoring of an intermediate-level ESL essay.

value as "good writing." Rubrics need to be carefully written to avoid over-reliance on ambiguously subjective terms, but tend to fall back on such descriptors as "fairly," "quite," and "reasonably" to describe writing features in intermediate bands. A sample rubric for a holistically scored essay is given in Figure 8.1 and a more detailed type in Appendix 8.1. Further examples can be found in Cohen (1994), Hamp-Lyons (1991), and White (1994).

More sophisticated rubrics can be devised for more complex forms of writing, tailored not only to genre and topic but to the fact that students may also have to express and counter different viewpoints or draw on suitable interpersonal strategies. But while more delicate holistic rubrics are feasible, they are also more difficult to apply as the reader is likely to encounter texts that simultaneously display characteristics from more than one category. Even the simple rubric in Figure 8.1 may fail to provide an obvious basis for scoring where, for instance, a text has a clear thesis statement and displays appropriate staging for the genre but contains numerous significant grammatical errors, so that features from B and C grades overlap. In such circumstances scorers might choose to make finer distinctions with + and − subdivisions, electing to grade the problematic paper as a B− or C+.

Reflection 8.10

It is sometimes argued that holistic scoring methods are only really effective with fairly advanced levels of writing. Why do you think this might be and do you agree?

Analytic scoring methods

Analytic scoring procedures require readers to judge a text against a set of criteria seen as important to good writing. The fact that raters must give a score for each category helps ensure features are not collapsed into one and so provides more information than a single holistic score. Analytic scoring more clearly defines the features to be assessed by separating, and sometimes weighting, individual components and is therefore more effective in discriminating between weaker texts. Widely used rubrics have separate scales for content, organization, and grammar, with vocabulary and mechanics sometimes added separately, and these are assigned a numerical value. Appendix 8.2 provides an example of an analytic scoring rubric.

Analytic methods can assist rater training by encouraging teachers to reflect on specific features of writing quality, while the fact that they give more detailed information means they are also useful as diagnostic and teaching tools. The use of explicit and comprehensible descriptors, which relate directly to what is taught, allows teachers to target writing weaknesses precisely and provides a clear framework for feedback and revision. These criteria can be introduced early in the course to show students how their writing will be assessed and the properties their teachers value in writing. Critics, however, point to the dangers of the halo effect, where results in rating one scale may influence the rating of others, while the extent to which writing can be seen as a sum of different parts is controversial. Table 8.4 summarizes these advantages and disadvantages (Cohen, 1994: 317; McNamara, 1996).

Trait-based scoring methods

Trait-based approaches differ from holistic and analytic methods in that they are context-sensitive. Rather than presupposing that the quality of a text can be based on a priori views of "good writing," trait-based instruments are designed to clearly define the specific topic and genre features of the task being judged (Hamp-Lyons, 1991). The goal is to create criteria for writing

Table 8.4: *Advantages and disadvantages of analytic scoring*

Advantages	Disadvantages
Encourages raters to address the same features	May divert attention from overall essay effect
Allows more diagnostic reporting	Rating one scale may influence others
Assists reliability as candidate gets several scores	Very time consuming compared with holistic method
Detailed criteria allow easier rater training	Writing is more than simply the sum of its parts
Prevents conflation of categories into one	
Allows teachers to prioritize specific aspects	Favors essays where scalable info easily extracted
	Descriptors may overlap or ambiguous

that are unique to each prompt and the writing produced in response to it, using either primary-trait or multiple-trait systems.

Primary-trait scoring represents a sharpening and narrowing of criteria intended for holistic scoring as it involves rating a piece of writing by just one feature relevant to that task. The primary trait is identified by the task designers and allows teachers and students to focus on a critical feature of the task, such as appropriate text staging, creative response, effective argument, reference to sources, audience design, and so on. But while the approach recognizes that it is not possible to respond to everything at once, raters may find it hard to focus exclusively on the one specified trait and inadvertently include others in their evaluation. The fact that this approach lacks generalizability and requires a very detailed scoring guide for each specific writing task means that it is most widely used in courses where teachers need to judge learners' command of specific writing skills rather than more general improvement.

Multiple-trait scoring is often regarded as an ideal compromise by teachers as it requires raters to provide separate scores for different writing features, as in analytic scoring, while ensuring that these are relevant to the specific assessment task. Multiple-trait scoring treats writing as a multifaceted construct which is situated in particular contexts and purposes, so scoring rubrics can address traits that do not occur in more general analytic scales. These might include the ability to "summarize a course text," "consider both sides of an argument," or "develop the move structure of an abstract." The method is thus very flexible as each task can be related to its own scale with scoring adapted to the context, purpose, and genre of the elicited writing. This also encourages raters to attend to relative strengths and weaknesses in an essay and provides opportunities for detailed feedback to students and for test results to assist washback

Task: Write a factual recount of your visit to the university language center last week. Remember that the purpose of a factual recount is to "tell what happened," so be sure to include the main things you saw and did and who you met. You can use your notes and photographs to help you.

Score	Content	Structure	Language
4	Event explicitly stated Clearly documents events Evaluates their significance Personal comment on events	Orientation gives all essential info All necessary background provided Account in chronological/ other order Reorientation "rounds off" sequence.	Excellent control of language Excellent use of vocabulary Excellent choice of grammar Appropriate tone and style
3	Event fairly clearly stated Includes most events Some evaluation of events Some personal comment	Fairly well-developed orientation Most actors and events mentioned Largely chronological and coherent Reorientation "rounds off" sequence	Good control of language Adequate vocab choices Varied choice of grammar Mainly appropriate tone
2	Event only sketchy Clearly documents events Little or weak evaluation Inadequate personal comment	Orientation gives some information Some necessary background omitted Account partly coherent Some attempt to provide reorientation	Inconsistent language control Lack of variety in choice of grammar and vocabulary Inconsistent tone and style
1	Event not stated No recognizable events No or confused evaluation No or weak personal comment	Missing or weak orientation No background provided Haphazard and incoherent sequencing No reorientation or includes new matter	Little language control Reader seriously distracted by grammar errors Poor vocabulary and tone

Figure 8.2: A multiple-trait scoring rubric for an elementary factual recount.

into instruction directly. Figure 8.2 shows an example of a multiple-trait rubric.

Multiple-trait scoring therefore provides rich data that can inform decisions about remedial action and course content. On the minus side, however, the method can consume enormous amounts of time to devise and administer. Teachers often reduce this workload by sharing the responsibility of writing new rubrics or by modifying a basic "Content, Structure, Language" analytic template to the specific demands of each assignment. More problematic, however, is that even though traits are specific to the task, teachers may still fall back on traditional general categories in their scoring (Cohen, 1994: 323). One way to overcome this is to ensure that all teachers are involved in the process of identifying the traits to be assessed and that categories are justified in terms of the task that will generate them. Raters also need to participate in a benchmarking exercise to agree on the score to be awarded to essays of different quality. Such processes can help ensure that assessments are agreed upon and relate to the purpose of the writing task and the objectives of the course.

Reflection 8.11
What advantages can you see multiple-trait methods having over analytic ones for you as a teacher of L2 writing? Do you think these advantages outweigh any potential problems?

Reducing assessment anxiety

Despite the ideal of the *teaching* → *assessing* → *teaching* relationship, assessment discussions are often framed as testing and product judging, rather than as responding and progress-tracking, and this conflicts with teachers' desires to guide students' understanding of writing. Students also often have a strong unease about assessment and the way that grades seem to replace learning as the goals of instruction. Teachers can reduce learner anxieties by making their assessment tasks and scoring procedures as fair and transparent as possible and by fully preparing learners for what the assessment will involve and how it will be scored. Figure 8.3 suggests strategies for reducing anxiety.

One way to accomplish many of these goals simultaneously is to fully integrate teaching and assessment with the use of portfolio projects as discussed in the next section.

Reflection 8.12
In addition to creating anxiety among learners, the acts of setting, negotiating, and scoring writing assessment tasks and monitoring learner progress also often cause stress among teachers and raters. Can you list some strategies for reducing teacher anxiety?

- Inform learners from the outset of the course that they will be assessed.
- Openly discuss the purposes for an assessment and the criteria used in terms they will understand.
- Assess against explicit criteria.
- Provide ways for students to appraise their own writing and those of others (see Chapter 7).
- Involve learners in regular dialogic assessments by modeling techniques for simple text analysis – for example by discussing strengths and weaknesses of a text on an OHT.
- Provide model texts, with key language features highlighted, which students can use to analyze their own writing.
- Encourage each student to collate a portfolio of their writing for comparison and analysis.
- Ensure, as far as possible, achievement tests are conducted when learners are likely to succeed.
- Consider reliability and validity issues in assessment construction.
- Make assessments as relevant, purposeful, and specific to the coursework and the students as possible by ensuring an integration of teaching and assessment.
- Give students feedback on results, highlighting their progress and what needs to be done next.

Figure 8.3: Strategies for reducing learner anxiety in assessment.

Portfolio assessments

Portfolios are multiple writing samples, written over time, and purposefully selected from various genres to best represent a student's abilities, progress, and most successful texts in a particular context. Portfolios in ESL writing contexts are a response to testing situations which ask students to produce a single piece of timed writing with no choice of topic and no opportunities for revision, seriously disadvantaging L2 writers who often require much longer to perform such tasks. In contrast, portfolio evaluation reflects the practice of most writing courses where students use readings and other sources of information as a basis for writing and revise and resubmit their assignments after receiving feedback from teachers or peers.

Features of portfolios

A good example of a portfolio structure for an L2 writing class is given by Johns (1997), who describes a portfolio devised by secondary school teachers in Singapore for final-year students preparing for a public exam (Figure 8.4). The model illustrates how a portfolio can be used even in a

A timed essay (argumentative or expository).
Reflection questions include: Why did you organize the essay in this way? What phrases or parts of the essay do you particularly like? Are you satisfied with this? Why or why not?
A research-based library project (all notes, drafts, and materials leading to the final paper).
What difficulties did you encounter writing this? What did you learn from writing it?
A summary (one summary of a reading).
Why did you select this particular summary? How is it organized? Why is it organized like this? What are the basic elements of all the summaries you have written?
A writer's choice (any text in the L1 or L2 that has been important to the student).
What is this? When did you write it? Why did you choose it? What does it say about you?
An overall reflection of the portfolio (a letter to the teacher integrating the entries).
What were the goals of this class? Describe each entry and why it was important for achieving these goals.

Source: Johns, 1997: 140–41.

Figure 8.4: A portfolio structure for advanced secondary school students.

highly constrained curriculum by drawing on the genres required by the school and encouraging students to reflect on these genres, on their task experiences, and on their writing practices and attitudes. Such reflections are often seen as a major strength of portfolios as they make visible what students see in their work, in their development, and what they value about writing.

Essentially, the purpose of portfolios is to obtain a more prolonged and accurate picture of students writing in more natural and less stressful contexts. They can include drafts, reflections, readings, diaries, observations of genre use, teacher or peer responses, as well as finished texts, thus representing multiple measures of a student's writing ability. The texts are typically selected by students, often in consultation with a teacher, and comprise four to six core items in categories which reflect the goals of the writing course. They can serve to either showcase a student's best work or display a collection of both drafts and final products to demonstrate process and highlight improvement. By assembling their texts over time, students are able to observe changes in their work, compare different genres and writing experiences, and discover something about the entries and their learning. Portfolios thus encourage students to reflect on their writing and the criteria employed for judging it; it is an assessment that promotes greater responsibility for writing (Belanoff and Dickson, 1991; Purves et al., 1995).

Reflection 8.13

Would you consider the use of portfolios as an assessment option in your teaching context? What items would you ask students to include and how would you link the collection to the course?

Advantages and disadvantages of portfolios

Portfolio assessments appeal to teachers of L2 writing because of the increased validity provided by multiple samples and the fact that evaluation can be matched with teaching objectives. Hamp-Lyons and Condon (2000) point out that portfolios strongly support pedagogies which involve multidrafting, revision, peer review, collaborative learning, and reflective writing. This not only helps students to more clearly see a direct connection between what they are taught and how they are assessed, but can also provide more data on individual writing progress, enabling teachers to offer more support in their weaker areas (Brown and Hudson, 1998). Multi-genre portfolios, perhaps including both narrative and expository genres, can also highlight how texts are organized differently to express particular purposes. Similarly, a portfolio can illustrate how one genre often relates to or interacts with others, as in cases where students assemble all the genres for a formal job application.

But, as White (1994: 127) observes, "a portfolio is not a test; it is only a collection of materials," and teachers still have to evaluate what is collected. Scoring a portfolio may, in fact, actually be harder than dealing with a single piece of writing because of the heterogeneous nature of what is assessed and the greater complexity in ensuring reliability across raters and rating occasions. Standardizing a single score to fairly express a student's ability from a variety of genres, tasks, drafts, and perhaps different subject discipline material can be extremely difficult. There is the problem of controlling the variability which can arise from different tasks assigned by different teachers, particularly if some are intrinsically more interesting, or easy, to write about (Grabe and Kaplan, 1996: 417). Teachers also need to consider the difficulties of establishing grade equivalence across raters and their own decisions in rating different portfolios. In fact, portfolios place huge cognitive and time loads on raters, which means they may take shortcuts in making decisions (Hamp-Lyons and Condon, 1993). Table 8.5 summarizes these issues.

Table 8.5: *Some potential advantages and disadvantages of portfolio assessments*

Advantages	Disadvantages
Represents program goals	Produces heavy workload for teachers
Reflects progress over time, genres, and conditions	May encourage "teaching the portfolio"
More broad, comprehensive, and fair than exams	Difficult to compare tasks set by different teachers
Closely related to teaching and students' abilities	Difficult to assign a single grade to varied collection
Students see portfolio as a record of progress	Problems with plagiarism or outside assistance
Focuses on multidrafting, feedback, revision, etc.	Problems with reliability across raters
Assignments build on each other and show genre sets	
Allows different selection and assessment criteria	
Students reflect on their improvement and weaknesses	

Reflection 8.14

To what extent would the disadvantages of portfolio assessment dissuade you from using this approach in your writing classes? How might you seek to overcome these problems?

Designing, managing, and assessing portfolios

Portfolios differ widely as they reflect the goals of different courses and the needs of different learners, but all require careful thought from the outset. When designing a portfolio assessment, a number of questions can be addressed as a concrete starting point:

1. What do we want to know about the writer – progress? genre awareness? self-reflection?
2. What texts will best achieve this purpose – what genres? drafts or final only? peer reviews?
3. Who will choose the entries? teachers only? students only? teacher and student together?
4. What should the performance criteria be and how will these be linked to course objectives?

Table 8.6: *A checklist for managing a writing portfolio*

1. Determine what the portfolio is to include based on course objectives and student needs analysis.
2. Ask students to buy a ring binder for the portfolio. They should paste a sheet in the front with the submission texts and due dates and divide the binder with labeled tabs.
3. Discuss the purposes and procedures of the portfolio with students throughout the course.
4. Agree on assessment decisions and scoring criteria with other teachers and communicate these, both formally and informally, through feedback comments to students throughout the course.
5. Set aside days to conduct checks to monitor progress and help learners reorganize their portfolios.
6. Provide opportunities for students to display their work through portfolio presentations, design competitions, readings, and so on.
7. Encourage reflection on entries by asking students to write an introduction to their portfolios and diary entries or letters to readers on its contents.

5. Should the entries receive a preliminary initial grade or the portfolio only be graded as a whole?
6. What part will students' reflections and self-assessments play in the assessment?
7. How will consistent scoring and feedback be achieved – what rater training is needed?
8. How many people will grade the portfolio and how will scoring disagreements be resolved?
9. How will the outcomes of the evaluation process washback into students' learning?
10. What mechanisms should be set up for evaluating the program and making changes to it?

Once a portfolio system is agreed upon, it needs to be implemented and managed, with an initial emphasis on teacher and learner training. Students will need explicit guidance in selecting items and learning to write reflective comments on their choices, while raters must have clear criteria to ensure consistency and reliability in compiling and assessing these choices. It is important that students understand their responsibilities in choosing texts and that they are aware of the rating process. It is also important that teachers participate in benchmarking sessions to familiarize them with the scoring rubric to be used. This is to improve reliability and to ensure that students receive formative commentary based on course performance criteria. A checklist for managing a portfolio might include the points in Table 8.6.

Consistently
present or high

Consistently
absent or low

←========= **Characteristics of the Writer** =========→
Fit between reflection and portfolio evidence
Awareness beyond immediate task
Perspective on self as a writer
Quality of reflection about writing

←== **Characteristics of the Portfolio as a Whole** ==→
Variety of tasks
Awareness of reader/writer context
Sense of purpose and task
Choice and management of genres

←====== **Characteristics of Individual Texts** ======→
Engagement with subject matter
Significance of subject matter
Resources used
Amount of writing
Quality of development and analysis
Critical perspective on subject matter

←============== **In-Text Features** ==============→
Control of grammar and mechanics
Management of tone and style
Coherence/flow/momentum
Control and variety of syntax

Source: Based on Hamp-Lyons and Condon, 2000: 144.

Figure 8.5: Dimensions for assessing portfolios.

As noted above, the heterogeneity of portfolios makes them difficult to score, but there are two main approaches to grading them:

1. Holistic: Previously scored portfolio samples are used as models representing certain score levels and student work is measured against these to provide a single grade.
2. Multiple-trait: Can include text features of specific genres, but may also include criteria for draft stages, awareness of processes, self-reflection, cooperative interaction, content knowledge.

Whereas the holistic method may be effective with smaller samples, it is unlikely to be reliable with longer and more open portfolios which display considerable variation. The multiple-trait option more faithfully reflects the complexities of both the products and the processes involved, but may become unwieldy if too many different criteria are scored. Hamp-Lyons and

Condon (2000) suggest a useful heuristic for devising criteria based on the main elements to be assessed (Figure 8.5).

When assessing portfolios, or any kind of writing task, it is important that there are some accountability processes involved so that the basis for a particular score can be given. Multiple-trait systems seem to offer the most effective means of accomplishing this, while simultaneously developing raters' appreciation of the features of good writing. It should be pointed out that portfolios do not necessarily bring greater accuracy to assessment, but they do promote a greater awareness of what good writing might be and how it might be best achieved. The advantages lay principally in that the validity, and value, of assessment is increased if it is situated in teaching and based on a clearer understanding of writing.

Summary and conclusion

Performance assessment is a crucial aspect of the writing teacher's job, providing information on students' progress and weaknesses and feeding back into new tasks, materials, and syllabus revisions. This chapter has provided a practical overview of the principles and practices of writing assessment relevant to classroom teachers, stressing its essentially pedagogical role. While institutional constraints may not always allow teachers to administer the assessment tasks they would prefer, the use of clear rubrics and prompts anchored in needs and course objectives, attention to issues of validity and reliability, and the application of explicit and systematic scoring criteria can help ensure fair and effective assessment. The main points made in this chapter have been:

- Although a stigma attaches to "teaching to the test," every assessment task should reflect the objectives of a course and relate to the writing skills and understandings that have been taught.
- Assessment is not a disembodied aspect of education but is an integral element of the curriculum, feeding back into and influenced by needs analysis, course design, and selection of tasks and materials.
- Teachers should be clear about the reason for any writing assessment and ensure that results are not used for inappropriate purposes.
- It is important to implement the principles of reliability and validity to ensure that the assessment is as fair and meaningful as possible.
- Teachers should consider rubrics and prompts carefully to create tasks that are clear, engaging, and relevant to students' needs and what they have been taught.
- Different scoring methods have their own advantages and problems and correspond to different views of writing and assessment. The choice of

method should be made bearing in mind issues of reliability, validity, practicality, and the information it can provide on students' writing abilities.

- Devising and implementing scoring criteria is a demanding task best done as a collaborative exercise with all raters and involving the benchmarking of texts to achieve consistency.
- Portfolio assessments have advantages over single essays by providing students with an opportunity to demonstrate their abilities in different genres and their understanding of different writing processes.

Discussion questions and activities

1 What is the essential difference between formative and summative assessment? How do these two categories relate to the broad purposes for assessing student writing discussed in the opening section of this chapter?

2 What do reliability and validity refer to and why are they important in the design and interpretation of L2 writing assessment tasks? Validity is said to be more important than reliability in assessing writing. Why?

3 What can writing assessment tasks tell us about learners that could feed back into curriculum decisions concerning needs, lacks, course design, task specification, materials production, and subsequent assessments? Can you anticipate any problems in this washback process? How might they be overcome?

4 Many teachers worry that their assessment practices are essentially subjective and can vary from one essay to the next or may be different from those of other teachers. How can teachers ensure greater consistency and reliability in judging performance?

5 In what ways can teachers make their writing assessments an integral feature of their courses? What advantages does integration offer course participants?

6 Evaluate the following task from what you know about prompt and rubric construction and assessment validity. Devise an appropriate scoring prompt for the assessment.

Write an essay which examines your progress as a writer in light of the assignments you have completed during this course. In your essay you should consider how at least two of the following have contributed to your development: genre, reader awareness, pre-writing, revising, or using feedback. Be sure to plan your essay carefully and allow time for this. Bear in mind the need for logical structure, introduction and conclusion, focusing statement, topic-led paragraphs, links, and appropriate tone. You have 60 minutes to write approximately 500 words.

7 Construct a writing assessment task for either an imaginary group of students or a class you are familiar with. Explain why this is an appropriate task for the learners in terms of their needs and class objectives and show how it meets the criteria given for task rubrics and prompts.

8 Devise an holistic and an analytic scoring rubric for the assignment you designed in 6 above.

9 A number of studies have shown that the judgments made by raters using both holistic and analytic scales are unreliable and that even experienced raters may differ in the importance they give to different criteria. Conduct a small-scale research project to test this finding. Allocate a number of student essays and a scoring rubric to three or four colleagues or fellow-students and examine the similarities and differences in their ratings. Write up your results in a short essay.

10 Devise a portfolio that would be an appropriate course assessment for a particular group of students you are familiar with. List the items you require students to include and the reflection questions they should respond to. Provide a written justification for your choices.

11 A significant difficulty for many new teachers is managing the distribution of assessment tasks through a course and keeping on top of the marking load. What do you think the main issues might involve here and what strategies would you use to deal with them?

Appendix 8.1: Holistic marking scheme

Rubric for a report written in response to listening and reading sources:

Score	Descriptors
86–100	**Outstanding work**: excellence clearly in evidence through correct selection of content and its ordering under the appropriate headings of the report; ability to summarize and rephrase wordings of input content; overall coherence of the report structure, internal cohesion of each of the three sections; linguistic accuracy and the use of a variety of structures and vocabulary; and the sustained employment of an appropriate tone and style
71–85	**Very good work**: all relevant points from the inputs identified and incorporated under appropriate headings; a mostly successful attempt is made to rephrase the wordings of the main points from the inputs; overall coherence is good and ideas are logically and clearly connected; syntactic variety may be limited but there is no more than a sprinkling of (nonserious) grammatical errors; only occasional lapses in tone and style, mainly through inappropriate selection of vocabulary

Appendix 8.1 *(continued)*

Score	Descriptors
56–70	**Satisfactory work**: incorporation of relevant points from the reading and listening inputs mostly satisfactory but some minor points may be missing and some phrases may be taken verbatim from the inputs; overall coherence is quite good but cohesion within and between sentences may be faulty in places; variety of structures/choice of vocabulary is limited and more than a sprinkling of grammatical errors is in evidence but these do not seriously impede reader comprehension
41–55	**Marginally satisfactory work**: some relevant points not incorporated, and some points copied verbatim and/or not subsumed under the appropriate headings of the report; connections between sections of the report and the linkage of ideas within sections of the report are relatively poor but can be read without causing the reader serious strain; grammatical mistakes are frequent but do not cause excessive strain for the reader; frequent lapses in tone and style
26–40	**Unsatisfactory work**: inadequate incorporation of relevant material from the inputs and/or direct copying of wordings; poor overall coherence and local cohesion leading to strain in reader comprehension; numerous grammatical errors, some serious and impeding comprehension; no consistent attempt to establish appropriate tone and style; some attempt to fulfill task requirements but at an unacceptably low level
1–25	**Very unsatisfactory work**: relevant points missing and/or irrelevant material included; may be strong evidence of extensive copying from the inputs; coherence and cohesion are consistently poor and cause serious strain for the reader; text is littered with grammatical errors of all kinds and there is little or no attempt to produce the appropriate tone or style; the work clearly fails to fulfill task requirements

Appendix 8.2: An analytic scoring rubric

Mark	Format and content 40 marks
31–40 *excellent to* *very good*	Fulfills task fully; correct convention for the assignment task; features of chosen genre mostly adhered to; good ideas/good use of relevant information; substantial concept use; properly developed ideas; good sense of audience
21–30 *good to* *average*	Fulfills task quite well although details may be underdeveloped or partly irrelevant; correct genre selected; most features of chosen genre adhered to; satisfactory ideas with some development; quite good use of relevant information; some concept use; quite good sense of audience
11–20 *fair to poor*	Generally adequate but some inappropriate, inaccurate, or irrelevant data; an acceptable convention for the assignment task; some features of chosen genre adhered to; limited ideas/moderate use of relevant information; little concept use; barely adequate development of ideas; poor sense of audience
1–10 *inadequate*	Clearly inadequate fulfilment of task; possibly incorrect genre for the assignment; chosen genre not adhered to; omission of key information; serious irrelevance or inaccuracy; very limited ideas/ignores relevant information; no concept use; inadequate development of ideas; poor or no sense of audience
Mark	**Organization and coherence 20 marks**
16–20 *excellent to* *very good*	Message followed with ease; well organized and thorough development through introduction, body, and conclusion; relevant and convincing supporting details; logical progression of content contributes to fluency; unified paragraphs; effective use of transitions and reference
11–15 *good to* *average*	Message mostly followed with ease; satisfactorily organized and developed through introduction, body and conclusion; relevant supporting details; mostly logical progression of content; moderate to good fluency; unified paragraphs; possible slight over- or under-use of transitions but correctly used; mostly correct references
6–10 *fair to* *poor*	Message followed but with some difficulty; some pattern of organization – an introduction, body, and conclusion evident but poorly done; some supporting details; progression of content inconsistent or repetitious; lack of focus in some paragraphs; over- or under-use of transitions with some incorrect use; incorrect use of reference
1–5 *inadequate*	Message difficult to follow; little evidence of organization – introduction and conclusion may be missing; few or no supporting details; no obvious progression of content; improper paragraphing; no or incorrect use of transitions; lack of reference contributes to comprehension difficulty

Appendix 8.2 *(continued)*

Mark	Sentence construction and vocabulary 40 marks
31–40 *excellent to very good*	Effective use of a wide variety of correct sentences; variety of sentence length; effective use of transitions; no significant errors in agreement, tense, number, person, articles, pronouns and prepositions; effective use of a wide variety of lexical items; word form mastery; effective choice of idiom; correct register
21–30 *good to average*	Effective use of a variety of correct sentences; some variety of length; use of transitions with only slight errors; no serious recurring errors in agreement, tense, number, person, articles, pronouns and prepositions; almost no sentence fragments or run-ons; variety of lexical items with some problems but not causing comprehension difficulties; good control of word form; mostly effective idioms; correct register
11–20 *fair to poor*	A limited variety of mostly correct sentences; little variety of sentence length; improper use of or missing transitions; recurring grammar errors are intrusive; sentence fragments or run-ons evident; a limited variety of lexical items occasionally causing comprehension problems; moderate word form control; occasional inappropriate choice of idiom; perhaps incorrect register
1–10 *inadequate*	A limited variety of sentences requiring considerable effort to understand; correctness only on simple short sentences; improper use of or missing transitions; many grammar errors and comprehension problems; frequent incomplete or run-on sentences; a limited variety of lexical items; poor word forms; inappropriate idioms; incorrect register

9 Researching writing and writers

Aims: This final chapter departs from exclusively pedagogic issues to focus on links between teaching and research. It offers a practical guide to ways of researching L2 writing processes, texts, and classrooms and suggests areas of research suitable for teachers and students.

Teaching and research are often seen in opposition, one practical and the other theoretical, leading many teachers to regard research as an activity conducted by scholars and unrelated to their everyday lives. Research, however, is central to what we know and do as teachers. I have argued that the most effective teachers are those able to make informed classroom choices from an awareness of current perspectives on second language writing. Keeping abreast of ideas and developments in the field is a key professional activity and many teachers make a point of reading the research published in the *Journal of Second Language Writing* and other journals that carry relevant articles such as *Language Teaching Research, TESOL Quarterly, Assessing Writing*, and *Research in the Teaching of Writing*.

But teachers are not simply consumers of others' research. They tend to be curious about their students and their subject; they actively experiment with different tasks and materials; and they reflect on their approaches and decisions. They know a great deal about teaching in the sense of formulating attitudes to the issues and events they encounter and have assumptions and beliefs about what they do. As professionals, they accept that their expertise should develop as they gain experience and look for ways to better understand what they teach and the ways they teach it.

In other words, as Stake (1995: 97) points out, "research is not just the domain of scientists, it is the domain of craftspersons and artists as well, all who would study and interpret." Because it stimulates curiosity, validates classroom observations, and helps develop a critical perspective on practice, research is at the heart of professional development since it helps to transform a personal understanding into an informed awareness. This chapter outlines how teachers can use research as a systematic and ongoing approach to solving problems and expanding their knowledge of writing, focusing on:

- Generating and designing research projects
- Collecting and analyzing data
- Reporting research

Orientation

What does "research" mean to you? What do you think makes good research? Can research into writing and learning to write be useful and if so, in what ways and to whom?

Some preliminaries and key steps

It is possible to study writing without detailed knowledge of the various procedures available, but equipped with an understanding of basic steps and methods, the process becomes more fruitful. "Good research" can be defined in many ways which reach beyond narrow conceptions of objectivity and validity. All research should interest the researcher, target a specific issue, have intellectual or practical value, be ethically and rigorously conducted, draw on appropriate data and methods of analysis, and produce credible results. The actual practices which can realize these broad criteria are extremely diverse, however, and an awareness of the options available can assist the researcher enormously.

Many "teacher as researcher" studies originate in the type of inquiry known as *action research*, the process of collecting and analyzing data to improve the quality of some action, typically a classroom practice (Wallace, 1998: 4). The emphasis is on concrete and practical issues of immediate concern and conducted in classroom settings by teachers working individually or collaborating in teams (Burns, 1999). But although this is a very accessible type of research, not all teacher studies are problem-driven and change-oriented. Research arises from a need to understand what people do in certain situations, and this may arise as much from a simple interest as to achieve a practical payoff.

It will become clear that there is no "one-size-fits-all" formula to carrying out research. Different topics, contexts, access to data, researcher preferences, and available time and resources will all influence the approach. Nor is research the tidy, linear, and efficient procedure often presented in completed studies. Topics often tend to evolve in an organic rather than a mechanical way, with accompanying dead ends, false starts, and new avenues subverting a simple stepwise approach. We can, however, identify the following ideal stages which help systematize the process while allowing for the possibility of change, recursion and redirection, and in the next sections I will enlarge on these basic steps:

Formulating➔Focusing➔Designing➔Collecting➔Analyzing➔Reporting

Generating research: Formulating and focusing a question

Formulating a topic

Almost anything can form a question for research, but basic prerequisites are that it should be viable, discrete, intrinsically interesting, and potentially involve collaboration with others (Hopkins, 1993: 64). Teachers should, initially anyway, only consider taking on small-scale and relatively limited topics that are interesting to them or relevant to their students and which have a chance of succeeding within a restricted time-scale. It is easy to underestimate the time that research demands, and formulating a specific issue at the outset can be time well spent.

This doesn't mean that research always begins with a clear idea or hypothesis. It often starts as an open-ended aspect of writing that seems interesting and slowly gains shape through jotting down observations or reflections. Teachers may be motivated by the desire to understand the texts they present, the effects of changing their teaching, the writing processes of their students, the ways students discuss writing, their preferences for particular expressions, or the genres of target communities. Some researchable topics are listed in Appendix 9.1, but an issue may evolve from one of these sources:

- A personal observation – why do two groups respond differently to the same assignment? How does the structure of a narrative differ from a report? Why don't students stay on task in peer review sessions?
- Something we find in a journal or a conversation – a surprising result or interesting suggestion.
- The behavior of students – why do they have trouble with transition paragraphs? What composing processes do they use? What do they say about their essays in peer groups? What kinds of writing do they engage in out of class?

- A claim about writing in a study guide or a textbook that seems questionable or interesting.
- An aspect of student needs analysis – How is this genre structured? How does it relate to other genres in this situation? What sources do students need to draw on in this context?

Reflection 9.1

While you may not have conducted any formal "research," what kinds of professional or classroom issues do you find interesting and would like to know more about? Why do these interest you?

Focusing

The original observation or practice which triggered an idea for research then needs to be more clearly focused in order to help define the kind of data that will be needed, the way it will be collected, and how it will be analyzed. The issue is reformulated more precisely as a result of a fact-finding and reflective process. This stage involves closer scrutiny of the topic through discussions with experienced colleagues, unstructured observation of the context, open-ended interviews with participants, or Internet and library searches to learn what others have said about the issue. Thus, if a teacher is interested in, say, the impact of teacher feedback, then he or she needs to be clear about the kind of behavior to include as feedback and what will count as a relationship between feedback and response. Is it worth looking only at written feedback? Should both margin and end comments be included? What counts as a revision? How are revisions to be related to feedback? Is the scope of a revision important or only its frequency? What should be done with revisions that originate outside feedback?

Focusing also involves thinking about how to *frame* the question. Some researchers prefer to formulate a specific question early in the process and then set out to answer it. This kind of tight framing reflects natural science procedures and involves stating an explicit hypothesis that the research can test to either confirm or disprove. Thus, the teacher concerned about students' use of feedback may hypothesize that offering more corrective advice in end comments will produce more form-focused revisions. He or she might then collect first and second drafts of student essays, identify all form-focused feedback, and match this against changes to students drafts.

An alternative is to work with general questions and take a more exploratory approach. This involves collecting and drawing on data to see where the issue leads, examining factors in the revising context, such as the help learners get from friends or the preferences they have for particular kinds of feedback. As we shall see below, the choice between these ways of framing the question has important implications for the design of the research itself.

Reflection 9.2
How would you focus the following general issue to make it possible to research: "Some of my students are reluctant to participate in peer-review sessions"? What specific questions might you need to frame to address your question? What sources could you turn to in order to learn more about the issue? What kinds of data would you want to collect?

Designing research

The next stage is to design a research plan by matching the topic to a feasible method of investigation. It involves three broad aspects:

1. Viability: Setting up a realistic way of carrying out the research.
2. Ethicality: Establishing principles and procedures to protect the participants in the research.
3. Validity: Ensuring that the research results are likely to fit with reality.

First of all, the research obviously needs to be feasible given situational constraints. While the choice of a particular method will depend on the individual's understanding of the issue and preference for a particular research approach, it is also a very practical matter involving mundane issues of access and management. The main issues here concern both the resources needed to collect data and get a project under way and those required to monitor and control it:

- acquiring access to texts, institutions, information, and participants
- gaining the cooperation and patience of students
- encouraging the cooperation of colleagues
- securing time to engage intellectually with the data and to reflect periodically on the changing shape of the project
- managing record-keeping and tracking progress

Table 9.1: *Some ethical considerations for research*

- Gain approval from participants – for documents, quotations, observations, transcripts – anything!
- Explain clearly – ensure those involved understand the aims, methods, and intended dissemination.
- Clarify consequences – guarantee that subjects are not penalized for involvement/noninvolvement.
- Maintain confidentiality – ensure participant's anonymity.
- Involve participants – encourage others with a stake in the work or contributing to it.
- Get feedback – allow contributors to see and discuss your accounts of their behavior.
- Report progress – keep the work visible and remain open to suggestions from colleagues.
- Negotiate release of information – different agreements may be needed at different levels.
- Retain rights – if participants are satisfied with fairness and accuracy, then accounts should not be vetoed later.

Ethical considerations are also a crucial dimension of design. Conducting a research project changes a teacher's relationships with his or her students and colleagues, and care needs to be taken to guard against exploiting those relationships through lack of negotiation or confidentiality. Of central importance are the potential issues of coercion, compromise, and misunderstanding which can arise because of the inherent power imbalance in the teacher-student relationship. The teacher's responsibility for assigning grades and other crucial decisions poses serious implicit challenges for conducting research in one's own class which need to be recognized and openly discussed. Students must understand that their participation or nonparticipation in the research will have no consequences for them.

In addition, participants should have the right to know the aims of the project, what information is sought, how it will be used, and who will have access to it. Even where the English proficiency of L2 students may not be high, every attempt should be made to ensure that they understand the purpose of the research and that they are aware that they have the right to anonymity, to withdraw, or to veto the release of data. Often students are keen to be involved in a study, but they should have a choice. Potential dilemmas arise, of course, when informing students may influence the data, but it might be possible here to ask students after the event and exclude data about those who are unwilling from the final results. Table 9.1 raises some key guidelines for ethical research (see also Cohen et al., 2000; Hitchcock and Hughes, 1995).

Table 9.2: *General features of quantitative and qualitative research*

Quantitative	Qualitative
Values objectivity and eliminates researcher bias	Sees behavior as subjective and context-bound
Data seen as measurable quantities	Interpretations through participant perspectives
Establishes and tests hypotheses	Theorizes issues via reflection on contextual data
May involve intervention to control the context	Explores natural contexts without controlling variables
Values reliability and replication of methods	Ensures validity through multiple data sources
Seeks to generalize beyond immediate context	Does not generalize but focuses on instances

Reflection 9.3

Imagine you want to conduct an experiment with two groups of writers to study the effects of feedback. One group will receive feedback on their drafts and the other only a grade, then each group will be tested on its improvement. What ethical issues does this raise? How could you modify the research to address these issues?

The third main aspect of design is to ensure that the research will answer the questions it has set itself, providing a credible explanation or characterization of the issue. In particular, this involves decisions concerning the researcher's understanding of the role of "objectivity" and the degree to which he or she will intervene to collect and analyze data. Data can be distinguished in various ways, and one familiar contrast is between *qualitative* and *quantitative* types. Until recently, educational research has favored quantitative scientific methods aimed at securing objectivity by testing hypotheses through structured and controlled procedures. Essentially the researcher approaches an issue from the outside, working to discover facts about a situation that can be measured and compared. Qualitative researchers, in contrast, argue that it is important to explore any situation from the participants' perspective and is more inductive, reflective, and exploratory. Denzin and Lincoln (1998) and Miles and Huberman (1994) provide authoritative discussions of the differences and these are summarized in Table 9.2.

This neat opposition, however, overlooks the fact that many studies employ both numeric and other kinds of data, and it is worth emphasizing that much writing research combines both quantitative and qualitative types of data, analysis, and interpretation to gain a more complete picture of a complex reality. There are, in fact, good reasons for incorporating several techniques in data gathering, and the concept of *triangulation*, the use of multiple sources, provides for greater plausibility in interpreting results. It obviously makes sense to view research pragmatically, adopting whatever tools seem most effective, and a researcher may, for example, gather student opinions about their writing practices through a questionnaire and supplement this with interview or diary data, mixing methods to increase the validity of the eventual findings.

Despite this, the qualitative-quantitative distinction does raise the interesting contrast between *elicited* and *naturalistic* data. The researcher has to consider whether data are to be gathered in controlled conditions, such as through questionnaires, structured interviews and experiments, or in circumstances not specifically set up for the research, such as via classroom observations or analyses of naturally occurring texts. No data can ever strictly be free of the effects of the researcher's intervention, and as we shall see below, all methods of collection and analysis allow varying degrees of open-endedness and control. In more interventionist research designs, however, the researcher has to take care that the data collected are authentic and not simply the product of an artificially contrived situation.

Reflection 9.4

Selecting either an interventionist or naturalistic approach, consider the tasks you might need to perform to investigate the impact of teacher written feedback on student revisions. Match these tasks with the resources required. What resource requirements are likely to be most problematic?

Collecting data

The previous two sections addressed the important steps of selecting a researchable issue and determining the mode of approach in terms of the degree of intervention and quantification to be used. With a focused research issue and a general plan, the next stage involves going deeper into the research process by collecting data. Space allows only a brief survey of the various data collection techniques used in writing research, and readers are referred to user-friendly introductions to classroom research by Bell (1999), Burns (1999), Hopkins (1993), McDonough and McDonough (1997), and

Table 9.3: *Main data collection methods for researching writing*

Questionnaires	Highly focused elicitations of respondent self-reports about actions and attitudes
Interviews	Adaptable and interactive elicitations of respondent self-reports
Verbal reports	Retrospective accounts and think aloud reports of thoughts while composing
Written reports	Diary or log accounts of personal writing or learning experiences
Observation	Direct or recorded data of "live" interactions or writing behavior
Text analyses	Study of authentic examples of writing used for communication in a natural context
Experiments	Controlled context to discover the effect of one variable on another
Case studies	A collection of techniques capturing the experiences of participants in a situation

Nunan (1992) for greater coverage. A profile of methods for researching writing would include those listed in Table 9.3.

Reflection 9.5

Which of the data collection methods listed above appeal to you most? Why do these seem most attractive and can you imagine circumstances where you might wish to use other methods?

Elicitation: Questionnaires and interviews

These are the two main methods for eliciting information and attitudes from informants. Questionnaires are widely used for collecting large amounts of structured, often numerical, easily analyzable self-report data, while interviews offer more flexibility and greater potential for elaboration and detail. Both allow researchers to tap people's views and experiences of writing, but interviews tend to be more quantitative and heuristic and questionnaires more quantitative and conclusive.

Questionnaire items vary in the kind of responses they elicit:

- Closed options from a set of fixed alternatives (yes/no/don't know)
- Structured items with opportunities to select or rank alternatives or scale agreement with statements
- Open-ended questions which prescribe no responses at all

The more predetermined questionnaire formats make them easy to administer and facilitate considerable precision in framing issues for large groups

254 Researching writing and writers

and assisting the analysis and quantification of data. The lack of opportunities for immediate followup and clarification, however, means that the researcher has to be confident that items can be interpreted independently and unambiguously, and that instructions for completing them are clear. These factors become particularly important when respondents are second language learners who may be intimidated by a long and daunting document. There is also the possibility that L2 students may restrict themselves to the options available and not consider perspectives that have not been proposed. As a result, teachers generally pilot their questions beforehand to ensure they are short, clear, and direct, and that learners have sufficient knowledge to respond.

Questionnaires are particularly useful for exploratory studies into writing attitudes and behaviors and for identifying issues that can be followed up later by more in-depth methods. One major use of questionnaires in writing research has been to discover the kinds of writing target communities require from students. Jenkins, Jordan, and Weiland (1993), for example, used a questionnaire to fine-tune the relevance of their technical writing course by learning more about the genres their L2 engineering students had to write and the attitudes their professors had about students' writing skills. Their questionnaire asked respondents to indicate the types of writing they asked students to do, judge the relative difficulty that L2 students had in writing them, rank the importance of different errors, and so on. In this case statistical tests were used to establish the significance of the differences between the responses for each question, but teachers often find that simple descriptive measures such as means and percentages are sufficient to identify general features of their results.

Reflection 9.6

What do you think might be the relative advantages and disadvantages of open and closed questions in questionnaires designed to research L2 writing? Consider both pros and cons for the researcher in designing and analyzing them, and for the subject in responding to them.

Interviews offer more interactive and less predetermined modes of eliciting self-report information. Although sometimes little more than oral questionnaires, interviews generally represent a very different way of understanding human experience, regarding knowledge as generated between people rather than as objectified and external to them. Participants are able to discuss their interpretations and perspectives, sharing what writing means to them rather than responding to preconceived categories. This flexibility and responsiveness means that interviews are used widely in L2 writing research and often supplement questionnaires as a means of clarifying and expanding potentially interesting answers. Like questionnaires, however, interviews can be divided according to the extent they constrain responses:

- Structured interviews: a relatively tight format and set of assumptions – preplanned questions given in a fixed order almost like a checklist.
- Semi-structured interviews: set of guidelines in no fixed order and allowing extensive followup.
- Unstructured interviews: loose outline of issues with direction following interviewee responses.

Once again, the researcher needs to weigh the relevant issues and the types of respondents involved to decide what kind of interview would be most appropriate for the research purpose.

Reflection 9.7

In what ways would the use of naturalistic, unstructured interview techniques be helpful as a research methodology and what difficulties might this also cause for the researcher?

Interviews can be undertaken with individuals or with small groups of three or four (often called focus groups) and in writing research typically address the following broad areas:

- *Writing practices*: to discover the genres people write and how they understand and go about writing (What kinds of texts do you write in this context? How is this text different from this one?).
- *Teaching and learning practices*: to discover people's beliefs and practices about teaching and learning (How many assignments do you set? How do you start planning an essay?).
- *Discourse-features*: to discover how text users see and respond to particular features of writing (Why did you use this here? Why do you think the writer changes direction here?).

Because they offer a flexible tool for gaining privileged access to others' writing beliefs and practices, interviews allow researchers to probe beyond preconceived explanations to refine categories and explore new perceptions. It is difficult, for instance, to predict the kinds of problems that students might have in understanding teacher feedback, but through interviews Hyland and Hyland (2001) learned that students often experienced considerable confusion in deciphering teachers' indirect feedback. Interviews are also effective means of discovering the kinds of writing that people do in different contexts and the meanings and challenges it holds for L2 writers. Thus, through interviews Chang and Swales (1999) found that their L2 student writers were disturbed by the appearance of informal features such as sentence fragments, sentence-initial *but*, and first person pronouns in published writing, while Flowerdew's (1999) Hong Kong L2 academics believed their weak facility of expression and poorer argument skills hindered their writing for publication in English.

Reflection 9.8

Suppose you want to conduct research into the writing done in a particular setting to ensure you are providing your students with appropriate preparation for the tasks that face them. To what extent would (a) questionnaires and (b) interviews be appropriate methods of investigation? What other kinds of data might you also need?

Introspection: Verbal and written reports

While elicited self-report data are central to much writing research, many interesting issues can be addressed through more introspective methods such as verbal and diary reports.

The idea of *verbal reports* as data rests on the belief that the process of writing requires conscious attention and that at least some of the thought process involved can be recovered, either as a retrospective recall or simultaneously with writing as a think-aloud protocol. Protocols involve participants writing in their normal way but instructed to verbalize all thinking at the same time so that information can be collected on their decisions, their strategies, and their perceptions as they work.

Think-aloud data have been criticized as offering an artificial and incomplete picture of the complex cognitive activities involved in writing. For one thing, many cognitive processes are routine and internalized operations and therefore not available to verbal description while, more seriously, the act of verbal reporting may itself distort the cognitive process being reported on (Stratman and Hamp-Lyons, 1994). Subjects' verbalizations tend to slow task progress and may interfere with the way they perform the task or explanations they give. In particular, the procedure can overload second language students who may only be able to describe their thinking in their L1. In fact, the technique is difficult even in one's first language, and may require considerable training to accomplish. But despite these criticisms, the method has been widely used (e.g., Smagorinsky, 1994), partly because the alternative is to deduce cognitive processes solely from subjects' behavior, and this would obviously be far less reliable.

Think-aloud techniques have been extremely productive in revealing the strategies writers use when composing, showing that writing is not simply a series of actions, but a series of decisions which involve setting goals and selecting strategies to achieve them. Much of this work has explored what students do when planning and revising texts, and in one study de Larios et al. (1999) used the method to examine what students did when they were blocked by a language problem or wanted to express a different meaning, tracing the patterns they used in searching for an alternative syntactic plan. The procedure has also been used to discover something about teaching processes. F. Hyland (1998), for example, asked teachers to conduct think-aloud protocols as they gave written feedback on student essays to reveal the reasoning processes behind the comments and the meanings they intended to convey by them (see Figure 9.3 for an example transcript). So, while think aloud is a potentially difficult technique, it can offer the researcher a source of considerable insights about writing and writing response practices.

Reflection 9.9
Record yourself thinking aloud while performing a language learning or teaching task (such as marking a paper, writing an essay, or engaged in a comprehension exercise). Does the tape tell you anything you weren't previously aware of about your behavior? What could be usefully explored further?

Diaries offer an alternative, and more straightforward, way of gaining introspective data. Bailey (1990: 215) defines diary studies as "a first-person account of a language learning or teaching experience, documented through regular, candid entries in a personal journal and then analyzed for recurring patterns or salient events." They can be kept by students, teachers, expert text users, or researchers themselves, and are often followed up with interviews. Individuals are encouraged to enter all relevant activities on a regular basis and, when a sufficient amount of material has been produced, the researcher examines it for patterns which are then interpreted and discussed with the writer. Diaries therefore provide a rich source of comparatively uncontrolled and reflective data which can reveal social and psychological processes that might be difficult to collect in other ways. While some diarists may resent the time and intrusion of making entries, journal writing is now a familiar feature of many writing classes and the use of this data can be a useful way of gathering information about ongoing writing practices.

Again, the procedure can be structured or open. Diarists may be given the opportunity to produce "narrative" entries which freely introspect on their learning or writing practices and experiences, or be set guidelines to restrict the issues addressed. Such guidelines help L2 learners to keep "on task" and supply a metalanguage to talk about their experiences. These can be in the form of detailed points to address ("write about what you found most/least interesting about this class"; "write about your interactions with group members") or a loose framework for response ("note all the work you did to complete this assignment"). Alternatively, researchers may ask diarists to concentrate only on "critical incidents" of personal significance or to simply maintain logs which record dates and times of reading and writing.

Diaries have been widely used as introspective tools by teachers to record their own writing experiences or the effects of their teaching on students' writing. More commonly though, studies have focused on students' reactions to their writing classes or the strategies they employ to accomplish particular tasks. Thus, Nelson (1993) used diaries to discover how her students went about writing a research paper. She told them that the entries could include notes on their trail through the library, how they evaluated sources and took notes, the conversations they had with others, insights that occurred to them at any time, decisions about planning the paper, and so on. The students understood that they were expected to explain in as much detail as possible how their research evolved, from the time they were given the assignment to the handing in of their paper. This approach provided a rich account of writers' reflections, suggesting why they acted as they did and how they saw contextual influences. They also highlighted the features of successful strategies that Nelson could use in her teaching.

Reflection 9.10

For many people, keeping a diary is not easy and can be time-consuming and burdensome, perhaps even leading to negative attitudes toward what is reported on. What strategies do you think might help to involve diarists in a study and increase their motivation to participate?

Observations

While elicitation and introspective methods provide reports of what people say they think and do, they do not offer any actual evidence of it. Direct observation methods attempt to bridge this gap by systematic documentation and reflection of participants engaged in writing and learning to write. They are based on conscious noticing and precise recording of actions as a way of seeing these actions in a new light. Observation of students is something teachers engage in constantly and, as a result, is a mainstay of classroom research, although the focus of research observation can be much broader and may include:

- Ourselves as teachers: the teaching methods and classroom practices employed to teach writing
- Students: the behavior of students engaged in writing, conferencing, or other learning tasks
- Contexts: the classroom layout, group arrangements, writing stimuli, uses of source materials
- Experts: the actions of expert writers in relevant target contexts

For research purposes observation needs to be systematized and narrowed to ensure that relevant data are recorded. McDonough and McDonough (1997: 105) distinguish observation as an "intentional activity" from the more usual "reactive noticing" and point out that while the latter can be useful for generating research issues, the former implies planning and prior decisions about what to record. The literature contains a wide variety of different approaches to classroom observation and the researcher needs to consider the extent to which a prior coding scheme will be useful as a way of highlighting significant events from the mass of data that taped or live observation can produce. Once again, the researcher has options about the degree of coding to employ, from simply checking pre-defined boxes at fixed intervals or every time a type of behavior occurs (Figure 9.2), to writing a full narrative of events (Figure 9.5).

For novice researchers, a clear structure is easier to apply and yields more manageable data, increasing the likelihood that a new perspective might be gained on a familiar situation. Burns (1999: 81) favors structured observation and provides the following guidelines for teachers:

1. Decide a focus relevant to the research. Don't try to record everything.
2. Identify a specific location for the observation (classroom, common room, library).
3. Identify the group or individual to be observed (class, peer-group, teacher-student conference).

4. Record the events (video, audio, or checklist).
5. Be as objective and as precise as possible and avoid evaluative descriptions.
6. Record complete events or incidents for a more inclusive or holistic picture.
7. Develop a recording system that fits in with other events in the context of observation.

Obviously coding schemes are easier to use than on-the-spot descriptions, but such pre-selection necessarily reduces the data and may ignore relevant behavior that wasn't predicted. All observation will necessarily privilege some behaviors and neglect others, as we only record what we think is important and so for beginning researchers it may be a good idea to identify appropriate observational categories as explicitly as possible. These categories may originate from a variety of sources: from background reading of the subject, from discussions or brainstorming sessions with colleagues, from initial unstructured observations of the activity, or from our own teaching experiences. They can also range from relatively low inferential categories ("uses chalk board," "asks question," "reads draft") to items that are highly interpretive or project attitudes on to participants ("offers compliment," "daydreams," "expresses irritation"). Clearly a balance has to be drawn between ease of recording and richness of analysis, and the teacher may need to first experiment with different schemes.

Reflection 9.11

Select a writing activity that you would like to observe and consider how you would observe it. Would you adopt a coding scheme and if so, what categories would you record? What would you hope to discover and how could you use the information you obtain?

Text data

A major source of data for writing research is writing itself: the use of communicative texts as objects of study. Research on texts can be done in a variety of ways and for many different purposes, but all modern text analyses seek to discover how people use language in specific contexts. Textual data allow us to see how texts work as communication and may comprise the writing that learners produce, the texts they need to produce, or simply texts that seem intrinsically interesting. Analysis of such texts can help identify the features of effective writing in different genres or among different groups of users and perhaps also the influences that contribute to these features, extending our understanding beyond the text itself to the multidimensional constraints of its context.

Selection of discourse data requires careful thought. Sometimes researchers work with a single text, either because it is inherently interesting or because it seems representative of a larger set of texts or particular genre. A major policy speech, a newspaper editorial, or an important scientific article can offer a rich source of insights into forms of persuasion, the distribution of particular syntactic or lexical choices, or the views of text writers. A sample student essay or exam writing may provide awareness about student uses of particular forms or the assumptions underlying different choices. In either circumstance, the data form a "case study" or "an instance in action" (Walker, 1985) and while this is a widely recognized approach, it also raises questions about the extent to which the text is actually representative of a larger set of texts. The view of an expert text user may be helpful here and the teacher may be able to call upon the judgment of another teacher familiar with the genre or student writer in question, an experienced journalist, a faculty member, or so on.

Support for the representativeness of textual data is obviously stronger if several texts are compared, and the random selection of texts from a corpus is one important approach here. A number of texts can be collected, from a newspaper or target workplace for example, and examined for recurring patterns of features, or a larger sample representative of a particular genre assembled in electronic form and analyzed using a concordance program (see Chapter 6). While this facilitates the acquisition of information for needs analysis, a major source of data is obviously students' written texts, perhaps essays or assignments submitted to the teacher as attachments or on disk, archives of LAN or Internet discussion sessions or asynchronous email exchanges. Small collections of texts of this sort, gradually built up week by week, can provide interesting frequency information and open up new research questions about students' progress as a group.

Reflection 9.12
Imagine you believe your students are overusing first person pronouns in their academic essays. What data would you collect to confirm or disprove this suspicion? How could you ensure that the texts you select are representative of the genre and writers you wish to study? What would you do with the data?

Experimental data

Experimental methods involve a deliberate intervention to isolate and study a single feature under controlled conditions. Experimental researchers are particularly concerned with external validity and design experiments to enable the results to be generalized to other populations, typically by minimizing threats to the reliability and validity of the research. Experimental techniques explore the strength of a relationship between two variable features of a situation such as test scores, proficiency, instruction, and so on. The idea is that the researcher seeks to discover if one variable influences another by holding other factors constant and varying the treatment given to two groups. Statistical tests are then carried out on the data to find if differences between the control and the experimental groups are significant.

While experiments have been largely rejected in writing research in favor of more qualitative, natural, and "thicker" data collection techniques, there are contexts in which they may be appropriate. A good example of an experimental approach in writing research is Berg's (1999) study on the influence of peer response training on the quality and type of text revisions made by peers. Berg studied her own students in two intermediate and two advanced level groups. One group from each level (the experimental group) received instruction in the language needed for peer response (e.g., asking questions, using specific words, giving opinions, etc.) and in rhetorical aspects of meaning, while the other classes (the control group) received no training. Both the trained and the untrained classes received similar writing instruction, used the same course text, and participated in similar composing and revising activities. Pre-peer first drafts and post-peer second drafts were then examined for meaning changes and graded holistically by two raters. The results showed that the students trained in peer response made significantly more meaning revisions and their writing improved more than untrained students over the two drafts.

Although this is a good example of how experimental research can apply to writing and feed back into teaching, results of experimental studies should be treated cautiously. Classrooms are not laboratories and there are serious difficulties of holding variables constant in two contexts. Differences in teaching styles, learner preferences, teacher attitudes, peer relationships, and so on can all influence results, and experimental methods are best combined with other forms of data for a fuller understanding of writing.

Reflection 9.13
How might you control the different influences on learners in a classroom in order to conduct an experiment on their use of one writing feature.

Case studies

Case studies are not an actual technique but the investigation of a single instance, usually a learner, a group or set of texts, explored as a totality using a range of methods for collecting and analyzing data. Case studies seek to provide a rich and vivid description of real people acting in real situations, blending description and analysis to understand actors' perceptions and experiences. This makes them an accessible type of research for teachers investigating their own classes because practitioners can identify with the individuals and issues and often have access to a range of data. Their strength lies in their potential for revealing the wholeness or integrity of human systems working in particular contexts, and while this often means they are of limited generalizability, others may recognize them as representing aspects of their own experience. On the minus side, the very richness and variety of data collected can mean that cases are difficult to organize and the fact they are not easily open to cross-checking makes them vulnerable to researcher bias (Cohen, Manion, and Morrison, 2000: 182).

Case studies can take a variety of forms and do not exclude quantitative or structured approaches, but typically they are interpretative and draw on qualitative data collection methods, particularly:

- Naturalistic and descriptive observation
- Narrative diaries
- Unstructured interviews
- Verbal reports
- Texts and documents

Given the potential breadth and complexity of contextual influences on writing, one of the main problems for the researcher is actually deciding where to set the boundaries of the case (McDonough and McDonough, 1997: 205). A teacher investigating a student's writing development must decide whether to include only the teaching aspects of the environment or to expand it to include institutional factors, the student's social networks, the physical conditions in which he or she typically writes, writing done outside an academic context, and so on. The researcher will be guided by what is relevant to the problem being studied, but might choose to limit the research to what seem (to the researcher and student) to be key people and incidents. All this data must then be coherently organized, either chronologically, as themes emerging from the data, or in relation to theoretical issues which scaffold the study.

A classic case study research of ESL writing is that by Zamel (1983), who used interviews, observations of students' writing, and analyses of their essays to track six students through a composing cycle. A more rigorous, exploratory, and longitudinal approach was adopted by Haas (1994), who followed one student through her entire four-year undergraduate career to trace the development of the student's academic reading and writing and her beliefs about these. Haas conducted a series of extended interviews, observed reading and writing sessions, analyzed essays and teacher comments, recorded think-aloud protocols while the student composed, and examined her log of all her writing and reading and of the activities she engaged in to complete assignments. Even though the study was conducted with an L1 student, it not only reveals how one student changed her understandings of texts and writers as she became familiar with her discipline, but illustrates the detail and richness that is possible using case studies.

Reflection 9.14

Select a student or a program as a possible case. What would be an interesting aspect to study? Sketch out a research design to show what research methods would be most appropriate.

Analyzing writing data

The purpose of data analysis is to clarify our understanding of the situation we have researched, exploring the data for patterns which make the situation meaningful, and perhaps provide a basis for action. This is not to say that data collection and analysis are separate activities. Figure 9.1 shows how the two are interrelated, ongoing, and often cyclical processes. Researchers always need to think about their data as it is collected: what it means, how it can be usefully supplemented, how to exploit interesting points, and so on.

Clearly the data that have been collected will differ both in form and in the degree of analytical structure the collection method has already imposed

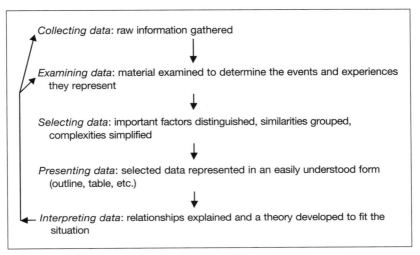

Figure 9.1: The analytical process.

on it. Data gathered by tightly structured procedures such as controlled observation codings, ticked questionnaire boxes, or transcripts of structured interviews are systematic in terms of the researcher's initial formulations of the issue and often produce precisely targeted categories that can be manipulated quantitatively. More open-ended data, including most interview responses, field notes, narrative observations, verbal protocols, and diary entries, call for more interpretation, and data will need to be reduced and grouped into categories in some way. Textual data, including essays, corpus data, and verbal transcripts of different kinds, can be analyzed in terms of its content or language.

Analyzing structured data

Most questionnaires and structured observations are designed to be analyzed numerically and allow fairly simple counting and tabulation techniques. The first step usually involves summarizing the figures with other figures, reducing the numbers to a more easily understood general picture. With small numbers of items, each questionnaire response can be plotted on a table with questions down one side and respondents along the top, allowing frequencies for each field to be plotted, grouped, and summarized. Similarly with data from check-box observation sheets, such as that shown in Figure 9.2, the frequencies of particular behaviors marked on the sheets can be combined in different ways to address the research problem.

Peer review task Student: *Vincent* Class: 4 Date: *Wed 19* Time: *2-2.20* observation		
	Frequencies	Total
Student talks in L1	*IIII*	4
Student uses reference material		
Student writes on feedback sheet	*I*	1
Student talks to teacher		
Student questions peer		
Student offers suggestion		
Student offers praise	*IIIII*	5
Student offers criticism		
Student reads essay aloud	*II*	2
Student listens to peer	*IIIII*	5
Student engages in off-task activity	*II*	2

Figure 9.2: Data from a structured observation sheet.

Reflection 9.15

What problems might arise in using the scheme in Figure 9.2 to code peer review behaviors? Can you see any patterns in this data? What higher-level categories might help provide insights into peer review?

Numerical data can be reduced to figures for central tendencies (means or modes), to the degree of dispersion around the midpoint (e.g., standard deviation), to how far figures for one feature are related to another (association and correlation), and to how strong these relationships are (significance tests). Powerful computer statistical packages such as *SPSS* and *Minitabs* offer relatively user-friendly means of dealing with these calculations. The role of statistics in language research is often questioned and it is certainly not always appropriate to use them. Decisions about the value of quantitative data more generally need to be made with particular research questions in mind and the contribution they can make to answering them, but while numbers lead away from real language use, they can be useful in showing relationships and connections which can then be explored in qualitative ways to reveal more interactive and affective dimensions of a situation.

Analyzing unstructured data

It is likely that most teacher-researchers will be confronted with unstructured data in various forms which need to be organized into categories through coding. Categories are conceptual tools that help researchers to organize their data and to reveal its major themes and relationships in order to build theories and explanations about it. This involves repeatedly reading the transcripts, diaries, and other texts and assigning sections of data codes that seem significant to the focus of the study. The categories used to code therefore emerge from the data itself, influenced by the researcher's theoretical knowledge and experience. They are chosen because of their relevance to the research questions and the fact that they represent the content of the data. Categories are therefore key concepts which form the nucleus of ideas about the data and should be:

1. Conceptually useful: help to answer research questions
2. Empirically valid: come from the data itself
3. Analytically practical: easy to identify, specific, nonoverlapping

One way of approaching coding is through *content analysis*, which involves identifying the meanings of structures or expressions by categorizing parts of texts, whether words, phrases, sentences, turns, etc. Coding can be quite challenging and it is a good idea to pass through the data several times, beginning with obvious or recurring topics, vocabulary, registers, and so on looking for themes. Subsequent passes through the data will help to generate and refine categories, identify core categories, find links, and gradually build a picture of the data. A simple procedure for novice researchers is suggested below:

1. Read through the text highlighting passages or phrases that seem important to get an overview.
2. Read through the marked passages and decide on categories – one word or phrase that expresses the content of each passage.
3. Read through the entire text again to find further examples of the categories and to expand them. Annotate the passages with category labels in the margin and the text in different colors – possibly double coding for more than one category.
4. Order, reject, combine, and separate the categories. Review the rationale for coding, list categories on a sheet of paper, count them, draw links between them, express them hierarchically as tree diagrams, and generally explore ways to see connections, core behaviors, and themes.
5. Reflect on the categories and their contents, using your insider knowledge to develop interpretations and note, in particular, the frequency

(Note: Italics = reading from the essay; underlining = written response)

– mm I don't think I'll read that – I haven't got time – so I'll read what she called draft first /

Mmm very strange – yes actually I have had a look at this before – I remember now – it's a very interesting beginning – and then she's – ah she's making some kind of promise to the reader I think about – mmm yep that introduction has potential but – yes – that definitely needs some work um yeah I think I'll make a positive comment about that sentence about culture and festivals – um the promise to the reader cos we've dealt with that today – that phrase – *I would like to think about how related to between culture and festivals* – underline <u>think</u> because that's not appropriate – yeah ignoring the spelling that's pretty amazing – um have a drink of tea – OK – <u>this is good</u> – a bit too strong – ha <u>promise to the reader</u> – um – the next sentence is very general actually – so I'll mark that <u>very general</u> – suggest it goes up the top – <u>maybe it should be earlier in the introduction</u> – that's not a real – not a grammatical sentence – <u>not a complete sentence</u> – um shall I – the first sentence – me is <u>too personal</u> – but is it? – I just don't know where to begin – mm um – it's that word – attractive – just imagine? – catches reader's attention there – <u>this is a very interesting beginning that catches the reader's attention</u>

– I feel that I'm giving quite detailed feedback here, but she is a quite serious student so I feel that it is worthwhile – what does this sentence mean? (pause 7 seconds) – *what about a long time ago* – that's – oh OK – *I'm very interested in that time. And also it is necessary – necessity to know* – about that time I suppose – not exactly clear is it? – it's not really connected – the physical wealth and the psychological wealth – how's this related to festivals? I don't see the connection – I suppose I should try and read it all through – I might just write a comment about that paragraph – <u>I don't see the connection with festivals</u> – just so she knows there's a problem in it – I might just quickly read through the whole thing. . . . .

Figure 9.3: Extract from teacher think-aloud protocol while responding to a paper.

with which they occur, their saliency in terms of the strength of the expression, and their distribution across the text and other texts collected in the research.

6. Discuss the categories with colleagues and ask them to check them against the data for reliability.

Software such as *WinMax, NUDIST*, and *Inspiration* can assist with these tasks. They are designed to help researchers keep track of their ideas and analyze unstructured data by retrieving data, labeling segments as variables, hyperlinking different parts of the data, brainstorming connections, and so on. As an example we can consider a possible approach to the transcript in Figure 9.3. This is a record of a teacher thinking aloud while correcting a

Tuesday 12. Today I took a writing test. I could not write well. I'm very worried about it. At first I though the test would be easy because we were given 40 minute. But I could not write as usual. I guess because too much pressure on by myself. It is so silly. 40 minute was not enough at all. As time past I was so impatient which made myself confused. If I had enough study I would have had less pressure. I'm going to forget about it, I decided that. However I'm very happy this moment because I have got a B+ mark! From last Friday's test writing. B+! How glad! I always dislike my writing but better mark is wonderful. It does help to prevent to get disappointment.

Figure 9.4: Entry from a learning diary in a writing class (F. Hyland, unpublished data).

student paper, and was collected as part of an investigation of feedback and revision (F. Hyland, 1998). A first sweep of the transcript might produce these categories:

Form response (spoken)   *Form response (written)*
Meaning response (spoken)   *Meaning response (written)*

This, however, captures only a limited aspect of what is happening, and subsequent readings might lead to a range of more specific categories. The researcher might notice, for instance, that the teacher focuses on either the *Writer* or the *Text*; that she responds with *Criticism, Praise*, and *Suggestion* and that these might be double coded according to the focus of the statement (*form* or *meaning*) and perhaps mode (*Written* or *Spoken*). While these categories might be expanded, collapsed, or rejected later, they provide a way of reducing the data to meaningful categories that help explain the teacher's process of responding to the essay.

While the categories suggested for the think-aloud data illustrate a person's response to their immediate situation, codes can refer to processes over time, activities, events, strategies, settings, participant perspectives, or anything that provides a handle on the data. A great deal of self-report data indicates respondents' definitions of the broader situation, their goals and aims, or their experiences. The extract from a student's learning diary in Figure 9.4, for instance, reveals a number of perspectives on writing including learning and writing anxiety, the effects of positive feedback, and the impact of testing.

Reflection 9.16

Look at the diary entry in Figure 9.4. What interesting lines of inquiry does this entry suggest to you and how might you follow them up?

Analyzing linguistic data

Finally, discourse data of various kinds, transcripts as well as texts, can be analyzed for the linguistic choices writers and speakers make to convey their meanings. Texts can be analyzed descriptively (revealing what occurs), analytically (interpreting why it occurs), or critically (questioning the social relations which underlie what occurs). Thus, we can seek to identify not only what is on the page or the tape, but also to establish what led the writer to make those choices. Analysis of transitivity, theme, or modality in a Systemic Functional framework, for instance, can reveal how the diarist or interviewee sees the topic he or she is discussing. Text analytic studies can focus on text-internal features such as tense or lexis, cohesive elements, move structure, interpersonal devices, and so on, and the work can be examined in isolation or compared with that of different proficiencies, genres, time periods, first language backgrounds, or social contexts. We know little about the characteristics of many genres or the influence that different cultural experiences, community expectations, teaching environments, social purposes, or proficiency levels have on writing, and all offer areas for small-scale research.

Reporting research

Disseminating the findings of writing research is important to prevent the knowledge gained from simply disappearing and to maintain the momentum of professional or curriculum development which got the research under way in the first place. Reporting can range from loose anecdotal accounts to formally published papers, but there are good reasons for writing up the research since it can:

- Increase the amount and the quality of reflection on both the research and practice.
- Increase the clarity of the topic through discussion with other teachers.
- Act to "repay" collaborators, participants, and sponsors.
- Facilitate further research, by the researcher or others, by providing models and ideas.

- Influence institutional or curriculum change.
- Increase teacher self-confidence, reporting skills, and professional development.
- Improve the reputation and profile of the profession through participation in public debate.

While teachers often underestimate the possible interest that others may have in their research, the potential audiences for it might be quite considerable, including students, colleagues, administrators, participants at in-service workshops, parents, employers, faculty members, course assessors, expert practitioners, and so on. The choice of methods for reporting are also varied, particularly as access and use of the Internet grows, and while teachers should not automatically reject the idea of scholarly publication, particularly in more teacher-oriented journals, they are not restricted to these. In fact, because much teacher writing research deliberately sets out to address local pedagogic, curriculum, or workplace writing practices and issues, rather than academic problems, other outlets may actually be more appropriate. Burns (1999) discusses distribution formats and venues in more detail, but potential venues for teacher research include:

Internet lists and Use group postings	In-house newsletters and staff bulletins
Personal or institutional Websites	In-service workshops and summer schools
Online journals	Videos of classroom/workplace practices
Conference presentations	Exhibitions and displays
Teacher journals (*Forum, Prospect, ELT Journal*)	Conference poster sessions

While these different sources imply different genres of reporting, all presentation of research needs to be both appropriate and persuasive to its audience. Engaging with these different audiences helps to free teachers from the constraints of formal academic styles and formats and offers colleagues and students greater access to the research. Web and other forms of visual presentation allow creativity and imagination in representing research activities and findings, while written formats provide opportunities for more narrative and personal texts which recognize the sequence of activities and emphasize concrete detail rather than academic abstractions. In these ways research can be seen as relevant to those most likely to be interested in it and to make use of it.

Reflection 9.17

Select two of the methods listed above for reporting research and consider how they might differ as genres. What adjustments must the researcher make in reporting in these two formats?

Summary and conclusion

This chapter has stressed the importance of research as a central form of professional development for writing teachers, enhancing their understanding of writing and how they teach it. It has also set out ways of carrying out research projects. The main points of the chapter can be summarized as follows:

- Teachers need not limit themselves to the issues and approaches of "action research," but employ whatever methods they see as appropriate and feel comfortable with to address questions that may originate from a range of sources.
- Time invested in clearly formulating a research question and designing a viable and valid means of investigating it helps to ensure successful and productive research.
- Teacher-researchers need to consider the ethical implications of their research and have a clear commitment to professional integrity and the interests of participants.
- Teacher-researchers should assess the relative merits of different ways of collecting and analyzing data for a particular question. This involves issues of validity and the degree of structure and control used to gather data and the extent analysis will involve quantification.
- There are good reasons for sharing research with others and a variety of ways to do this.

Discussion questions and activities

1 Write a short essay to discuss what you see as the main consequences of adopting a qualitative or quantitative approach to writing research. Sketch the relative advantages and disadvantages of these two broad approaches.

2 Keep a teaching or learning diary for two weeks. Set aside some specific times every day or so to record fairly freely your experiences in a particular

class, recording what you did and how you felt about the activity. After two weeks, reflect on the entries and look for patterns. Do any salient features emerge? How do you interpret these in terms of your teaching/learning in this class? How could you focus the study further to address these issues in more detail?

3 Decide on a feature of writing instruction that interests you and arrange to observe an L2 writing class to study it. Either (a) brainstorm the behaviors that might provide insights about the feature and devise a systematic observation scheme to use or (b) observe the class and write as comprehensive field notes as possible. Do any significant patterns emerge from your data?

4 Which methods of collecting data might you use to address the following writing questions? Select one question and consider (a) how different methods could make a contribution to answering it; (b) the effect of each method on the findings of the research.

   a. What are the effects of peer comments on revisions?
   b. What do readers regard as an effective text in a particular context?
   c. What is the typical move structure of a particular genre?
   d. How do writers go about planning and preparing to write a particular genre?
   e. How often do teachers give writing assignments and what kinds of assessments do they use?
   f. What do students write about outside of class?
   g. What writing tasks are typically required of participants in a target context?
   h. Does using a word processor make a difference to the quality and quantity of revisions?
   i. Does a student's culture or L1 make a difference to their attitudes to writing instruction?
   j. What do particular students think about group writing projects?

5 Select a research issue, either from those listed in Appendix 9.1 or another question that interests you. Focus the question and draw up a research design to investigate it including a time schedule. Outline the kinds of data you will need, how you will collect and analyze it, who the participants will be, how you will address issues of ethics, reliability, and validity, and how you will disseminate the results of the study.

6 Consider the narrative classroom observation notes in Figure 9.5. Do you think the observer has already formulated issues of potential interest? Using a content analysis, identify potentially useful categories in the notes and search for patterns which might help characterize the lesson. What productive lines of inquiry does the description suggest? How might these be followed up?

Class B   11 A.M.–12 A.M.

11:10 A.M.
T tells the students to choose a question.

11:13 A.M.
Tasks if they have decided but there is no response. She asks those who are doing question 1 to put up their hands. There is no response to this or to question 2. Many people choose question 3. Jo and Di on table A then say they are doing question 1. Polly says so is she. Polly is told to move to table A and all the other students are told to work in a group or pairs.

T says that the second thing that you do is to brainstorm ideas. She tells them to do this in a group but to write down their own ideas. She tells them to move. Polly moves to table A and the two Thai girls on table A move to table B.

11:15 A.M.
Tables A, B, and C are talking in English. On table D students are reading their theme booklets. T sits with table A and listens as Mo talks about the question in relation to Thailand and the other students listen. T says "You have to understand exactly what the question says." They discuss this together. Polly gets some paper.

Table C start talking in Chinese. They whisper and one takes notes. They switch from Chinese to English and back again. Lydia speaks more English than the others. The students on table D start to talk in English. They are discussing ideas. Li says "advantages and disadvantages. Anything else?" Table B are still talking in Thai. Mo says "Speak English" and they switch. "Plan OK, plan " one says and they get out some paper. They laugh and talk in English. They also write from time to time.

11:20 A.M.
By now all tables are talking and English is dominating. Table D is quieter than the others and Li and BJ are doing nearly all the talking.

T is still sitting with table A and they are talking about the difference between general ideas and specific examples. T is telling the students they will need to start in general terms. The students interrupt and ask questions. All three students are contributing.

11:24 A.M.
T leaves table A and stands in front of table D. The students talk quietly. She moves away to table C and asks " How are we doing here?" She sits down. Fa is consulting his dictionary. T jokes with him telling him to put it away as it makes her blood pressure rise. He goes red and does so. Lam reads the question aloud. T asks them what compare means. They are unable to tell her immediately and start to read the relevant sheet to find out. T asks them what they are going to do and Lam says they will talk about similarities. T asks to see their list. They say that they are sorry but they don't have one. T says that this is slack but she laughs as she says it. Lam gets out a piece of paper. They decide to think of a definition.

Groups D and A are talking a lot, with contributions from nearly all students. Li is leading table D. Table B are leaning forward and writing. They look absorbed.

Source: F. Hyland, unpublished data.

Figure 9.5: Extract from observational field notes of an L2 writing class.

Apppendix 9.1: Some topics and issues in writing research

Researching writers

- What strategies does this group of writers use to write or revise a specific writing task?
- How do they interpret prompts, plan, draft, edit, make use of sources and other students, etc.?
- What sources of feedback do students make use of?
- Do L2 learners transfer composing strategies from their L1?
- Are the processes of writing on computer different from writing on paper?
- What intervention strategies can teachers use to make these processes more effective?
- What are the effects of teacher/peer written/oral feedback on writing?
- What do teachers/peers focus their feedback on in given contexts?
- What interactions occur in teacher-student/peer conferences and how do these influence revision?
- Are there individual/cultural/proficiency differences in use of teacher feedback?
- What kinds of feedback do particular learners prefer and why?
- What are students' attitudes to particular forms of instruction, texts, materials, or assignments?

Researching texts

- What lexical/syntactic/discoursal features characterize a given genre?
- What are the main stages of this genre and how are these realized?
- How does a set of texts differ from those in another genre or in the same genre in other contexts?
- What writing tasks are typically required of this group of learners in the target context?
- What features characterize the texts of this specific group of learners?
- Do these features differ from those in texts produced by other writers?
- Can these differences be explained by reference to language proficiency or L1 conventions?
- In what ways do genres link with other genres in a given context?
- What instructional strategies are most effective in this particular context?

Researching readers

- What does this audience typically look for in a text and how do they read it?
- What do writers need to know about the target audience to write successful texts?
- What text features are important to engage a particular audience?
- In what ways are expert texts more "reader-friendly" than those of novice L2 writers?
- What do readers regard as an effective text in a particular context?
- What strategies are most effective in helping students learn to address audiences in their writing?

References

Akar, D., and Louhiala-Salminen, L. (1999). Towards a new genre: a comparative study of business faxes. In F. Bargiela-Chiappini and G. Nickerson (eds.), *Writing business: genres, media and discourses*. London: Longman.

Allison, D. (2002). *Approaching English language research*. Singapore: Singapore University Press.

Altman, H. (1980). Foreign language teaching: focus on the learner. In H. Altman and C. Vaughan James (eds.), *Foreign language teaching: meeting individual needs*. Oxford: Pergamon.

Aston, G. (1997). Involving learners in developing learning methods: exploiting text corpora in self access. In P. Benson and P. Voller (eds.), *Autonomy and independence in language learning* (pp. 204–14). London: Longman.

Bachman, L. (1990). *Fundamental considerations in language testing*. Oxford: Oxford University Press.

Bachman, L., and Palmer, A. (1996). *Language testing in practice: designing and developing useful language tests*. Oxford: Oxford University Press.

Bailey, K. (1990). The use of diary studies in teacher education programs. In J. Richards and D. Nunan (eds.), *Second language teacher education*. Cambridge: Cambridge University Press.

Ballard, B., and Clanchy, J. (1991). Assessment by misconception: cultural influences and intellectual traditions. In L. Hamp-Lyons (ed.), *Assessing second language writing in academic contexts* (pp. 19–35). Norwood, NJ: Ablex.

Bargiela-Chiappini, F., and Nickerson, G. (eds.). (1999). *Writing business: genres, media and discourses*. London: Longman.

Barnett, M. (1989). *More than meets the eye. Foreign language reading: theory and practice*. Englewood Cliffs, NJ: Prentice Hall.

Barton, D., and Hamilton, M. (1998). *Local literacies*. London: Routledge.

Bates, L., Lane, J., and Lange, E. (1993). *Writing clearly: responding to ESL composition*. Boston: Heinle & Heinle.

Bazerman, C., and Russell, D. (eds.). (1994). *Landmark essays on writing across the curriculum*. Davis, CA: Hermagoras Press.

Belanoff, P., and Dickson, M. (eds.). (1991). *Portfolios: process and product*. Portsmouth, NH: Heinemann.

Bell, J. (1999). *Doing your research project* (3rd ed.). Milton Keynes, UK: Open University Press.

Bell, J., and Gower, R. (1998). Writing course materials for the world: a great compromise. In B. Tomlinson (ed.), *Materials development in language teaching* (pp. 116–29). Cambridge: Cambridge University Press.

Benesch, S. (2001). *Critical English for academic purposes*. Mahwah, NJ: Erlbaum.

Benesch, S., Rakijas, M., and Rorschach, B. (1987). *Academic writing workshop*. Belmont, CA: Wadsworth.

Bereiter, C., and Scardamalia, M. (1987). *The psychology of written composition*. Hillsdale, NJ: Erlbaum.

Berg, E. C. (1999). The effects of trained peer response on ESL students' revision types and writing quality. *Journal of Second Language Writing*, 8 (3), 215–37.

Bernhardt, S., Edwards, P., and Wojahan, P. (1989). Teaching college composition with computers: a timed observation study. *Written Communication*, 7, 342–74.

Berwick, R. (1989). Needs assessment in language programming: from theory to practice. In R. Johnson (ed.), *The second language curriculum*. New York: Cambridge University Press.

Bhatia, V. K. (1993). *Analysing Genre: Language use in professional settings*. London: Longman.

Bhatia, V. K. (1997). The power and politics of genre. *World Englishes*, 17(3), 359–71.

Bialystok, E. (1985). The compatibility of teaching and learning strategies. *Applied Linguistics*, 6, 255–62.

Bizzell, P. (1992). *Academic discourse and critical consciousness*. Pittsburgh: University of Pittsburgh Press.

Blass, L., and Pike-Baky, M. (1985). *Mosaic I: a content-based writing book*. New York: Random House.

Board of Studies. (1998a). *K-6 English Syllabus:* Sydney, NSW: Board of Studies.

Board of Studies. (1998b). *K-6 English Syllabus: Modules*. Sydney, NSW: Board of Studies.

Braine, G., and Yorozu, M. (1998). Local Area Network (LAN) computers in ESL and EFL writing classes: promises and realities. *JALT Journal*, 20(2), 47–59.

Breen, M. (2001). Syllabus design. In R. Carter and D. Nunan (eds.), *The Cambridge guide to teaching Engish to speakers of other languages* (pp. 151–9). Cambridge: Cambridge University Press.

Brown, J. D. (1995). *The elements of language curriculum: a systematic approach to program development*. Boston: Heinle & Heinle.

Brown, J. D., and Hudson, T. (1998). The alternatives in language assessment. *TESOL Quarterly*, 32(4), 653–75.

Brown, K., and Hood, S. (1989). *Writing matters: writing skills and strategies for students of English*. Cambridge: Cambridge University Press.

Bruffee, K. (1986). Social construction: Language and the authority of knowledge. A bibliographical essay. *College English*, 48, 773–9.

Bruner, J. S. (1986). *Acts of meaning*. Cambridge, MA: Harvard University Press.

Burns, A. (1990). Genre-based approaches to writing and beginning adult ESL learners. *Prospect*, 5(3), 62–71.

Burns, A. (1999). *Collaborative action research for English language teachers*. Cambridge: Cambridge University Press.

Butt, D., Fahey, R., Feez, S., Spinks, S., and Yallop, C. (2000). *Using functional grammar: an explorer's guide* (2nd ed.). Sydney: NCELTR.

Buttjes, D., and Byram, M. (eds.). (1991). *Mediating languages and cultures: towards an intercultural theory of foreign language education*. Clevedon, UK: Multilingual Matters.

Byrne, D. (1988). *Teaching writing skills*. Harlow, UK: Pearson Education.

Canagarajah, S. (1999). *Resisting linguistic imperialism in English teaching*. Oxford: Oxford University Press.

Canale, M., and Swain, M. (1980). Theoretical bases of communicative approaches to second language teaching and testing. *Applied Linguistics*, 1(1–47).

Carson, J., and Leki, I. (eds.). (1993). *Reading in the composition classroom*. Boston: Heinle & Heinle.

Carson, J., and Nelson, G. (1996). Chinese students' perceptions of ESL peer response group interaction. *Journal of Second Language Writing*, 5(1), 1–19.

Chang, Y.-Y., and Swales, J. (1999). Informal elements in English academic writing: threats or opportunities for advanced non-native speakers? In C. N. Candlin and K. Hyland (eds.), *Writing: texts, processes and practices* (pp. 145–67). London: Longman.

Clarke, D. (1989). Communicative theory and its influence on materials production. *Language Teaching*, 73–86.

Clyne, M. (1987). Cultural differences in the organisation of academic texts. *Journal of Pragmatics*, 11, 211–47.

Coe, N., Rycroft, R., and Ernest, P. (1992). *Writing: A problem solving approach*. Cambridge: Cambridge University Press.

Cohen, A. (1994). *Assessing language ability in the classroom* (2nd ed.). Boston: Heinle and Heinle.

Cohen, M., Manion, L., and Morrison, K. (2000). *Research methods in education* (5th ed.). London: Routledge.

Connor, U. (1996). *Contrastive rhetoric*. Cambridge: Cambridge University Press.

Connor, U., and Asenavage, K. (1994). Peer response groups in ESL writing classes: how much impact on revision? *Journal of Second Language Writing*, 3, 257–76.

Connors, R., and Lunsford, A. (1993). Teachers' rhetorical comments on student papers. *College Composition and Communication*, 44, 200–223.

Cook, G. (1989). *Discourse*. Oxford: Oxford University Press.

Crookes, G., and Gass, S. (eds.). (1993). *Tasks in a pedagogical context: integrating theory and practice*. Clevedon, UK: Multilingual Matters.

Cumming, A. (1985). Responding to the writing of ESL students. *Highway One*, 8, 58–78.

Cumming, A. (2003). Experienced ESL/EFL writing instructors' conceptualizations of their teaching: curriculum options and implications. In B. Kroll (ed.), *Exploring the dynamics of second language writing* (pp. 71–92). New York: Cambridge University Press.

Cunningsworth, A. (1995). *Choosing your coursebook*. Oxford: Heinemann.

Daedalus. (1997). *Integrated Writing Environment* [Computer Software]. Austin, TX: The Daedalus Group.

Davies, A., Brown, A., Elder, C., Hill, K., Lumley, T., and McNamara, T. (1999). *Dictionary of language testing*. Cambridge: CUP/UCLES.

Davis, B., and Thiede, R. (2000). Writing into change: style shifting in asynchronous electronic discourse. In M. Warshauer and R. Kern (eds.), *Network-based language teaching: concepts and practice* (pp. 87–120). Cambridge: Cambridge University Press.

Day, R., and Bamford, J. (1998). *Extensive reading in the second language classroom*. Cambridge: Cambridge University Press.

de Larios, J., Murphy, L., and Manchon, R. (1999). The use of restructuring strategies in EFL writing: a study of Spanish learners of English as a Foreign Language. *Journal of Second Language Writing*, 8, 13–44.

DeMauro, G. (1992). *An investigation of the appropriateness of the TOEFL test as a matching variable to equate TWE topics*. Princeton, NJ: Educational Testing Service Report No. 37.

Denzin, N., and Lincoln, Y (eds.). (1998). *Collecting and interpreting qualitative materials*. Thousand Oaks, CA: Sage.

Douglas, D. (2000). *Assessing languages for specific purposes*. Cambridge: Cambridge University Press.

Dudeny, G. (2000). *The internet and the language classroom*. Cambridge: Cambridge University Press.

Dudley-Evans, T., and St John, M.-J. (1998). *Developments in English for specific purposes*. Cambridge: Cambridge University Press.

Elbow, P. (1998). *Writing with power: techniques for mastering the writing process*. New York: Oxford University Press.

Ellis, R. (1987). Contextual variability in second language acquisition and the relevancy of language teaching. In R. Ellis (ed.), *Second language acquisition in context* (pp. 179–94). Englewood Cliffs, NJ: Prentice Hall.

Ellis, R. (1994). *The study of second language acquisition*. Oxford: Oxford University Press.

Ellis, R. (1999). Input-based approaches to teaching grammar: a review of classroom-oriented research. *Annual Review of Applied Linguistics*, 19, 64–80.

Faigley, L. (1986). Competing theories of process: a critique and a proposal. *College English*, 48, 527–42.

Fathman, A., and Whalley, E. (1990). Teacher response to student writing: focus on form versus content. In B. Kroll (ed.), *Second language writing: research insights for the classroom* (pp. 178–90). Cambridge: Cambridge University Press.

Feez, S. (1998). *Text-based syllabus design*. Sydney: Mcquarie University/ AMES.

Ferris, D. (1997). The influence of teacher commentary on student revision. *TESOL Quarterly*, 31(2), 315–39.

Ferris, D. (2002). *Treatment of error in second language student writing*. Ann Arbor: University of Michigan Press.

Ferris, D., and Hedgcock, J. S. (1998). *Teaching ESL composition: purpose, process, practice*. Mahwah, NJ: Erlbaum.

Ferris, D., Pezone, S., Tade, C., and Tinti, S. (1997). Teacher commentary on student writing: descriptions and implications. *Journal of Second Language Writing*, 6, 155–82.

Flower, L. (1989). Cognition, context and theory building. *College Composition and Communication*, 40, 282–311.

Flower, L. (1994). *The construction of negotiated meaning: A social cognitive theory of writing*. Carbondale: Southern Illinois University Press.

Flower, L., and Hayes, J. (1980). The cognition of discovery: defining a rhetorical problem. *College Composition and Communication*, 31, 21–32.

Flower, L., and Hayes, J. (1981). A cognitive process theory of writing. *College Composition and Communication*, 32, 365–87.

Flowerdew, J. (1999). Problems in writing for scholarly publication in English: the case of Hong Kong. *Journal of Second Language Writing*, 8 (3): 243–64.

Freadman, A. (1994). Anyone for tennis? In A. Freadman and P. Medway (eds.), *Genre and the new rhetoric* (pp. 43–66). London: Taylor & Francis.

Friere, P. (1974). *Education for critical consciousness*. London: Sheed and Ward.

Gere, A. (1987). *Writing groups: history, theory, and implications.* Carbondale: Southern Illinois University Press.

Gerrard, L. (1989). Computers and basic writers: a critical view. In G. Hawisher and C. Selfe (eds.), *Critical perspectives on computers and composition instruction* (pp. 94–108). New York: Teachers' College Press.

Goldstein, L., and Conrad, S. (1990). Student input and negotiation of meaning in ESL writing conferences. *TESOL Quarterly*, 24(3): 443–60.

Grabe, W. (2001). Reading-writing relations: theoretical perspectives and institutional practices. In D. Belcher and A. Hirvela (eds.), *Linking literacies: perspectives on L2 reading and writing connections* (pp. 15–47). Ann Arbor: University of Michigan Press.

Grabe, W. (2003). Reading and writing relations: L2 perspectives on research and practice. In B. Kroll (ed.), *Exploring the dynamics of second language writing* (pp. 242–61). New York: Cambridge University Press.

Grabe, W., and Kaplan, R. (1996). *Theory and practice of writing*. Harlow: Longman.

Grellet, F. (1996). *Writing for advanced learners of English*. Cambridge: Cambridge University Press.

Haas, C. (1994). Learning to read biology: One student's rhetorical development in college. *Written Communication*, 11(1), 43–84.

Hadfield, J. (1992). *Classroom dynamics*. Oxford: Oxford University Press.

Halliday, M. A. K. (1994). *An introduction to functional grammar* (2nd ed.). London: Edward Arnold.

Halliday, M. A. K., and Hasan, R. (1989). *Language, context and text: aspects of language in a social semiotic perspective*. Oxford: Oxford University Press.

Hamp-Lyons, L. (ed). (1991). *Assessing second language writing in academic contexts.* Norwood, NJ: Ablex.

Hamp-Lyons, L., and Condon, W. (1993). Questioning assumptions about portfolio-based assessment. *College Composition and Communication*, 44(2), 176–90.

Hamp-Lyons, L., and Condon, W. (2000). *Assessing the portfolio: principles for practice, theory and research.* Cresskill, NJ: Hampton Press.

Hamp-Lyons, L., and Heasley, B. (1987). *Study writing.* Cambridge: Cambridge University Press.

Harmer, J. (2001). *The practice of English language teaching.* Harlow: Pearson Education.

Hawisher, G., and Selfe, C. (eds.). (1989). *Critical perspectives on computers and composition instruction.* New York: Teachers' College Press.

Heath, S. B. (1991). The sense of being literate: historical and cross-cultural features. In R. Barr, M. Kamil, P. Mosentahl, and P. Pearson (eds.), *Handbook of reading research*, vol. II (pp. 3–25). New York: Longman.

Hedgcock, J., and Lefkowitz, N. (1992). Collaborative oral/aural revision in foreign language writing instruction. *Journal of Second Language Writing*, 1, 255–76.

Hedge, T. (2000). *Teaching and learning in the language classroom.* Oxford: Oxford University Press.

Henry, A., and Roseberry, R. (2001). A narrow-angled corpus analysis of moves and strategies of the genre: "letter of application." *English for Specific Purposes*, 20(2), 153–67.

Hinds, J. (1987). Reader versus writer responsibility: A new typology. In U. Connor and R. B. Kaplan (eds.), *Writing across languages: analysis of L2 text.* Reading, MA: Addison-Wesley.

Hinkel, E. (ed.). (1999). *Culture in second language teaching and learning.* Cambridge: Cambridge University Press.

Hitchcock, G., and Hughes, D. (1995). *Research and the teacher.* London: Routledge.

Hoey, M. (1983). *On the surface of discourse.* London: Allen & Unwin.

Holliday, A. (1994). *Appropriate methodology and social context.* Cambridge: Cambridge University Press.

Holliday, A., and Cook, T. (1982). An ecological approach to ESP. *Issues in ESP. Lancaster Papers in ELT*, 5, 123–43.

Holst, J. K. (1993). *Writ 101: Writing English.* Wellington, NZ: Victoria University.

Hopkins, D. (1993). *A teacher's guide to classroom research.* Buckingham, UK: Open University Press.

Hughes, A. (1989). *Testing for language teachers*. Cambridge: Cambridge University Press.

Hunt, K. (1983). Sentence combining and the teaching of writing. In M. Martlew (ed.), *The psychology of written language: a developmental approach* (pp. 99–125). New York: Wiley.

Hutchison, T., and Waters, A. (1987). *English for specific purposes*. Cambridge: Cambridge University Press.

Hyland, F. (1998). The impact of teacher-written feedback on individual writers. *Journal of Second Language Writing*, 7(3), 255–86.

Hyland, F. (2000). ESL writers and feedback: giving more autonomy to learners. *Language Teaching Research*, 4(1): 33–54.

Hyland, F. (2001). Providing effective support: investigating feedback to distance language learners. *Open Learning*, 16(3), 233–47.

Hyland, F., and Hyland, K. (2001). Sugaring the pill: praise and criticism in written feedback. *Journal of Second Language Writing*, 10(3), 185–212.

Hyland, K. (1990). Providing productive feedback. *ELT Journal*, 44(4), 279–85.

Hyland, K. (1993). ESL computer writers: what can we do to help? *System*, 21(1), 21–30.

Hyland, K. (1994). The learning styles of Japanese students. *JALT Journal*, 16(1), 55–74.

Hyland, K. (1998). *Hedging in scientific research articles*. Amsterdam: John Benjamins.

Hyland, K. (1999). Talking to students: metadiscourse in introductory textbooks. *English for Specific Purposes*, 18(1), 3–26.

Hyland, K. (2000). *Disciplinary discourses: Social interactions in academic writing*. London: Longman.

Hyland, K. (2002). Genre: language, context and literacy. In M. McGroaty (ed.), *Annual review of applied linguistics*, vol. 22: 113–35.

Hyland, K. (2003). Genre-based pedagogies: a social response to process. *Journal of Second Language Writing* 12(1), 17–29.

Janopoulos, M. (1992). University faculty tolerance of NS and NNS writing errors. *Journal of Second Language Writing*, 1, 109–22.

Jenkins, S., Jordan, M., and Weiland, P. (1993). The role of writing in graduate engineering education: a survey of faculty beliefs and practices. *English for Specific Purposes*, 12, 51–67.

Johns, A. M. (1997). *Text, role and context: developing academic literacies*. Cambridge: Cambridge University Press.

Johnson, K., and Johnson, G. (1999). *Teachers understanding teaching*. Boston: Heinle & Heinle.

Jolly, D., and Bolitho, R. (1998). A framework for materials writing. In B. Tomlinson (ed.), *Materials development in language teaching* (pp. 90–115). Cambridge: Cambridge University Press.

Jordan, B. (1990). *Academic writing course*. London: Collins.

Kachru, Y. (1996). Culture in rhetorical styles: contrastive rhetoric and world Englishes. In N. Mercer and J. Swann (eds.), *Learning English: development and diversity* (pp. 305–14). London: Routledge.

Kahtani, S. (1999). Electronic portfolios in ESL writing: an alternative approach. *Computer Assisted Language Learning*, 12, 261–68.

Kaplan, R. (1966). Cultural thought patterns in intercultural education. *Language Learning*, 16, 1–20.

Kaplan, R. (1987). Cultural thought patterns revisited. In U. Connor and R. Kaplan (eds.), *Writing across languages*. Reading, MA: Addison-Wesley.

Kaplan, R., and Shaw, P. (1983). *Exploring academic discourse*. Singapore: HarperCollins.

Knapp, P., and Watkins, M. (1994). *Context-text-grammar: teaching the genres and grammar of school writing in infants and primary classrooms*. Sydney: Text productions.

Knobel, M., Lankshear, C., Honan, E., and Crawford, J. (1998). The wired world of second language education. In I. Snyder (ed.), *Page to Screen: taking literacy into the electronic era* (pp. 20–50). London: Routledge.

Knoblauch, C., and Brannon, L. (1981). Teacher commentary on student writing: the state of the art. *Freshman English News*, 10, 1–4.

Knoblauch, C., and Brannon, L. (1984). *Rhetorical traditions and the teaching of writing*. Upper Montclair, NJ: Boynton/Cook.

Kramsch, C. (1993). *Context and culture in language teaching*. Oxford: Oxford University Press.

Krapels, A. (1990). An overview of second language writing process research. In B. Kroll (ed.), *Second language writing: insights for the writing classroom* (pp. 37–56). Cambridge: Cambridge University Press.

Krashen, S. (1993). *The power of reading: insights from the research*. Englewood, CO: Libraries Unlimited.

Kroll, B. (2002). Considerations for teaching an ESL/EFL writing course. In M. Celce-Murcia (ed.), *Teaching English as a Second or Foreign Language* (3rd ed.). Boston: Heinle & Heinle.

Kroll, B., and Reid, J. (1994). Guidelines for designing writing prompts: clarifications, caveats and cautions. *Journal of Second Language Writing*, 3(3), 231–55.

Lankshear, C., and Snyder, I. (2000). *Teachers and techno-literacy*. St. Leonards, Australia: Allen & Unwin.

Lantolf, J. P. (1999). Second culture acquisition: cognitive considerations. In E. Hinkel (ed.), *Culture in second language teaching and learning* (pp. 28–46). Cambridge: Cambridge University Press.

Larsen-Freeman, D., and Long, M. (1991). *An introduction to second language acquisition research*. London: Longman.

Lave, J., and Wenger, E. (1991). *Situated learning: Legitimate peripheral participation*. Cambridge: Cambridge University Press.

Leki, I. (1990). Coaching from the margins: issues in written response. In B. Kroll (ed.), *Second language writing: insights from the language classroom* (pp. 57–68). Cambridge: Cambridge University Press.

Leki, I. (1992). *Understanding ESL writers: a guide for teachers*. Portsmouth, NH: Boynton/Cook.

Leki, I., and Carson, J. (1997). Completely different worlds: EAP and the writing experiences of ESL students in university courses. *TESOL Quarterly*, 31: 231–55.

Lock, G., and Lockhart, C. (1999). Genres in an academic writing class. *Hong Kong Journal of Applied Linguistics*, 3(2), 47–64.

Lockhart, C., and Ng, P. (1995). Analysing talk in peer response groups: stances, functions and content. *Language Learning*, 45, 605–55.

Macken-Horarik, M. (1996). *Construing the invisible: specialized literacy practices in junior secondary English*. Ph.D. thesis: University of Sydney.

Macken-Horarik, M. (2002). "Something to shoot for": a Systemic Functional approach to teaching genre in secondary school science. In A. Johns (ed.), *Genre in the classroom: multiple perspectives* (pp. 21–46). Mahwah, NJ: Erlbaum.

Mager, R. (1975). *Preparing instructional objectives*. Palo Alto: Fearon.

Markus, H., and Kitayama, S. (1991). Cultures and the self: implications for cognition, emotion and motivation. *Psychological Review*, 98, 224–53.

Martin, J. R. (1989). *Factual writing: exploring and challenging social reality*. Oxford: Oxford University Press.

Martin, J. R. (1992). *English text: system and structure*. Amsterdam: John Benjamins.

Master, P. (1995). Consciousness raising and article pedagogy. In D. Belcher and G. Braine (eds.), *Academic writing in a second language* (pp. 183–205). Norwood, NJ: Ablex.

Mauranen, A. (1993). Contrastive ESP rhetoric: Metatext in Finnish-English Economics Texts. *English for Specific Purposes*, 12, 3–22.

McCarthey, S. J. (1992). The teacher, the author, and the text: variations in form and content of writing conferences. *Journal of Reading Behaviour*, 24(1), 51–82.

McDonough, J., and McDonough, S. (1997). *Research methods for English language teachers*. London: Arnold.

McDonough, J., and Shaw, C. (eds.). (1993). *Materials and methods in ELT*. Oxford: Blackwell.

McNamara, T. (1996). *Measuring second language performance*. London: Longman.

Mendoca, C., and Johnson, K. (1994). Peer review negotiations; revision activities in ESL writing instruction. *TESOL Quarterly*, 28(4), 745–68.

Messick, S. (1989). Validity. In R. Linn (ed.), *Educational measurement* (3rd ed.) (pp. 13–103). New York: Macmillan.

Messick, S. (1996). Validity and washback in language testing. *Language Testing*, 13, 241–56.

Miles, M. and Huberman, A. (1994). *Qualitative data analysis*. Thousand Oaks, CA: Sage.

Milton, J. (1997). Providing computerized self-access opportunities for the development of writing skills. In P. Benson and P. Voller (eds.), *Autonomy and independence in language learning* (pp. 204–14). London: Longman.

Milton, J. (1999a). Lexical thickets and electronic gateways: making text accessible by novice writers. In C. N. Candlin and K. Hyland (eds.), *Writing: texts, processes and practices* (pp. 221–43). London: Longman.

Milton, J. (1999b). *WordPilot 2000* (Computer program). Hong Kong: CompuLang.

Mittan, R. (1989). The peer review process: harnessing students' communicative power. In D. Johnson and D. Roen (eds.), *Richness in writing: empowering ESL students* (pp. 207–19). New York: Longman.

Moffett, J. (1982). Writing, inner speech and mediation. *College English*, 44, 231–44.

Mohan, B. (1986). *Language and content*. Reading, MA: Addison-Wesley.

Murray, D. (1985). *A writer teaches writing* (2nd ed.). Boston: Houghton Mifflin.

Nation, P. (1990). *Teaching and learning vocabulary*. New York: Heinle & Heinle.

Nelson, J. (1993). The library revisited: exploring students' research processes. In A. Penrose and B. Sitcoe (eds.), *Hearing ourselves think: cognitive research in the college writing classroom*. New York: Oxford University Press.

Newkirk, T. (1995). The writing conference as performance. *Research in the Teaching of English*, 29, 193–215.

Nunan, D. (1989). *Designing tasks for the communicative classroom*. Cambridge: Cambridge University Press.

Nunan, D. (1992). *Research methods in language teaching*. Cambridge: Cambridge University Press.

O'Keefe, J. (2000). *Invitation to reading and writing*. Englewood Cliffe, NJ: Prentice Hall.

Ohta, A. (2000). Rethinking interaction in SLA: developmentally appropriate assistance in the zone of proximal development and the acquisition of L2 grammar. In J. Lantolf (ed.), *Sociocultural theory and second language learning*. Oxford: Oxford University Press.

Oshima, A., and Hogue, A. (1999). *Writing academic English* (3rd ed.). London: Longman.

Oxford, R., and Anderson, N. (1995). A crosscultural view of learning styles. *Language Teaching*, 28(201–15).

Oxford R., Hollaway, M., and Horton-Murillo, D. (1992). Language learning styles: Research and practical considerations for teaching in the multicultural tertiary ESL/EFL classroom. *System*, 4, 439–56.

Paltridge, B. (2001). *Genre and the language learning classroom*. Ann Arbor: University of Michigan Press.

Partington, A. (1998). *Patterns and meanings: using corpora for English language research and teaching*. Amsterdam: Benjamins.

Patthey-Chavez, G., and Ferris, D. (1997). Writing conferences and the weaving of multi-voiced texts in college composition. *Research in the Teaching of English*, 31, 51–90.

Pemberton, R., and Toogood, S. (2001). Expectations and assumptions in a self-directed language-learning programme. In M. Mozzon-McPherson and R. Vismans (eds.), *Beyond language teaching towards language advising*. London: CILT.

Pemberton, R., Toogood, S. Ho, S., and Lam, J. (Forthcoming). Learner and advisor expectations in a self-directed language-learning programme: a case study of four learners and four advisers. In D. Bickerton and M. Gottin (eds.), *5th CercleS Conference Proceedings*.

Pennington, M. C. (1993). A critical examination of word processing effects in relation to L2 writers. *Journal of Second Language Writing*, 2, 227–55.

Pennington, M. (1996). *The computer and the non-native writer: a natural partnership*. Cresskill, NJ: Hampton.

Pennington, M., and Brock, M. (1989). Use of computers in the teaching of ESL writing: effectiveness of text analysis and word processing. *University of Hawaii Working Papers in ESL*, 8(1), 155–83.

Pennycook, A. (1996). Borrowing others' words: text, ownership, memory and plagiarism. *TESOL Quarterly*, 30, 201–30.

Peyton, J. K., and Staton, J. (eds.). (1993). *Dialogue journals in the multilingual classroom: building language fluency and writing skills through written interaction*. Norwood, NJ: Ablex.

Phillipson, R. (1992). *Linguistic imperialism*. Oxford: Oxford University Press.

Phinney, M. (1991). Computer assisted writing and writing apprehension in ESL students. In P. Dunkel (ed.), *Computer assisted language learning and testing: Research issues and practices*. New York: Newbury House.

Polio, C. (2003). An overview of what we investigate and how. In B. Kroll (ed.), *Exploring the dynamics of second language writing*. New York: Cambridge University Press.

Pratt, D. (1980). *Curriculum design and development*. New York: Harcourt Brace.

Purves, A. C. (ed.). (1988). *Writing across languages and cultures: Issues in contrastive rhetoric*. Newbury Park, CA: Sage.

Purves, A., Quattrini, J., and Sullivan, C. (eds.). (1995). *Creating the writing portfolio*. Lincolnwood, IL: NTC Publishing.

Radecki, P., and Swales, J. (1988). ESL student reaction to written comments on their written work. *System*, 16, 355–65.

Raimes, A. (1991). Out of the woods: emerging traditions in the teaching of writing. *TESOL Quarterly*, 25(3), 407–30.

Raimes, A. (1992). *Exploring through writing: a process approach to ESL composition* (2nd ed.). New York: St. Martin's Press.

Ramanathan, V., and Atkinson, D. (1999). Individualism, academic writing and ESL writers. *Journal of Second Language Writing*, 8(1), 45–75.

Reid, J. M. (1987). The learning style preferences of ESL students. *TESOL Quarterly*, 21(1), 87–109.

Reid, J. M. (1993). *Teaching ESL writing*. Englewood Cliffs, NJ: Regents/Prentice Hall.

Reid, J. M. (1994). Responding to ESL students' texts: the myths of appropriation. *TESOL Quarterly*, 28, 237–92.

Reid, J. M. (2000). *The process of composition* (3rd ed.). New York: Longman.

Reid, J., and Kroll, B. (1995). Designing and assessing effective classroom writing assignments for NES and ESL students. *Journal of Second Language Writing*, 4(1), 17–41.

Richards, J. (2001). *Curriculum development in language teaching*. Cambridge: Cambridge University Press.

Richards, J., and Lockhart, C. (1994). *Reflective teaching in second language classrooms*. Cambridge: Cambridge University Press.

Riley, P. (1997). The guru and the conjurer: aspects of counselling for self-access. In P. Benson and P. Voller (eds.), *Autonomy and independence in language learning* (pp. 114–31). London: Longman.

Rothery, J. (1986). *Teaching writing in the primary school: a genre-based approach to the development of writing abilities.* Working Papers in Linguistics: University of Sydney.

Rowntree, K. (1991). *Writing for success: A practical guide for New Zealand students.* Auckland: Longman.

Sawyer, W., and Watson, K. (1987). Questions of genre. In I. Reid (ed.), *The place of genre in learning: current debates.* Deakin: Deakin University Press.

Schriver, K. (1992). Teaching writers to anticipate readers' needs. *Written Communication*, 9(2), 179–208.

Seal, B. (1997). *Academic encounters: content focus human behaviour.* Cambridge: Cambridge University Press.

Sheldon, L. (1987). *ELT textbooks and materials: problems in evaluation and development.* London: Modern English Pubs and British Council.

Silva, T. (1990). Second language composition instruction: developments, issues, and directions. In B. Kroll (ed.), *Second language writing: research insights for the classroom* (pp. 11–23). Cambridge: Cambridge University Press.

Silva, T. (1993). Toward an understanding of the distinct nature of L2 writing: the ESL research and its implications. *TESOL Quarterly*, 27, 665–77.

Silva, T. (1997). Differences in ESL and Native-English-Speaker writing: the research and its implications. In C. Severino, J. Guena, and J. Butler (eds.), *Writing in multicultural settings* (pp. 209–19). New York: Modern Language Association of America.

Silva, T., Leki, I., and Carson, J. (1997). Broadening the perspective of mainstream composition studies: some thought from the disciplinary margins. *Written Communication*, 14, 398–428.

Silva, T., and Reichelt, M. (2003). Second language writing up close and personal: some success stories. In B. Kroll (ed.), *Exploring the dynamics of second language writing* (pp. 93–114). Cambridge: Cambridge University Press.

Skehan, P. (1989). *Individual differences in second language learning.* London: Edward Arnold.

Smagorinsky, P. (ed). (1994). *Speaking about writing: reflections on research methodology.* Thousand Oaks, CA: Sage.

Snyder, I. (1993). Writing with word processors: a research overview. *Educational Research*, 35, 49–68.

Snyder, I. (ed). (1998). *Page to screen: taking literacy into the electronic era*. London: Routledge.

Sommers, N. (1982). Responding to student writing. *College Composition and Communication*, 33, 148–56.

Spack, R. (1996). *Guidelines* (2nd ed.). New York: St. Martin's Press.

Stake, R. (1995). *The art of case study research*. Thousand Oaks, CA: Sage.

Stoddard, B., and MacArthur, C. (1993). A peer editor strategy: guiding learning disabled students in response and revision. *Research in the Teaching of English*, 27(1), 76–103.

Stratman, J., and Hamp-Lyons, L. (1994). Reactivity in concurrent think-aloud protocols: issues for research. In P. Smagorinsky (ed.), *Speaking about writing* (pp. 89–112). Thousand Oaks, CA: Sage.

Straub, R. (2000). The student, the text, and the classroom context: a case study of student response. *Assessing Writing*, 7, 23–55.

Susser, B. (1998). The mysterious disappearance of word processing. *Computers and Composition*, 15, 347–71.

Swaffer, J., Romano S., Markley, P., and Arens, K. (eds.). (1998). *Language learning online*. Austin, TX: Labyrinth.

Swales, J. (1990). *Genre analysis: English in academic and research settings*. Cambridge: Cambridge University Press.

Swales, J., and Feak, C. (1994). *Academic writing for graduate students: essential tasks and skills*. Ann Arbor: University of Michigan Press.

Swales, J., and Feak, C. (2000). *English in today's research world: a writing guide*. Ann Arbor: University of Michigan Press.

Taylor, T., and Ward, I. (eds.). (1998). *Literacy theory in the age of the Internet*. New York: Columbia University Press.

Tomlinson, B. (ed.). (1998). *Materials development in language teaching*. Cambridge: Cambridge University Press.

Tribble, C. (1996). *Writing*. Oxford: Oxford University Press.

Tribble, C., and Jones, G. (1997). *Concordances in the classroom*. Houston, TX: Athelstan.

Truscott, J. (1996). The case against grammar correction in L2 writing classes. *Language Learning*, 46, 327–69.

Tyler, R. (1949). *Basic principles of curriculum and instruction*. New York: Harcourt Brace.

Tyner, K. (ed.). (1998). *Literacy in a digital world: teaching and learning in the age of information*. Mahwah, NJ: Erlbaum.

Ur, P. (1996). *A course in language teaching: practice and theory*. Cambridge: Cambridge University Press.

Valero-Garces, C. (1996). Contrastive ESP rhetoric: Metatext in Spanish-English Economics texts. *English for Specific Purposes*, 15(4), 279–94.

Vanett, L., and Jurich, D. (1990). A context for collaboration: teachers and students writing together. In J. K. Peyton (ed.), *Students and teachers writing together* (pp. 51–62). Alexandria, VA: TESOL.

Villamil, O., and de Guerrero, M. (1996). Peer revision in the L2 classroom: social-cognitive activities, mediating strategies, and aspects of social behaviour. *Journal of Second Language Writing*, 5, 51–75.

Vygotsky, L. (1978). *Mind in society: The development of higher psychological processes*. In M. Cole, V. John-Steiner, S. Scribner, and E. Souberman (eds.). Cambridge, MA: Harvard University Press.

Walker, R. (1996). *Doing research: a handbook for teachers*. London: Routledge.

Wall, D. (1997). Impact and washback in language testing. In C. Clapham (ed.), *The Kluwer encyclopedia of language in education, vol. 7: testing and assessment*. Dordrecht: Kluwer.

Wallace, M. J. (1998). *Action research for language teachers*. Cambridge: Cambridge University Press.

Warschauer, M. (1995). *E-mail for English teaching: bringing the Internet and computer learning networks into the language classroom*. Alexandria, VA: Teachers of English to Speakers of Other Languages.

Warschauer, M. (2002). Networking into academic discourse. *Journal of English for Academic Purposes*, 1: 45–58.

Warschauer, M., and Kern, R. (eds.). (2000). *Network-based language teaching: concepts and practice*. Cambridge: Cambridge University Press.

Watson-Reekie, C. (1982). The use and abuse of models in the ESL writing class. *TESOL Quarterly*, 16, 5–14.

Weigle, S. (2002). *Assessing writing*. Cambridge: Cambridge University Press.

White, E. (1994). *Teaching and assessing writing* (2nd ed.). San Francisco: Jossey-Bass.

White, R., and Arndt, V. (1991). *Process writing*. Harlow, UK: Longman.

Wichmann, A., Fligelstone, S., McEnery, T., and Knowles, G. (eds.). (1997). *Teaching and language corpora*. London: Longman.

Windeatt, S., Hardisty, D., and Eastment, D. (2000). *The Internet*. Oxford: Oxford University Press.

Wright, T. (1987). *Roles of teachers and learners*. Oxford: Oxford University Press.

Wu, M. H. (1992). Towards a contextual lexico-grammar: An application of concordance analysis in EST teaching. *RELC Journal*, 23(2), 18–34.

Yalden, J. (1987). *The communicative syllabus*. Englewood Cliffs, NJ: Prentice-Hall.

Zamel, V. (1983). The composing processes of advanced ESL students: six case studies. *TESOL Quarterly*, 17, 165–87.

Zamel, V. (1985). Responding to writing. *TESOL Quarterly*, 19(1), 79–101.

Zamel, V. (1997). Towards a model of transculturation. *TESOL Quarterly*, 31, 341–52.

Zhang, S. (1995). Reexamining the affective advantage of peer feedback in the ESL writing class. *Journal of Second Language Writing*, 4, 209–22.

Author Index

Subject Index